JOHN LOCKE

TWO TRACTS ON GOVERNMENT

JOHN LOCKE

TWO TRACTS ON GOVERNMENT

EDITED
WITH AN INTRODUCTION, NOTES
AND TRANSLATION

BY

PHILIP ABRAMS

*Fellow of Peterhouse and Lecturer in Economics and
Politics in the University of Cambridge*

CAMBRIDGE
AT THE UNIVERSITY PRESS
1967

Published by the Syndics of the Cambridge University Press
Bentley House, 200 Euston Road, London, N.W. 1
American Branch: 32 East 57th Street, New York, N.Y. 10022

© Cambridge University Press 1967

Library of Congress Catalogue Card Number: 66–19603

Printed in Great Britain
at the University Printing House, Cambridge
(Brooke Crutchley, University Printer)

TO

PETER LASLETT

CONTENTS

FOREWORD

This volume is the first English publication of John Locke's earliest writings on politics.* It contains the texts of these works, one in English, the other in Latin, with a translation of the Latin document, notes on the texts and their intellectual and political environment, and an introductory essay.

The writings deal with a question of religious toleration: the question whether freedom of practice should be allowed in indifferent matters of ceremony and ritual or whether governments had the authority to impose a set form. Although this issue appeared to be the 'Great Question' of the age to Locke and his contemporaries in the winter of 1660–1, it is hardly compelling today. Such interest as the two works have now springs rather from the fact that the issue forced Locke to take up a number of more fundamental problems concerning the nature of government. By the time he had finished he had committed to paper an elaborate and quite rigorous statement of a complete political philosophy. Even were this philosophy not strikingly at odds with that implicit in his later writings, these first works would therefore deserve some scrutiny.

Locke gave no title to his papers on indifferent things. Their only heading is a statement of the problem to be discussed. Some convenient short title was required and I have named them Locke's *Tracts on Government*. Their polemical character, their similarity of form with the *Two Treatises*, and their underlying concern with questions of law and obligation will, I hope, justify this choice.

I should like to thank those who have helped me: first my wife for help so tireless and varied that the book is almost as much hers as mine; then St Antony's College, Oxford, and Peterhouse, Cambridge, for time and stimulation; Peterhouse, again, for a historical education; the Faculty of Economics and Politics at Cambridge for a timely grant; E. J. Kenney for the care and scholarship he devoted to rescuing me from many difficulties

* An Italian edition appeared in 1961: C. A. Viano, *John Locke: Scritti Editi e Inediti sulla Tolleranza*, Taylor Torino, Collezione di Filosofia, Documenti e Ricerche.

with the Latin translation; Dr W. von Leyden for his meticulous criticism of the entire work at two stages of its development; Dr Kenneth Dewhurst for information and advice about Locke's work in chemistry and medicine; Jill Steinberg for nobly reading proofs and helping with the index; and Maurice Cranston, E. S. de Beer, Ernesto de Marchi, J. W. Gough, Christopher Hill, Philip Long, W. E. Molyneux, Elizabeth Papanikolaou, Peter Thirlby and Brian Wormald for help on many points of detail and for conversations which encouraged and guided me at successive stages of the work. My greatest debt is acknowledged in the dedication.

September 1965   P. A.

INTRODUCTION

I

JOHN LOCKE AS A CONSERVATIVE

Why should John Locke at the age of thirty have written two heavy-handed defences of authoritarian government? Having written them, why should he then have suppressed them? That he did both, and in doing so provided further evidence of the fragile and conditional nature of liberalism, is the occasion for this book. The importance of the two tracts which were Locke's first contribution to moral and political philosophy is twofold: they encourage a thorough reappraisal of Locke in his familiar role as the great English liberal; and they are in themselves records to a consequential moment in intellectual history—a moment when the received tools of political thought proved inadequate to resolve the problems posed by experience. At thirty Locke chanced to be faced with an intolerable situation. He met it in a characteristically Lockeian way—by retreating under pressure from reason to faith and from liberty to authority.

The argument that leads me to these conclusions is a simple one. It is powerfully supported by the evidence of Locke's papers—if we will only read them without requiring them in advance to reveal a liberal. But it has to be developed in a piecemeal and circuitous manner.

THE LOCKE PAPERS

First, what are the raw materials we have to identify and interpret? The Lovelace Collection of Locke manuscripts acquired by the Bodleian Library in 1947 contains some 2,700 letters and about 1,000 miscellaneous items including notebooks, journals, accounts, academic exercises and drafts of several of Locke's published works.[1] Among them is a set of early writings on political and philosophical subjects. One group of these, dealing with the status and obligation of natural law, has been published by W. von Leyden. There are also two texts in Locke's hand about the power of government over 'indifferent' things, the nature of magistracy and the obligation of subjects. It is these texts, unpublished for 300 years, that are edited here.[2] They were Locke's first attempt at sustained political and ethical argument. I shall refer to them henceforth as Locke's *Tracts on Government*. They are in every sense profoundly conservative works.

One of these writings (MS Locke e. 7) is in English and has the title, *Question: whether the Civill Magistrate may lawfully impose and determine the use of indifferent things in reference to Religious Worship*. The other (MS Locke c. 28, fols. 3 ff.) is in Latin with the title, *An Magistratus Civilis possit res adiaphoras in divini cultus ritus asciscere, eosque populo imponere? Aff:* There are thirty-six manuscript pages and slightly under 20,000 words of the English work and just over 10,000 words and eighteen pages of the Latin one. The last page and a half of the English work are in the form of a letter addressed to an unnamed correspondent and dated 11 December 1660.

These two *Tracts* are our main concern. The Locke manuscripts are full of supplementary items which give them meaning and context. On the reverse pages of a notebook headed *Lemmata* ('themes') there is a draft version of the Latin work which differs in many details from the final text and has twenty-two lines missing from the beginning. This notebook (MS Locke e. 6) also contains drafts of six of the writings on natural law. Then there is a manuscript headed *The Preface to the Reader* (MS Locke c. 28, fol. 1) which is unquestionably meant as an introduction to a published version of the English work. Some tendentious extracts from this *Preface* were printed by King in his biography of Locke.[3] It is published here in full. There is a long, undated but obviously early letter in which Locke criticizes a defence of religious toleration just published by his correspondent, 'S.H.'. Other letters exchanged by Locke and his family and friends between 1659 and 1662 throw light on the date and intention of the tracts and on the mood in which Locke wrote them. Among them are three in which a project to publish at least one of the writings is debated. Finally, there is the rich evidence of the commonplace books, the medical and scientific notebooks and the reading lists—evidence that maps the elaborate and unsatisfactory intellectual system with which Locke was burdened in 1660. A number of these items and the problems of interpretation that they raise are discussed in detail in Appendix II.

The English *Tract* is a point-by-point refutation of a pamphlet published in Oxford in 1660 by Edward Bagshaw the younger, *The Great Question Concerning Things Indifferent in Religious Worship*. Bagshaw urges, mainly on scriptural grounds, that the individual should be allowed to observe or disregard religious ceremonial according to his conscience. Since ceremonies are agreed to be 'indifferent' it cannot be a matter of any ultimate moral consequence whether they are observed or not. A man who has a conscientious objection to a particular ceremony should not be forced to perform it.

In refuting this dangerous argument Locke works his way through the text of the *Great Question* meticulously. With only a few opportune omissions he quotes and scrutinizes the whole of Bagshaw's argument sentence by sentence. His own alternative opinion emerges piecemeal through the piling up of his objections to Bagshaw. He treats his own observations on general questions of power and obedience as digressions. His purpose is to isolate the problem of indifferent things in the most specific and narrowly limited way possible. He avoids fundamental questions of political theory by blandly asserting their irrelevance:

> But I too forwardly intrude myself into the council chamber and like an impertinent traveller which am concerned only which way the hand of the dial points, lose time in searching after the spring and wheels that give it motion. It being our duty not curiously to examine the counsels but cheerfully to obey the commands of the magistrate in all things that God hath left us free.

But Locke was a conscientious intellectual craftsman. In the Latin work he takes up the general theoretical problems which he had previously set aside. Bagshaw is not mentioned. The conclusions of the English work are drawn together in a formal, rigorously argued general defence of the authority of governments to impose ceremonies or any other indifferent acts on their subjects. He sets out an impeccably structured exercise in deductive reasoning—a monument to the scope and internal cogency of scholastic thought even in its last days.

Nevertheless, the evasions of the English work remain as critical weaknesses in the argument of the Latin writing as well. They are most apparent in Locke's efforts to close the case for imposition by exploiting the concept of natural law. He does not, of course, admit the difficulties that this stratagem created. But I think he recognized them. And if he did we may say that the problems he faced in 1660 were the foundation of his entire intellectual career.

AN INTERPRETATION

In 1660 John Locke, a Student of Christ Church, was embarked on a routine clerical career.[4] He had received, without conspicuous complaint, the orthodox education of a schoolman. His world lay between his father's home at Pensford in Somerset and his circle of friends at the university. A surprising number of these friends were themselves Somerset men or had connexions there. Bristol and Oxford were the poles of his little world. His life exemplified the traditional small-scale social order of the professional classes of a feudal society. He had been educated to share the skills and assumptions of a traditional scholarship. But he had lived through two decades in which both the traditional way of life and the traditional ways of thought had been under continual attack. The theme of his early letters is the theme of insecurity: 'Where is that great Diana of the world Reason?... there is not a man but thinks he alone hath this light within and all besides stumble in the dark.'[5] His first reaction was a defensive one. In 1660 he reiterates the old certainties. And he does so, in his own words, with just 'that regulated motion which a pedantical fencer would prescribe'.[6]

Locke's intellectual development thus embodies a sweeping reconstitution of ideology. He started by invoking the resources of a traditional academic world-view. He sought to discipline a troublesome political issue by referring it to the moral norms and epistemological axioms of an elaborate, formally structured and established system of ideas. But the issue escaped and in doing so exposed a critical gap in traditional moral argument. Most of his contemporaries and predecessors had lapsed into assertiveness rather than recognize this gap. Locke recognized it, examined it and was led to dismantle the old intellectual structure. His initial need for access to natural law triggered off a long exploration of the sources of knowledge and produced eventually a new conception of the status of moral laws, a new conception of political society. From a late statement of the old ideology in the 1660s he arrived in the 1690s at an authoritative adumbration of the new.

The momentum for this revolution in thought was supplied by his own intellectual curiosity and by his continuing search for principles of moral authority. More than any other issue of seventeenth-century politics, the great question of indifferent things had made the need for such principles an urgent one. But, to effect the transformation, it needed a man as sensitive to ambiguity as Locke and as determined as he to prove 'morality as well as mathematics capable of demonstration'. It needed an ideologist. But in setting out at this stage the elements of my general interpretation I, also, 'too forwardly' anticipate an argument. We must begin with more immediate matters of evidence and context. How did Locke come to write the tracts? What is in them? And in so far as their content is authoritarian, how can it be squared with our image of Locke as the presiding genius of liberal democracy?

LOCKE'S AUTHORITARIANISM

One obstacle to answering these questions can be cleared at once: we can establish the exact quality of Locke's early authoritarianism. It was both more fundamental and less extreme than has been supposed.

In 1830 King printed some sections of *The Preface to the Reader* and on the strength of these described the young Locke as a champion of an arbitrary authority. Later writers have followed him; it is the illiberal aspect of the *Tracts* that has been most remarked; he is described as a 'man of the Right', an 'extreme authoritarian', 'definitely Hobbesian'. But King also published a number of other writings of a plainly liberal character which he identified as coming from Locke's 'Commonplace Book for 1661'. And again later writers have followed his lead: it is held that the letter to 'S. H.' reveals him as, in his own term, an 'admirer' of the notorious champion of toleration, Henry Stubbe, in 1659; the 'theoretical outlines' of his mature liberal philosophy are perceived by several authors in his writings as early as 1661.[7]

And, since Locke is thought of as somehow a liberal in both 1659 and 1661, the *Tracts*, for all their supposed extreme authoritarianism, are seen as a temporary aberration, a lapse, even by one author as a *volte face*. In 1660, it is argued, Locke abandoned his normal liberalism under the pressure of an ephemeral political crisis, only to recover equally quickly as the crisis passed. The English *Tract* with its *Preface* was obviously meant to be published. Why did the project fail? An obvious answer is that by 1661, when the question of publication became urgent, Locke had become, or become again, a liberal. He suppressed the *Tract* because he no longer endorsed its arguments.[8]

7

These views are not unfounded. But their foundations are shaky ones. There is no evidence that Locke was a liberal prior to 1660—however that word is defined. And there is ample evidence that the defence of authority he produced in 1660 was tempered by 'no less a love of liberty'.

All we can say with confidence about Locke's political thinking prior to December 1660 is that he wanted to be left alone. He was sceptical and timorous: 'I would be quiet and I would be safe', he writes and adds, 'but if I cannot enjoy them together the last must certainly be had at any rate.' His sense of insecurity was explicitly intellectual—it is the uncertainty of knowledge, the chaos of opinions, that make him anxious. The authority for which he feels a need is therefore intellectual authority: ''Tis our passions that brutish part that dispose our thoughts and actions...when did ever any truth settle itself in any one's mind by the strength and authority of its own evidence?', 'we are all Centaurs...and every one's *recta ratio* is but the traverses of his own steps.' And from here it is but a short step to the view from which the nervous energy of the two *Tracts* flows: 'If private men's judgments were the moulds wherein laws were to be cast 'tis a question whether we should have any at all.' To be safe, as Locke saw the world, was to discover an authority that could override private men's judgments. The problem was epistemological as much as it was political.[9]

I can find no reason to call Locke's thought liberal (in the sense that the *Letters Concerning Toleration* are liberal) before 1667. The admiration expressed in the letter to 'S.H.' is ambiguous. The letter itself reveals an enthusiasm for the idea of toleration severely hedged about with doubts as to its practical effects; will it, he asks, 'consist with the security of the nation'? What he admires is the agility and learning with which Stubbe swept aside the complexities of the problem. But for him the problem remained: 'Seeing you yourself', he tells his correspondent,

make the apprehensions of interest and the justice of the cause the rule and measure of constance to, activity for, and obedience under any government, you can never hope that they should cordially concur with you to any establishment whose consciences and concernments both for this world and hereafter shall always bias them another way.

In any event, Stubbe's *Essay in Defence of the Good Old Cause* (which is almost certainly the book discussed in the letter), although it argues for toleration, is itself not exactly a liberal work. Stubbe's proposal was for a compulsory toleration imposed by the 'good people...possessed with the Militia'.[10]

The only other important evidence for Locke's early liberalism is the so-called 'Commonplace Book for 1661' quoted by King. So far as I can tell, no such book exists. The passages printed by King come from two separate notebooks and all of them are plainly dated by Locke as entries made after 1680. Thus, the notes on 'Virtue', which King says 'must have been written very early', are dated 1681; those on the Church are dated 1681 and 1698. In short there is nothing in the Locke papers earlier than 1667 which suggests any sort of support for the practice of religious toleration or for any other form of permissive government.[11]

The interpretation of the *Tracts* as expressions of an extreme authoritarianism can also be disposed of. King's selection of passages from *The Preface to the Reader* which initiated this interpretation is quite startlingly misleading. Locke describes the world and his own sympathies as 'perpetually kept tumbling' between the extremes of liberty and authority. King printed only those passages in which the advantages of authority are enumerated. The distinctive Lockeian sense of balance, tension and ambiguity is obliterated. Later writers have followed King's treatment, noting the dramatic aspect of the *Tracts* (the tipping of the balance on the side of authority) rather than their total structure. Yet Locke's position is plain enough: his defence of authority reflects the intensity of his sense of insecurity: 'I no sooner perceived myself in the world but I found myself in a storm, which hath lasted almost hitherto, and therefore cannot but entertain the approaches of a calm with the greatest joy and satisfaction.' He asserts the need for authority specifically and exclusively in respect of issues which the champions of liberty themselves 'confess to be little and at most are but indifferent'. The authority he upholds is that of laws and of established legislators without regard to the basis of the legislators' power and in a field where it is agreed that the content of law is irrelevant, where the choice is between any law and no law: ''Tis therefore in defence of the authority of these laws that against many reasons I am drawn to appear in public.' His commitment is to the necessity for law in the face of a rampant and logically irreducible individualism: 'Were every indifferent thing left unlimited nothing would be lawful.'[12]

The authoritarianism of the *Tracts* is, then, a limited defence of a special form of authority. Their extreme quality derives more from the logical absolutism of the concept of indifferency than from any enthusiasm for civil power as such. If indifferent things were allowed to escape from the restraints of law all social order could in theory be dissolved, 'magistracy itself will at last be concluded anti-Christian'. Because these things *were* indifferent it seemed reasonable to Locke, as well as politically essential, that they should be bound by law. Experience confirmed the logic of his position: 'He must be a stranger to England that thinks that meats and habits, that places and times of worship, etc., would not be... sufficient occasion of hatred and quarrels amongst us.' But it was the logic of the position that most interested him, his 'design being only the clearing a truth in question'.

THE ENGLISH 'TRACT'

In preparing his work for publication Locke decided to spare his readers 'the history or occasion of its original'. The only certain information he has left us is the date, 11 December 1660, on the letter at the end of the English work. On that date the *Tract* was finished and sent to an unidentified correspondent. All the other evidence is circumstantial.

Locke had 'discoursed of' Bagshaw's pamphlet with his correspondent and wrote his own *Tract* at the latter's instigation. It is just possible that the work was commissioned by the new Dean of Christ Church, John Fell, who was himself involved in a running fight with Bagshaw in the winter of 1660–1. More probably it was the product of discussions with a friend and it seems likely that that friend was Gabriel Towerson of All Souls. Towerson and Locke seem to have exchanged letters about the politics of toleration fairly regularly at this date. In 1663 Towerson published a work of his own on a linked theme.[13]

Bagshaw's pamphlet was published on 15 September 1660. Locke may have seen the text before publication as Bagshaw was himself a Student of Christ Church at this time and the practice of circulating manuscripts before publication was a standard one. We do not however know where Locke was in the early autumn of 1660. He spent a good deal of time at Pensford throughout this period as his father was mortally ill there. On 23 October Towerson wrote to Locke at Pensford giving him news of events in Oxford in previous weeks. Bagshaw is not mentioned but the mutual interest of Locke and Towerson in ecclesiastical politics was evidently already overt. Towerson notes the publication of John Pearson's *No Necessity of Reformation* (Oxford, 20 August 1660), which, he says, 'will I believe give you much content...for the assurance he there gives of a sudden and just reply to all their exceptions against the doctrine, discipline and ceremonies of the Church of England'.

It seems likely that Locke returned to Oxford soon after receiving this letter. He was certainly there in mid November and it was probably at this time that he encountered Bagshaw's work and had the conversations in which he was 'engaged' to write a reply. There is some evidence that he went again to Pensford in late November or early December and that he wrote the English *Tract* there. The deleted address on the letter of 11 December that accompanies the tract is more likely to be Pensford than Oxford. Locke speaks of being 'careful to sequester my thoughts both from books and the times' when he wrote the *Tract*. Pensford, which he always refers to as an intellectual backwater, would certainly have provided such sequestration. There is a half page of notes bearing on the argument of the *Tract* on the back of a letter of May 1660 from a family friend, John Strachey, to Locke's father at Pensford. Towerson was in Oxford at this time and distance would explain (if Towerson was indeed the recipient of the *Tract*) why Locke added the formal letter of 11 December to his text.[14]

In any event, Locke was in Oxford again by 20 December when he wrote urging his father to consult his doctor. On the 22nd he was elected into his first official post in Christ Church.

It seems that the *Tract* took something up to six weeks to write and that Locke and Towerson then pursued the problems it raised in correspondence and conversation for another year. Towerson twice urged Locke to publish the *Tract* in the spring of 1661. 'Mr Bagshawe's book', he wrote on 12 March, 'is so well liked ...that it is probable it may pass a second impression', 'you may perhaps do God and the Church a piece of seasonable service if you...print your answer to it.' (Bagshaw's book, in fact, went through three impressions in the course of the year.) And a month after Towerson's second appeal to Locke we find the publisher James Allestry writing on 14 May 1661 'in answer to yours of the

7th instant' to announce that 'the treatise you left in my hand will be put to the press tomorrow and all expedition used in its dispatch'.[15]

Allestry's letter is not addressed to Locke himself but to his close friend (and Somerset neighbour) Samuel Tilly of Hart Hall. It is preserved in Locke's papers, however. And there is independent evidence in letters between Locke and Tilly that the latter had a copy of the *Tract* in 1661 and was interested in its publication. No work by Tilly was published (or written?) that year. It is virtually certain that the treatise mentioned by Allestry was in fact Locke's English *Tract*. Locke, in other words, was serious in his declared intention to publish anonymously and entrusted the business to Tilly as a further precaution. This procedure is quite in conformity with the way he went about publishing his later works.[16]

April–May 1661 was perhaps the ideal time for such a publication. No religious settlement had yet been achieved although the machinery for building one had been set up. The Savoy Commission was called to review the 'forms of prayer' on 25 March, and it met on 15 April. By the end of May it had provoked a pamphlet war as virulent as any in the previous twenty years. But it was not yet clear that this was all it would achieve. In Oxford Bagshaw was still well enough placed on 26 March to preach in the University Church, making it 'a mark of Anti-Christ to impose ceremonies', as Towerson informed Locke. And Locke allowed himself to be persuaded to publish; the parliamentary references in *The Preface to the Reader* show that he could not have written it earlier than 8 May 1661. Allestry's urgent request for 'the title page and what other additions you shall think fitting to make it complete' was made on the 14th.

Why, then, was the *Tract* not published? Several answers have been suggested. King and Gough argue that Locke was repelled by the policy of 'rigidly Anglican uniformity' adopted and imposed by the government in the summer of 1661, that this policy was too authoritarian for him and led him to have second thoughts about his argument. Von Leyden suggests that by mid 1661 Locke's 'theory of consent' had developed to a point where it superseded the authoritarian opinions of the *Tract*. Alternatively, he argues that the publication of works by Sanderson and Ussher had given the world such authoritative statements of the case for imposition that Locke felt his own contribution had been made superfluous. Cranston holds that with the expulsion of Bagshaw from Christ Church Locke lost interest in the discussion—and that in any event Bagshaw had been 'answered' adequately by Bishop Morley.[17]

None of these explanations will suffice. The dispute between Bagshaw and Morley was about a different issue. Bagshaw was expelled, in his own view, 'for no reason at all that I know of unless for the impartial and unbiased discovery of my judgment about indifferent or rather doubtful things in religious worship'—but not until the winter of 1661. His *Second Part of the Great Question* was published in September 1661 when he was still able to sign himself 'Student of Christ Church'. The decisive failure to publish Locke's *Tract* must have occurred before this.[18]

The same reason tells against the arguments about Locke's 'development' and his revulsion from government policy. If Allestry had the *Tract* ready for the printer on 14 May the reason for the failure of the project must lie in some decision or inaction on his part, or on Locke's, very soon after that date. But immediately before that date we find Locke penning his most explicit endorsement of authority and imposition in *The Preface to the Reader*. It is unlikely that Locke developed from an authoritarian defender of imposed forms of religion into a liberal in the course of a week—especially as the harshness of the government's religious policy (which Locke implicitly welcomes in *The Preface to the Reader*) did not become apparent until midsummer or later.

There are other possibilities, however. It may be that it was Allestry and not Locke who decided against publication. At some time in his life Locke certainly acquired a strong dislike of publishers and booksellers as a class. An unhappy experience in an early attempt to publish might account for this. Or it is possible that it was Tilly who delayed matters by failing to forward Locke's last 'additions' to the publisher. Tilly's role is somewhat enigmatic. He seems to have won a reputation for unreliability. Despite repeated requests Locke could not get his manuscript back from him until the spring of 1662. By that time it is quite likely that some liberal development of his ideas or some revulsion from the practical effects of the Clarendon Code could have dissuaded him from publication.[19]

But my own impression is that Locke himself decided in May

1661 that the *Tract* need not be published and that he did so for more powerful reasons than that his argument had been voiced by more eminent authors. It was government action in the Parliament of that month that made the *Tract* superfluous. When Locke wrote in December 1660, the government had not yet given the nation laws in respect of indifferent things. The debate between him and Bagshaw was about what the magistrate ought to do at a time when he had not yet done anything. Both authors agreed that the question could be resolved by magisterial action. In a retrospective apology Bagshaw himself made this point: 'I handled the question when it was *res integra*. . .since parliament have decided the controversy and put the matter out of question I think myself discharged from meddling with it.'[20]

And if this argument carried weight for Bagshaw it must surely have carried much more for Locke. *The Preface to the Reader* speaks of the 'tenderness' shown by the monarch in opening Parliament as providing a basis for settlement. But this was a tenderness only towards the past. Speaking of the Act of Indemnity Charles made it clear on 8 May that the moderation of the previous winter was now at an end: 'In God's name provide full remedies for any future mischiefs. . .be as severe as you will against new offenders . . .and pull up those principles by the roots.' Clarendon's speech on the same occasion was blunter still. And the debates on Church Order that followed echoed his tone. On 13 May the Commons agreed that all Members should be compelled to take the sacrament according to the Liturgy. On the 17th they decided to burn the Covenant. Events and the government thus made the publication of Locke's *Tract* unnecessary, not by violating his trust but by fulfilling his hopes. By the end of May 1661 the lack of positive law which had made it legitimate and necessary to debate the status of indifferent things had been made good.[21]

This and his vehemently expressed distaste for public controversy would surely have been enough to lead Locke to abandon publication. Publication now could only exacerbate a dispute that was in principle ended. As he says in *The Preface to the Reader*, 'I now run upon the same guilt I condemned in others, disturbing the beginning of our happy settlement by engaging in a quarrel which it would be well if it were quite forgotten.' Locke shared the common opinion of intellectuals about the importance of ideas and writings in politics, accusing:

the pens of Englishmen of as much guilt as their swords judging that the issue of blood from whence such an inundation hath flowed had scarce been opened...had men been more sparing of their ink, and that these furies, war, cruelty, rapine, confusion, etc., which have so wearied and wasted this poor nation have been conjured up in private studies and from thence sent abroad to disturb the quiet we enjoyed.

Believing this, he had little reason after May 1661 'to hazard again the substantial blessings of peace and settlement in an over-zealous contention about things...indifferent'.

By the end of 1661 Locke's interest had probably moved forward from the debate on indifferent things as such to the broader problems that the great question opened up. The Latin *Tract*, which is certainly a later work than the English one, itself suggests a movement in this direction. In a letter to Locke in the autumn of 1661 Towerson looks back on an elaborate and detailed discussion between Locke and himself. He notes that the 'papers between us' have grown 'so voluminous that I conceive it more difficult to inform ourselves of the state of the controversy between us, than to retell what either of us hath said'. And he ends by urging Locke to turn his attention to new and more fundamental questions:

Consider but these two things which I have now to propose to you, whether (it being agreed on between us that there is such a thing as a law of nature...) it were not much more for our advantage to proceed in our enquiry touching the law of nature than to contend any longer about a secondary argument; 2, I would willingly know of you whether you think the law of nature can be evinced from the force of conscience in those men who have no other (divine) rule to square their actions by.[22]

The secondary argument was presumably that on indifferent things. Certainly indifferency occupies a secondary place in the theory of law Locke develops in the *Tracts*. And towards the end of 1661 Locke did turn his attention to problems of the competence and accessibility of natural law, as we know from the *Essays* edited by Von Leyden. The fifth *Essay* deals directly with Towerson's second question.

The correspondence with Towerson may thus have provided the chronological link between the English *Tract* and Locke's later interests. But the *Tract* itself suggests that there were also intrinsic logical connections. The ephemeral problem of indifferent cere-monies raised fundamental questions which Locke was to explore and re-explore for the rest of his life.[23]

THE LATIN 'TRACT'

The origin and occasion of the Latin *Tract* can be more briefly described. A reference to Robert Sanderson as Bishop of Lincoln tells us the extreme limits within which it was written. Sanderson was consecrated on 29 October 1660 and died on 27 January 1662/3. That it is a later work than the English *Tract* seems clear from the more generalized form of argument and from Locke's use of the writings of Sanderson and Hooker, which he claimed not to know when he wrote the English *Tract*. He now draws heavily on Sanderson's lectures *De Obligatione Conscientiae* (published, by Allestry, in February 1659/60) and on at least the first book of the *Laws of Ecclesiastical Polity*.

The fact that the draft version of the Latin *Tract* is found at the beginning of a notebook which contains drafts of the *Essays on the Law of Nature* suggests that it was penned at about the same time as the first of the natural law writings was begun, in 1661–2. A passing and jocular reference to the appointment of 'Rhetores' invites an association of the *Tract* with Locke's own appointment as Rhetor (Praelector Rhetoricus) in Christ Church on Christmas Eve 1662.

The form and content of the *Tract* make this association the more plausible—everything about it suggests a formal academic oration. It resembles nothing so much as the set-piece *Excercitationes* and *Orationes* published in Oxford by numerous college and university officials, including Edward Bagshaw, in the seventeenth century.[24] The formula of the title and the precisely structured argument, 'proceeding, as the schools do, *ad determinandum*', as Selden puts it, are in the orthodox convention of this type of exercise. In the light of Locke's professed aversion to scholastic terminology and methods, his slavish use of both in the Latin *Tract* also suggests that the work was meant for formal submission to an academic audience. As he had written to Stubbe, schoolmen had to be argued with in school terms.[25]

He speaks of himself at the beginning of the *Tract* as entering the 'gymnasium', as arriving 'proponere thesin'. Following Cicero he uses a terminology that applies ambiguously to battles and disputations. Nor is it likely that a piece so full of unacknowledged borrowing from the lately published work of Sanderson was itself meant for public consumption. In a private lecture on the other hand extensive plagiarism could pass as a legitimate dependence upon a familiar and revered authority. And why else should Locke have written in Latin?

The presence of the Latin draft in the same volume as drafts of the writings on natural law supports the idea of a conscious intellectual continuity between the *Tracts on Government* and the *Essays*. It suggests that all these works may have been in the first instance a single project—perhaps a course of lectures. James Tyrrell, a close friend of Locke's at this time, did later refer to the natural law writings as 'lectures'. Here again we glimpse the possibility of an unbroken thread of enquiry running from Locke's first conversations with Towerson to the *Essay on Human Understanding* and beyond.[26]

THE GREAT QUESTION

Formally, the debate between Locke and Bagshaw concerns the moral status of ceremonies associated with religious worship. Essentially, it is an argument about the nature of law: 'The question', as Bagshaw put it, 'is not of convenience but of lawfulness, not *cui bono?* but *quo iure?*' A summary in abstract of what each man had to say will be useful at this point.

There are five relevant works: Bagshaw's *Great Question*, published 15 September 1660; Locke's English *Tract*, finished by 11 December 1660; Bagshaw's *Second Part of the Great Question*, published in September 1661; Locke's Latin *Tract*; and Bagshaw's *Third Part*, published January 1662. Locke's English *Tract* apart, it is not clear that the two men ever wrote specifically against one another. Yet there is a sequential development of their arguments.

Both authors agree on four fundamental positions. They agree that it is meaningful to speak of a logically watertight sphere of morally neutral actions: 'I will suppose that there are some things in their own nature indifferent...I mean those outward circumstances of our actions which the law of God hath left free and arbitrary.' Both authors agree that this natural indifferency is in fact a relative and dependent condition; they are speaking of actions which are neither good nor evil in respect of *certain* rules. Indifferent things may be invested with a second-order necessity by moral authorities 'lower' than the revealed will of God, but derived from and authorized by it and so 'higher' than the indifferent acts themselves. Both authors thus agree in subscribing to a hierarchic and legalistic idea of moral obligation; they both allow

17

that decisive moral authority is embodied in and expressed as law; the problem for both of them was to identify those laws relevant to indifferent things and to establish in some unequivocal way their respective authority and competence; in particular to establish whether or not the civil magistrate was empowered to make laws making indifferent things necessary for his subjects. And finally both agree in an ostentatious enthusiasm for the restored monarchy; both look to the king to effect the political and ecclesiastical settlement they desire:

'None', writes Bagshaw, 'is more satisfied with the present government or hath a more loyal and affectionate esteem for his Majesty's person and prudence than this writer...he doth heartily wish that all parties would agree to refer the whole cause of ceremonies to his Majesty's single discretion.'[27]

Locke of course echoes the sentiment; and where he speaks of his 'submission for authority', Bagshaw repudiates both active disobedience, 'a practice he abhors' and passive 'repining' which 'he can by no means approve of'. Like Locke Bagshaw upholds an extensive and authoritarian competence of magistracy in all civil affairs; he claims liberty only in respect of religious ceremonial.

But here their agreement ends. The settlements they urge on the King are incompatible. The political and moral theories on which they ground their appeals to his discretion conflict at every point. Bagshaw maintains that neither the magistrate nor any Christian may determine the use of any indifferent thing of a religious character for any other Christian. Locke replies that the magistrate, and he alone, can and must determine the use of any or all indifferent things at his own discretion.

Bagshaw's argument starts from the theological assumption that a sense of spiritual integrity rooted in conscience is essential to the devout Christian and not to be violated at any cost. Moral status is assigned to all actions by the will of God expressed as law. This will is made known in Scripture. The basic distinction is between necessary and indifferent acts; indifferency is a category established by divine law and irreducible for that reason. Indifferent things can be subdivided in two ways; in terms of whether or not they are treated as indifferent; and in terms of whether their reference is civil or religious. We thus have four logically distinct types of indifferency:

	Civil	Religious
Treated as such	A	B
Not treated as such	C	D

It is type D that concerns us. Power over civil indifferent things is delivered to the magistrate by general precepts of the divine law; in this respect the magistrate 'bears not the sword in vain'. But it follows from the nature of indifferency that there ought not to be any actions in category D; any that are are there unlawfully. For Bagshaw the only relevant law in this respect is the law of God delivered in Scripture; his theological and legal arguments are inseparable. Scripture establishes that the defining characteristic of Christianity is liberty, expressed in the spontaneity of Christian worship. He demonstrates the nature and necessity of this liberty from the precepts of the Gospels, from the fundamental principle of charity that governs Christian behaviour, from the practice of Christ and the Apostles, and from the principle that what a man thinks sinful is sinful for him—to force a man to sin in a matter agreed to be indifferent is a sin in the imposer, i.e. unlawful.

He thus produces a general syllogistic case for liberty: Christians must be free; they cannot be free in things necessary; things are either necessary or indifferent; Christians must be free in things indifferent. For this category of acts the only law-giver, under God, is the conscience of the individual which, because the acts are indifferent and therefore 'answerable to inward impressions', gives commands which are properly laws for the individual. Thus, it will always be lawful for any individual to do or omit anything in this category in the light of his own beliefs about it. And it will never be lawful for the use of any such thing to be imposed by the magistrate and so treated as more than indifferent.

Locke's problem was thus to make a case for civil law which would allow its authority to be interposed between the revealed will of God which left ceremonies indifferent and the conscience of each and every individual. His argument has perforce to be more directly political than Bagshaw's.

He starts, appropriately, from a political assumption—that men are so depraved and partial in their own causes that if they are not bound to a common order in society they will destroy one another and themselves. A theory of law is the ostensible foundation of both *Tracts*. But it is not the rational weight of this theory that sustains and informs Locke's writing. Rather, it is an instinctive commitment to government as a means of order, a conviction that the free use of indifferent things spells civil chaos. He broods on the perversity, self-love and dissidence of men. It is a vivid sense of the sociological necessity of government that inspires the *Tracts*. The imposition of indifferent things by magistrates is treated as a necessary condition of government.

Now Bagshaw had in fact noted in the *Great Question* that the case for imposition was usually based on a second-order consequential argument about the political effects of freedom and not on the fundamental theological argument about the moral status of indifferent actions. He recognized the weight of the divine command to decency and order in religious practice. But he maintained that order and liberty could be reconciled. For Christians order is by consent, not constraint. Those who deny the compatibility of liberty and order do so on the strength of an unwarranted sinister view of human nature. The disorder they envisage so gloomily is not disorder but variety. And the order required by God is compact of variety; it entails personal sobriety and responsibility but not an imposed uniformity.

The argument from the necessity of order that Bagshaw controverts is of central importance in Locke's *Tracts*; and Bagshaw's criticism of it is the only major theme of the *Great Question* that Locke ignores in his reply. This is the most striking weakness of the *Tracts*. Perhaps it suggests the force of Locke's own sinister view of his fellows.

He opens his case by rejecting the distinctions made by Bagshaw within the category of indifferency. He asserts the logical indivisibility of the concept. If an act relevant to religion is indifferent, then it is indistinguishable from any other non-necessary act. An all-or-nothing ruling on indifferency is required; any indifferent thing may be treated by misguided people as necessary; no distinction between civil and religious indifferencies is viable. Indifferent things are all those things not specifically required or prohibited by God; any indifferent thing can be made relevant to either government or worship by the customs and prejudices of particular men or societies. What we have to decide is the legal status of *all* indifferent acts, not of a spurious sub-category. But to permit individual freedom in the use of all indifferent things is to open the door to chaos and disorder. It follows as a condition of order that all indifferent things ought to be susceptible to civil law.

Thus, where Bagshaw concentrates rather narrowly on the particular religious ceremonies in dispute in 1660—the time and place of meeting for worship, set forms of prayer, the wearing of surplices, kneeling at the Lord's Supper, making the sign of the cross in baptism, bowing at the name of Jesus, etc.—Locke constantly introduces purely civil ceremonies into the discussion. On what ground can one object to a set time for worship if one approves civil anniversaries—such as the anniversary thanksgiving enjoined by Parliament for the Stuart restoration?

Locke re-examines Bagshaw's scriptural evidence and concludes that it nowhere tells against the all-or-nothing application which the concept of indifferency requires. He finds that there are no general prohibitions in Scripture against the imposing of indifferent things by magistrates; that Christ and the Apostles used indifferent things as circumstances and considerations of convenience, decency and order prompted; that the liberty given to Christians is not a liberty of use; and that it is compatible with the imposition of set forms of worship by magistrates.

Christian liberty, he holds, is a liberty of belief, not of practice; of judgment, not use. Christians are freed from believing that any indifferent thing is necessary to their salvation. What matters for the preservation of Christian liberty in indifferent things is not, therefore, any particular actions but the conscientious conviction that no actions are in themselves morally necessary. The necessary liberty of Christians is the liberty of belief. There is also a liberty left men by the divine law in the use of indifferent things. But this latter freedom has no necessary practical consequences beyond the requirement that no use should be thought necessary.

Locke's examination of Scripture thus leads him to expose a serious gap in moral knowledge: it is not clear what use *ought* to be made of indifferent things. His theory of law is designed to close the gap. Meanwhile it follows from the nature of Christian liberty that if it *were* lawful for the magistrate to impose a set use of indifferent things Christian liberty would not be affected thereby—so long as subjects were not required to believe, or did not believe, that the use was intrinsically necessary either way. If subjects do treat such practices as necessary they sin. And if the magistrate tries to impose them as necessary he sins. But happily he cannot do this; the individual judgment is beyond his power of control and scrutiny. The necessary liberty of Christians is thus safe whether they obey the magistrate or not. It remains to show that he *may* impose and that subjects *must* then obey him.

He achieves this through his theory of law. His strategy is to show that magistrates are authorized to determine the use of indifferent things and that the nature of this authorization gives the rulings of magistrates a stronger obligation than those of the individual conscience. Because he is sufficiently authorized, the magistrate's commands are 'laws'. Because they are laws, they must be obeyed.

He defines law in a thoroughly voluntaristic manner. It is the will of its instigator that gives law its obligation. Law is the imperative expression of a competent will within its sphere of competence. A condition of lawlessness would be a condition of total indifferency; anyone could then do anything, not because any law empowered him to but because no law constrained his will. Whatever is not bound by law is indifferent—its use is a matter of arbitrary choice. The introduction of law ends this state of freedom or chaos by articulating an authoritative will and so establishing moral obligations. Who, then, is authorized to make laws affecting the use of indifferent things and how does he acquire his authority?

Locke distinguishes between four types of law-maker and four types of law standing in hierarchic relation to one another. At each level a law-making will creates moral necessities among acts left indifferent by the legislation of some higher authority.

At the highest level is divine law, that body of general norms and basic moral principles delivered directly by the will of God either as revelation (divine positive law) or as principles of reason (divine natural law). Whatever this law ignores remains indifferent and its use is free. But this residual area of indifferency creates a new situation in which any will is competent to determine any thing. Any determination and use of such things is lawful simply because a higher law has declared them all indifferent. Yet there are general injunctions of divine law, such as the command to 'decency and order' in worship, which seem to preclude lawlessness. There is need, rather, for a subsidiary level of law-making. This is the level of human or civil law: of those commands on the part of lawfully empowered human beings to their inferiors by

22

which the external aspects of human relationships are regulated. Evidently, such laws cannot affect things made necessary by the divine law; their matter, consequently, must be the things left indifferent by that law. Human lawgivers act under the divine law to give it concrete reference and application. They adjust the details of social life to the norms of the divine law.

At the level immediately below this we find what Locke calls the fraternal law. This is a law peculiar to Christianity. It is a law by which, under the general divine command to charity, Christians impose obligations on themselves out of respect for the conscientious feelings of their fellows. This law operates among things left indifferent by divine and human laws. Its effect is usually to produce voluntary abstention from acts which, although indifferent, might cause offence or scandal.

Finally, Locke recognizes a level of personal or private law: a body of obligations which a man may impose on himself in dealing with all or any of the things left indifferent by other laws. It has two forms, oath and contract. In either case it has the force of law because it is made by an act of will alienating rights in matters within the power of that will.

Thus, in every case the matter of a law is to be found among things left indifferent by some law above it. Over-arching and sanctioning the authority of each legislator is a higher legislator. In particular the argument requires that there should be human legislators invested with a power over all the indifferencies of the divine law. But this has still to be proved. It remains to show how and why the will of the civil magistrate is made authoritative, to show how power is vested in the magistrate and removed from everyone else.

Locke offers two theories of authorization. In the first the magistrate is directly authorized by God as an agent of the divine will. Things may be necessary, Locke argues, in two ways: because they are explicitly stated to be necessary by God; or because they are an indispensable means to achieving something explicitly stated to be necessary by God. Thus, although we are free to use indifferent things as we will, we are expressly bound to live in 'order'. Some uses of indifferent things will be more orderly than others. And order will vary from society to society, being in each a stable use of indifferent things suited to local habits, prejudices and institutions. Order is a necessity of the first kind and a set use of indifferent things thus becomes a necessity of the second kind. It is at once necessary and a matter for human discretion. The magistrate exists to determine the forms of order suited to his society and to impose them. The necessity of order transforms his commands into laws. The argument is *ex causa finale*. Within his sphere of action the magistrate is the 'vice-gerent' of God and a law-maker because he fulfils divine purposes. The sphere of action must be indifferent things and Locke has argued elsewhere that indifferent things cannot be properly split into civil and religious categories.

The weak point of this argument is that, while it postulates an unimpeachable source of authority for the magistrate, divine law is not in fact quite as explicit as the argument requires it to be. Rather, the terms of the divine will are either mysterious (natural law) or too accessible (Scripture); in either case they are excessively controversial. Locke therefore makes use of a second theory—a theory which lacks the manifestly moral authorization given to the magistrate by the first but which does effectively deprive subjects of their 'primitive' liberties.

It is essentially a Hobbesian argument that Locke deploys. The magistrate is man-made. The possible chaos implicit in the free use of indifferent things permitted by divine law is again Locke's point of departure. It has already been shown, he claims, that this free use, though permitted, is not necessary; it may consequently be alienated. Given the debauched nature of man it *must* be alienated if society is to survive. It is essential that some order should be distilled from the freedom all men have over all indifferent things. Being all equal in this respect, the will of each is a law for himself; but for no one else. No mutual obligation is possible unless each surrenders the competence of his own will over indifferencies and invests some other, the magistrate, with a competence to decide for him and thus for all. The magistrate emerges as a duly authorized law-maker because his will comprises and reconstitutes the wills of all his subjects. Thus, in respect of all those things over which the divine law initially gave individuals a lawful power, the magistrate's commands are, by virtue of the common and sociologically imperative surrender of rights, laws; they therefore oblige to obedience.

Locke presents these two arguments as alternatives, allowing the reader to make his own choice between them. Whichever is preferred, he argues, the effect is the same. In the Latin work he declares his own preference for a third view, combining both the others, in which the authority of magistracy in general is established by God while particular forms of government are created by the people. He concludes that any account of the origins of magistracy is thus also an account of the effective authorization of the magistrate to make laws about indifferent things.

CONTRACT AND NATURAL LAW IN LOCKE'S ARGUMENT

Locke claims that his use of a contract theory of government is hypothetical and a necessary rhetorical concession to the assumptions of his adversaries.[28] Neither claim stands up very well. Bagshaw, for example, does not invoke a contract theory. On the other hand Locke himself needed such a theory rather badly. The argument that a surrender of the free use of indifferencies is a necessary condition of government and that the magistrate is the product of that surrender had the advantage of at once granting the principle of individual freedom in indifferent things and simultaneously using that very freedom as the source of the magistrate's authority. More important, perhaps, by employing an argument from popular consent Locke was spared the more hazardous necessity of a close scrutiny of the law of God. In particular it was an alternative to an argument from natural law.

Locke's weakest arguments are those from Scripture. He seems to have been aware of this and tends, especially in the Latin *Tract*, to relegate scriptural arguments to the background of his thesis. But this creates a curious difficulty. His theory of law rests on the assumption that certain general injunctions of divine law can be treated as matters of established knowledge. The whole conception of derived authorizations which he uses as the sanction for magisterial power makes sense only if the will of the ultimate legislator, God, has some tangibility and specificity—which Scripture, in Locke's hands at least, could not give it.

This being so, it is very remarkable that Locke failed to provide any extended argument in terms of the second mode of divine law, the law of nature. Yet such an argument is not to be found in the *Tracts*. The 'particular conception of natural law' noted by Von Leyden in these works is a rudimentary one. References to natural law, where not actually suppressed in the manuscript, are invariably vague, conventional and assertive. Locke deleted the one passage in which he came near to developing the idea and giving it argumentative substance. In effect, although a theory of natural law and some demonstration of its accessibility were urgently required for his argument, the concept has no more than a symbolic weight in either tract. He invokes it as a 'principle' in T. D. Weldon's sense, as a convenient argumentative full stop, something axiomatic which he did not need to explore:

It was not therefore requisite that we should look for the magistrate's commission to be renewed in Scripture who was before even by the law of nature and the very condition of government sufficiently invested with a power over all indifferent actions.[29]

Where Owen, Stillingfleet, Sanderson, Locke's friend John Parry, and other of his contemporaries explored the idea of natural law at length in their efforts to reach political rulings on the question of indifferent things, Locke himself offers only such marginal and passing assurances. But, as Von Leyden points out, 'the ultimate support for his proof' of the need of magisterial imposition was 'derived from the concept of natural law'. The concept *ought* to have had more than the marginal status Locke allows it. Faced with the ambiguity of Scripture he infers that one cannot 'rationally conclude' that the magistrate has no power 'because we cannot find it in the Bible'. But where else could one look? Only to natural law. Powerful as is his argument from the consequences of freedom, it is not morally conclusive; as Bagshaw had already complained, 'truth is to be tried by the evidence and not by its consequences'. Nevertheless, in the *Tracts*, as later in the *Two Treatises*, Locke was content to take the evidence for granted and leave it unexplored so far as natural law was concerned. It was thus proper, and intellectually necessary, for him to turn from the *Tracts* to the detailed study of the law of nature.[30]

Meanwhile, since he skimped the arguments both from Scripture and from natural law, the case for magisterial authority based on contract or consent could not but gain weight in his thesis. He may have chosen to present that case hypothetically and to delete his only explicit commitment to it (p. 33),* but if it is removed the cogency and substance of the tracts is lost. The peculiar impor-

---

* Throughout, page references to the *Tracts* are to Locke's own pages as indicated in the printed text in this volume.

tance of the *consensus populi* argument in these writings will be clearer later on when we have discussed the relation of the young Locke to Thomas Hobbes.

NOTES

1 For a full discussion of these sources see Von Leyden, 1954, pp. 1–7; also my own unpublished dissertation, Abrams, 1961.

2 This is not, however, the first time they have been published; an Italian edition appeared in 1961, printing the *Tracts* along with the *Essay Concerning Toleration* of 1667 and the first *Letter Concerning Toleration* of 1689; cf. Viano, 1961. There are numerous misreadings of the Locke MSS in this text (discussed in Abrams, 1961) but these hardly detract from the importance of the volume, which for the first time brings together the complete range of Locke's thought on toleration.

3 King, 1830, pp. 74–86.

4 See the masterly account of this stage of Locke's career in Cranston, 1957, pp. 47–80.

5 MS Locke c. 24, fol. 182, in the Bodleian Library, Lovelace Collection.

6 MS Locke c. 27, fol. 12.

7 King, 1830, pp. 8–13; and cf. Fox Bourne, 1876, pp. 154–5; Bastide, 1907, ch. 1; Aaron, 1937, pp. 3–5; Maclean, 1947, appx. 1; Gough, 1950, ch. VII; De Marchi, 1953, *passim*; Cranston, 1957, pp. 67 ff.; Molyneux, 1957, ch. III.

8 Von Leyden, 1954, pp. 21–30.

9 Quotations in this paragraph are from MS Locke, c. 24, fol. 175, MS Locke c. 24, fol. 182, and English *Tract*, p. 9.

10 MS Locke c. 27, fol. 12; Stubbe, 1659, p. 158.

11 King, 1830, pp. 74–86, and Bodleian Library, MS Film 77; also Abrams, 1961, pp. 27–9, for a more detailed discussion.

12 MS Locke c. 28, fol. 1, *The Preface to the Reader*; Cranston, 1957, p. 59.

13 MS Locke e. 7, fol. 35, English *Tract*, p. 35; MS Locke c. 22, fols. 1–7 and c. 24, fols. 173–9; Towerson, 1663 and 1676.

14 For a parallel case of private circulation of controversial papers on the question of indifferent things see Jeanes, 1660; thirty years later Stillingfleet still sent his criticisms of Locke's *Essay* to Locke before publishing them. For the correspondence with Towerson see MS Locke c. 22, fols. 1–7; Von Leyden, 1954, p. 9; Abrams, 1961, pp. 31–8. The notes referred to are in MS Locke c. 18, fol. 196v and give references to the two statutes cited in English *Tract*, p. 22, and to the passages from Deuteronomy and St John discussed on p. 27.

For Locke's whereabouts at the time of writing see Gough, 1950, p. 177, and MSS Locke c. 18, fol. 197; c. 24, fol. 179.

15 MSS Locke c. 22, fols. 5 and 7; c. 20, fol. 179; c. 3, fol. 21 (reproduced below, Appendix 1).

16 Laslett, 1960, pp. 5–6; for Tilly see MSS Locke c. 20, fols. 173 and 179; Bagshaw's publisher, Hall, was 'Printer to the University' in 1659; Allestry replaced him in this semi-official role after the Restoration. In 1660 he published Matthew Wren's *Monarchy Asserted*, Sanderson's lectures on conscience, and works by Gilbert Clark and Thomas Willis. There is a further unexplained reference to Allestry in MS Locke f. 27, fol. 43, a notebook of 1664.

17 King, 1830, p. 13; Gough, 1950, p. 177; Von Leyden, 1954, pp. 27 and 34; Cranston, 1957, p. 64; Bishop Ussher's *The Power Communicated by God to the Prince* was republished by Ussher's grandson and Locke's friend, James Tyrrell, in 1661 with a *Preface* by Robert Sanderson.

18 Bagshaw's dispute with Morley occurred in 1662 and was about the authority of bishops; Richard Baxter, Samuel Holden and Roger l'Estrange were also involved in the controversy; cf. Bagshaw, 1661 (*a*), 1662 (*a*), 1662 (*b*); White Kennet, 1728, 1, p. 603.

19 Laslett, 1960, pp. 6–7; MS Locke c. 20, fols. 173 and 179; c. 22, fol. 173; Tilly speaks of 'instructions' given him by Locke on 5 November 1661 and apologizes for his failure to implement them.

20 Bagshaw, 1662 (*a*).

21 *Commons Journals*, VIII, pp. 408 ff.; *Lords Journals*, XI, p. 243, 'but still let there be a yoke...', etc.

22 MS Locke c. 22, fol. 3.

23 Von Leyden, 1954, pp. 160–79, 'An Lex Naturae Cognosci Potest ex Hominum Consensu? Negatur'. As Von Leyden comments (p. 30), 'There is a process of thought linking all [Locke's] early writings... All his three early writings form one single whole, as do the eight books of Hooker's *Laws of Ecclesiastical Polity* and the *Preface* containing his criticism of Puritanism.'

24 Bagshaw, 1661 (*b*).

25 'They are so general habituated to that play of primus, secundus, tertius, the only thing one may confidently presume they learned at school, that unless you deal with them in the same method and keep the same rule, they will not think themselves concerned' (MS Locke c. 27, fol. 12).

26 This idea is powerfully developed by Von Leyden, 1954, pp. 61 ff.; for Tyrrell's efforts to get Locke to publish his 'Treatise or lectures upon the Law of Nature' see MS Locke c. 22.

27 Bagshaw, 1660.

28 MS Locke e. 7, fols. 2, 3, 5, 35. Gough, 1950, ignores the hypothetical presentation of Locke's arguments; Von Leyden, 1954, by taking Locke's claims at face value possibly misses something of the fundamental importance of the argument from consent for Locke's whole case.

29 MS Locke e. 7, fol. 24. As Von Leyden, 1954, p. 26, comments, for the purposes of his argument in the *Tract*, Locke 'regarded this notion (of natural law) as fundamental'. But regarding a concept as fundamental is not the same as demonstrating the reality to which that concept refers.

30 Von Leyden, 1954, pp. 27–30.

II

THE CONTEXT OF CONSERVATISM: JOHN LOCKE IN 1660

The position adopted by Locke in the *Tracts* was a product of the coming together of three strands of historical experience. There was the political experience of the English Revolution, the philosophical experience of the long-standing debate on the concept of indifferent things, and the personal experience of Locke himself as a young intellectual making his way in an unstable world. I shall now fill out this three-dimensional, and determining, context of his conservatism.

THE POLITICS OF THE RESTORATION

To be concerned about indifferent things in 1660 was to be immersed in the whole political and moral crisis of the Restoration, to be caught up in that swift succession of systems of government that sought to impose order in England between 1659 and 1662. Oxford mirrored the national crisis step by step. In both Oxford and the nation as a whole the late autumn of 1660 was a peculiarly pregnant moment in that crisis—a new government had been created; it had not yet made itself felt. The new order had still to be dragged from the bowels of the old chaos. The initiative was taken, often, in a quite disorderly way. On 11 November 1660, Antony Wood reported: 'The Canons and Students of Christ Church (the Dean, Dr Morley, was absent) began to wear surplices and the organ played. Great resort by the rout, and Dr Fell...kept the door.'[1]

Locke and Bagshaw were both Students of Christ Church at the time of their dispute. Indeed, Locke's *Tracts* could be read as referring exclusively to the domestic politics of his college and university. Indifferent things, surplices in particular, had been an explosive issue in Christ Church long before 1660. From 1659 to 1662 the careers of Locke and Bagshaw reflect the impact of the Restoration on the Great Question with brutal clarity. After graduating from Christ Church in 1651 Bagshaw became second master at Westminster School; but his insistence on wearing his hat in the Abbey offended the Master, Busby, who ordered the boys to seize and remove him. He came back to Christ Church under John Owen and was Senior Censor there until December 1659. His orations on taking up and laying down this office reveal him as an uncompromising modernist in the great ideological struggle of ancients and moderns of his day. He denounced scholastic philosophy, which he said consisted of nothing but vain and idle disputations, and took particular exception to the servility of his contemporaries to the authority of Aristotle, who, he said, ruled supreme in Christ Church—'here a temple and altar have been built to the Stagyrite'. In no uncertain terms he demanded a liberty of philosophizing. A year later Bagshaw's works were still being published by the 'printer to the university'. In April 1661 he preached in the university church against the wearing of surplices. But he held no further office in Christ Church and left Oxford for Anglesey in the summer of 1661. He was deprived of his Studentship at the end of the year and in May 1662 he appealed to Clarendon against charges of disloyalty. On 30 December a warrant was issued for his arrest and in January he and his books were seized and he was thrown into prison.

Locke graduated Master of Arts in June 1658. He made no appearance in Oxford politics until July 1660 when he contributed to the official academic celebration of the return of the king. In December, when negotiations for a comprehensive church were already breaking down, his reply to Bagshaw was circulating privately. At the end of the month he received his first college preferment. Within three years he was himself Censor and was delivering polite academic, and properly Aristotelian, orations at the height of the persecution phase of the Restoration.[2]

In the interval the Students of Christ Church had had direct experience of what Bagshaw's principles could mean in practice. Between Christmas 1659 and Christmas 1660 the college had four Deans, each reflecting the changing tides of national politics. John Owen, who had presided since 1651, was replaced on 13 March by Edward Reynolds, Reynolds by George Morley on 27 July, and, following the elevation of Morley to the see of Worcester, John Fell became Dean on 30 November. Locke, in *The Preface to the Reader*, associates his own interests with those of the magistrate and insists that he has 'taken up arms' only to pursue the true end of the magistrate, peace. But this was of course the end pursued by each of the Christ Church magistrates under whom Locke lived in these years. Whatever their particular preferences as to surplices, academic dress and other indifferent things, each sought as best he could to establish and maintain order in the college.

But an enthusiasm for peace, however sincere, was an insufficient basis for peace in a polemical situation; especially when the dispute was about things indifferent. Each magistrate in turn, whether in Christ Church or at Westminster, was driven to seek some 'fundamentals' on which to ground and sanction the order he wished to impose.

Owen, who favoured the free use of indifferent things, took his stand on Scripture. But Scripture was open to all to read and could be variously interpreted. As a basis for civil authority over the externals of religious worship, it proved useless. Faced with vehemently asserted and mutually exclusive readings, he fell back on resources of a more purely political order. In 1656 he enlisted the members of his college to campaign on his behalf. Henry Stubbe, who was among their number, wrote to Hobbes that he had 'received orders' from Owen 'to study Church government and a toleration and so to oppose Presbytery'. A little later he reported that all the scholars from Westminster School (including Locke presumably) were entirely 'Dr Owen's creatures' and had 'promised to defend liberty of conscience and the other fundamentals of his government'.[3]

With the return to power of the Presbyterians Owen's position quickly deteriorated. In 1657 John Conant was made Vice-Chancellor and the issue of indifferent things, specifically of the wearing of academic 'formalities', was at once joined between him and Owen. Owen's appeals to Scripture and his use of his magisterial position both became increasingly arbitrary. Stubbe wrote to tell Hobbes he was 'so engaged in disputes of divinity in our private college' that he had had no time for anything else. Wood records the progress of the dispute:

Many [he writes] and especially those of Christ Church and particularly Mr Edward Bagshaw declaimed so eagerly against them [formalities] in full convocation that the modest vice chancellor sat down in peace and said no more. Those that abetted Bagshaw in this...were set on by Dr Owen.

As late as February 1659 Bagshaw in his capacity as Censor of Christ Church 'presented his bachelors *ad determinandum* without having on him any formalities, whereas every dean besides had formalities on'.[4] By the end of 1659 Owen was advocating a military dictatorship.

Lacking a general and voluntary recognition, the 'Saints' could only rule by the most arbitrary seizure of power; no proliferation of texts could demonstrate the unique scriptural legitimacy of their government to those who did not want to accept it. The need for fundamentals was greater than ever but the degeneration of Owen's regime into a petty and insoluble squabble with higher powers made it clear that they would have to be of a new type. The lesson of Owen's experience was not lost on Locke; Scripture could not suffice to establish political obligation: 'frustra expectares, frustra in Evangelio quaereres, unam eandemque venustatis normam'.

The appointment of Conant's father-in-law, Edward Reynolds, as Dean in March 1660 was a deliberate attempt to bring Christ Church into line with the rest of the university and nation. But the coming and going of Deans exacerbated the disorder within the college. Those who had supported Owen were faced now with a personal crisis of conscience. Were they to stand by their former principles and risk eviction, or were they to abandon those principles and don the new attitudes, and garments, now required by authority? Some, spotted and disliked by Wood as 'young pragmatics', took the latter course and trimmed their sails to each new regime. Others, like Stubbe and Bagshaw, held out for toleration, disrupted the life of the college and were in due season deprived of their Studentships. Neither course solved the problem of finding a basis for stable political and ecclesiastical order—the problem to which Locke was shortly to address himself.

Meanwhile the Presbyterians in their turn now faced the dilemma of exercising an 'un-founded' power. The 'free parliament', which was the external source of the Presbyterian regime in Oxford, was preparing to throw itself at the feet of the monarchy. The polemical initiative passed to the Independents and the Laudians. Reynolds's solution was to advocate good will. In *The Substance of Two Sermons* 'touching the composing of differences', which he published in the spring of 1659, he proposed a balance of gentle exhortation above and quietism below, 'an humble submission of judgment...some main fundamental doctrines wherein the dissenting parties do all agree...a willingness to walk exactly in order...and to hold the things wherein we agree in love, unity and constancy'.[5]

But in 1660 there were no fundamentals 'wherein the dissenting parties do all agree', and few were willing to 'shake off the opinion of their own righteousness' or accept Reynolds's exhortation to put Charity above Truth. In April the Common Prayer book reappeared in several college chapels. On 1 May the university authorities failed to have a maypole, set up by the 'loyal party', 'on purpose to vex them', pulled down. They did not protest later in the month at the '12 maypoles besides 3 or 4 morrises' that marked Holy Thursday. On the other side their efforts to restore 'formalities' were no more successful. Bagshaw and his friends still refused to wear surplice or gown and inveighed publicly against both the imposing of indifferent things and the indifferent practices of the Laudians.

The long passage at the end of the English *Tract* where Locke surveys the benefits of toleration echoes the tone used by Reynolds, and it may well reflect Locke's experience of Reynolds's regime:

If the believer and unbeliever could be content...to live together and use no weapons to conquer each other's opinions but pity and persuasion, if men would suffer one another to go to heaven every one in his own way...how much I say if such a temper and tenderness were wrought in the hearts of men our author's doctrine of toleration might promote a quiet in the world...I shall leave every one to judge.[6]

What is clear for Locke is that among a people 'apt to judge every other exercise of religion as an affront to theirs', forbearance was 'like to produce far different effects'. Reynolds had shown that government by good will merely opened a new door to chaos.

Was there no third course between the arbitrariness represented by Owen and the failure of government represented by Reynolds? Writing to his father in the spring of 1660 Locke seemed to have little hope of finding one:

It appears to us here altogether lowering and cloudy and I fear a storm will follow. Divisions are as wide, factions as violent and designs as pernicious as ever and these woven so intricately that few know what probably to hope and desire and the best and wisest are fain to wish for the general thing settlement, without seeing their way to it.[7]

John Fell saw the situation in the same way as Locke and wrote: 'The pretensions of no party now on foot in the nation are attainable; or if attained, are consistent with the good of other parts, or of the nation; or in fine their own.' But he also saw where the solution lay; government must be put into such hands 'as besides present force can plead a legal title to it'. Law would provide the objective basis for authority that previous regimes had so desperately lacked. The next phase of the Restoration was conducted under the banner of the 'law of 1648'. Office-holders evicted in 1648 were restored; serious efforts were made to negotiate a comprehensive church settlement; George Morley became Dean of Christ Church.[8]

Morley, like his predecessor, was a moderate, 'a very moderate, orthodox man'. But he was also able to refer disputes and challenges to his authority to an objective standard, that of 1648. Under this impartial standard the Laudian canons of Christ Church were restored; Sanderson was reinstalled as Divinity Professor; the legitimacy of Anglican ritual was proclaimed. But ceremonies were not yet directly imposed. And the intruded 'interval men' were in general treated kindly—in Christ Church only two of the five examined by the Visitors on 8 August were expelled and both were men of violent habits. As late as 4 October at least one of the chaplains of Christ Church had 'not yet read the Common Prayers in the Church'. What is striking about Fell's reintroduction of surplices and the organ is that it did not take place until November and that even then it was unofficial.[9]

But law moderately applied could not contain men committed to disputes about indifferent things. The lesson of this period was that law unless backed by coercion would rapidly lose its authority in the face of the Great Question. Bagshaw's pamphlet, one among many, appeared in September. On 8 October Paul Hood, the new Vice-Chancellor, issued a peremptory injunction to members of the university requiring conformity in matters of dress. Three weeks later the royal Declaration undermined this injunction by announcing that practices in dispute should be left undetermined and that a decision on ceremonies should be postponed until a national synod 'of both persuasions' could be called. The King entrusted the nation to the good will of the parties, 'exorbitant passion only retrenched', and refrained from enjoining any indifferent things—hoping in general for a willing obedience to the decrees of lawful authority. Opposition to imposed formalities and ceremonies at once redoubled. In January Bagshaw's party in Christ Church stole as many of the offending surplices as they could find and buried them in the college sewers.[10]

Clearly, law had to be backed by specific decisions, and decisions by coercion if law was not to perish. However reasonable the expectation of the dissenters in the summer of 1660 that, having recognized a common and lawful authority, they would be left considerable room for debate and manoeuvre in indifferent matters, it was plain from the moment of the Vice-Chancellor's injunction that in the end peace would depend upon a power which would not only lawfully decree but also lawfully coerce. The problem in Christ Church after Fell had made his intention of coercing manifest was simply to avoid the arbitrariness that coercion had represented under Owen. To keep order within his domain Fell as a magistrate had to make and impose decisions. But unless backed by the legal authority of the national magistrate his efforts would be either tyrannical or futile.[11] It had become essential that the national magistrate should give a legal sanction to such efforts. There was a momentary but urgent need for the case for magisterial determination and compulsion to be aired. There was a need, as Clarendon put it in opening Parliament in May 1661, for 'some law, that may be a rule to that indulgence, that under pretence of liberty of conscience men may not be absolved from all the obligations of law and conscience'. And there was a need for works like Locke's English *Tract*.

LAW AND IGNORANCE: THE HISTORY OF INDIFFERENT THINGS

The political problem which the debate on indifferent things was meant to solve was a real, troublesome and long-standing one. As Stillingfleet wrote: 'If any controversy hath been an increaser and fomenter of heart-burnings and divisions among us, it hath been about the determination of indifferent things.'[12] Yet the debate was curiously stylized and unfruitful. The argument Locke produced in 1660 was not an original one. Rather, it was a late statement of an old orthodoxy. The case on both sides had been rehearsed many times in the century before Locke wrote. On neither side had there been much argumentative development.

The question of the use of indifferent things was rightly felt to be of major political importance. Why was so little ground gained, after the first exchanges, in discussions of the question? Probably, because the debate provoked by the concept of indifferency was one that could only end in blank assertions or in an epistemological crisis, a crisis which no one prior to Locke was willing to face. Three things were given in this debate: that there were some things indifferent; that there was a system of moral laws established by God and accessible to the human understanding; and that the relation of conscience to these laws could be demonstrated. On these assumptions elaborate and inconclusive structures of argument were built.

No Protestant, of course, ever challenged the 'perfection' of Scripture. 'The religion of Protestants', it was agreed with Chillingworth, was the Bible, which provided a decisive rule, 'fit to end all controversies in things necessary'. But not in things indifferent. Disputes about particular ceremonies or other indifferencies were referred first to Scripture. But Scripture invariably proved ambiguous: Galatians i. 15; ii. 9; and iii. 6, as well as I Corinthians viii. 9–13, seemed to assert the authority of the individual conscience. But Acts xv. 28, I Corinthians xiv. 40 and II Corinthians i. 12 treated the conscience as liable to be overruled by superior moral duties. It was necessary to go beyond Scripture to explore the general relationship of conscience and law.[13] For to talk about indifferency implied the possession of reliable moral-philosophical knowledge. The idea of a system of universal law symbolized the sort of knowledge Christian philosophers had always supposed to be available to them. In appealing to law the object of each of the great line of seventeenth-century casuists was to interpose demonstrable principles of obligation between the conscience and the use of indifferent things. Each proceeds in his own way. Each, almost, has his own system of law; but what is agreed is that some such principles must be available and must have the force of law: 'This we must either maintain or else overturn the world and make every man his own commander.'[14]

The immediate effect of the appeal to law was thus to modify the moral and epistemological arbitrariness of earlier assertions about the right use of indifferent things. But, ultimately, that appeal did no more than postpone an investigation of the bases of moral knowledge—an investigation implicitly required all along by the very concept of indifferency. Among Locke's predecessors in the debate only Lord Brooke seems to have appreciated that the reference to law was a detour. Locke's interests shifted quite rapidly from problems of law to problems of knowledge after 1660. For most who engaged in the dispute the appeal to law was axiomatic and inescapable, however unsatisfactory or hazardous they felt it to be. John Burges, who in 1631 attempted 'a history of this dispute', deplored the endless introduction of legal arguments. To the time of Cartwright, he argued, a composition of parties was possible because those who attacked ceremonies did so only on the ground that they were inconvenient, 'but they which have written of later times undertake to prove them simply unlawful'. He regards the appeal to law as futile and circular; 'fuel is brought to the fire still and opposition begetteth more opposition'. But he himself then proceeds to a 74-page analysis of the legal status of ceremonies.[15]

The debate was conducted in the form of several series of parallel and overlapping arguments between more or less separate groups of authors. In the late sixteenth and early seventeenth centuries numerous distinct controversies were pursued. By the 1650s authors had become more conscious of a broader body of literature. The years 1658–60 saw a sudden acceleration in the output of pamphlets and a convergence of arguments. Twelve contributions to the debate were published in Oxford alone in six months in 1660.

Two levels of argument can be distinguished. There are general works which treat problems of indifferency in the context of an inclusive moral theology. The most important of these were William Ames, *Conscience with the Power and Cases Thereof* (1634), Henry Hammond, *Of Conscience* (1644), Robert Sanderson, *De Obligatione Conscientiae* (1660), Edward Stillingfleet, *Irenicum* (1660), Gabriel Powel, *De Adiaphoris* (1606), and various works of Roger Williams and John Milton. And then there are more sharply focused works inspired by particular disputes and exploiting the more fundamental writings for local and limited purposes. There are several sequences of such works. Typical is the one launched by the so-called *Lincoln Abridgement*. The *Abridgement*, which appeared in 1617, was itself a re-vamping of a statement presented by the ministers of Lincoln diocese to James I in 1605. It produced an answer from the Bishop of Lincoln, Thomas Morton, *A Defence of the Innocency of Three Ceremonies*, which was in turn answered by Ames, *A reply to Dr Morton's Defence of Three Nocent Ceremonies* (1622). After some minor tracts and broadsheets had appeared on each side a more elaborate answer to Ames was published by John Burges, *An Answer Rejoined...* (1631), and this shortly inspired Ames, *Triplication, a Fresh Suite against Ceremonies* (1633). After this the thread of this particular sequence of the debate is lost for some years in broader discussions. However, in 1659 a Somerset minister, Henry Jeanes, published *A Treatise Concerning Indifferency*, which is an explicit continuation of the former controversy and reiterates the case of Ames against Burges. In its turn this work provoked Henry Hammond, *A Vindication of Uniformity in... Ceremonies* (1659), and thus Henry Jeanes, *A reply unto Dr Hammond* (1660). Jeanes was a Somerset author who published in Oxford. At the same time another strand of the debate was also coming to roost in Oxford via Somerset. This was a broader but equally long-lived discussion which inspired Locke's neighbour Cornelius Burgess to publish *Reasons showing the Necessity of Reformation* (3 August 1660) and so to provoke John Pearson, *No Necessity of Reformation* (20 August 1660), Henry Savage, *Reasons Showing that there is no Need of Reformation* (5 September 1660), William Hamilton, *Some Necessity of Reformation* (11 September 1660), Cornelius Burgess, *A Postscript to Dr Pearson* (13 September 1660) and John Pearson, *An Answer to Dr Burgess* (20 September 1660).

The exacerbation of the debate in 1660 and the coming together of its several strands is evidenced again in the republication in that year of several major works on indifferency that had first appeared early in the century. Among these William Bradshawe's two volumes, *English Puritanism* and *Several Treatises of Worship*, originally published in 1604, were particularly influential. Bradshawe's case remained the most comprehensive and powerful working-out of the argument against an imposed use of ceremonies, matching the work of Sanderson on the other side.

For the most part the arguments in this debate resolved themselves under six heads. The propriety of each disputed ceremony was examined in relation to (*a*) its scriptural basis, the extent to which it could be derived from that 'perfect rule', (*b*) the nature of Christian worship, (*c*) superstition, (*d*) the powers of the magistrate in matters of religion, (*e*) Christian liberty, and (*f*) scandal and error.

The argument about the perfection of Scripture was central and, in any debate among Protestants, indispensable. The dissenting ministers of Morton's diocese objected to his insistence on the surplice on the simple ground that 'every ceremony should have a warrant from Scripture and this has none'. Morton, in reply, appeals to the authority of St Paul, holding that ceremonies are but part of the 'Decency enjoined by the Apostle' (in I Corinthians xiv. 40) and so 'altogether Divine'. The arguments of Burges and Sanderson are identical. But Bradshawe and others had already challenged this point. Granting that 'religion cannot stand without some ceremonies', they hold that 'this does not prove that the ceremonies now in question...are necessary'. And they went on to confront the injunction to the Corinthians with other, countervailing, Pauline pronouncements—with Romans xiv. 14, for example, 'but to him that esteemeth anything to be unclean, to him it is unclean'. They gained their point but in doing so they virtually forced their opponents to appeal beyond Scripture to a general theory of law.

From Hooker to Locke no Anglican denied the perfection of Scripture. But its ambiguity on questions of indifferency quickly led them to deny its adequacy. Thus Hammond ruled that Scripture is the supreme law and contains 'some fibres or strings of other laws', but that it is not a complete guide, not such a 'code or Pandect of laws' as to comprehend all situations. Happily, Anglicans argued, we have access to other laws 'beside the law of God'; and these laws, they thought, could be shown to be made by authorities superior to the individual and therefore able to oblige the conscience, albeit by a 'relative, derivative and inferior' obligation.[16]

An application of this doctrine appeared in the Anglican account of the nature of worship. Worship involves some acts that are wholly internal, others that are wholly external and circumstantial. The essence of worship is internal; it is a matter of adoration and faith. This is directly commanded by God and is necessary to salvation; here the conscience is explicitly bound to obedience. But this inner worship must be expressed in external actions. Some of these, such as prayer, are also directly prescribed by God. But unfortunately 'there can be no external acts without circumstances and these are not prescribed in the Gospel'. This contingent apparatus must not of course 'be esteemed equal with

God's law'.[17] The external circumstances of worship are indifferent under divine law and therefore susceptible to the same laws as any other indifferent things. But they are also thoroughly bound up with worship, inseparable from it and therefore susceptible to that general injunction of the divine law that requires decency and order. There must be ceremonies but not any particular ceremonies. At the same time, because the essence of worship is internal belief, it cannot be violated by anything the magistrate may impose in the way of ceremonies so long as these are not imposed 'under any opinion of efficacy, holiness or necessity, but only for decency'.[18]

The Puritan answer to this case accepted the dual nature of worship but denied that the use of outward forms was separable from or irrelevant to inner experience. A ceremony, they argued, is but a 'corporeal adumbration of some hidden thing in the mind'; it has value only if it complements and sets forth that 'hidden thing'. An indifferent act performed because it is part of a prescribed ritual is at best valueless; at worst it drives the worshipper into either hypocrisy or superstition. In addition it was argued that if the legitimacy of man-made rituals was once granted there could be no end to imposition: 'Those that bring in without special warrant from God, piping into his service, might as well bring in dancing also.'[19]

Once Anglicans had made it clear that ceremonies were not imposed because the magistrate believed them to have any religious significance but 'only for decency', the magistrate could not himself be charged with superstition. But his actions might still lead other 'weak' Christians into superstition, by making them believe, say, that it was wearing surplices and not faith that was important to God. And this would be contrary to the obligation of the magistrate as one of the 'strong', in St Paul's sense, to cherish the 'weak'. By the obstinate imposing of 'alterable gewgaws' despite this obligation, so Puritans argued, 'many Christians are compelled to sin against themselves and against Christ'.[20]

Anglicans met such arguments evasively. If it could be shown, they held, that the actual imposition of ceremonies was legitimate, then the magistrate could not be censured for the superstitious misapprehensions of the weak; he might be obliged to instruct them, but not to abolish ceremonies on their account.[21]

Though possibly good logic this argument was poor theology.

For the weak *were* bound by their own misapprehensions. A false belief about an indifferent thing carries an obligation to act—it is subjectively true. If a man holds an objectively false belief he must act as though it were objectively true. To multiply occasions for false belief was to inflate the chances of men being forced to 'sin against themselves'. Instruction was a poor remedy if the magistrate was himself the source of sin.

At this point the argument plainly became one about the competence of the civil magistrate as a 'lawful authority'. It came to rest on the standard Anglican assumption that 'things indifferent are the peculiar and proper matter of positive human laws'.[22] The problem of the competence or incompetence of the magistrate emerged inescapably from the discussion of worship and superstition.

The Anglican case has two stages. First, the place of the magistrate as a necessary agent in a system of moral legislation is argued. Then the idea of such a system is used to place all indifferent things at his disposal. In this respect Locke's case against Bagshaw, described above, reproduces in exact detail the arguments of Sanderson, Hooker, Hammond and Taylor. All arrive by inference and deduction at the common proposition, 'the peculiar field in which human laws can assert their power of obliging is in things indifferent, where there is no pre-existing obligation'.[23] Once it is clear that human laws about indifferent things can oblige without 'any change in the thing itself', the magistrate could in principle impose anything he thought fit.

The Puritan answer transferred the debate to yet another level. Though couched in the language of law the central idea of this answer was that of regeneration. And thus ultimate problems of knowledge were perennially intruded into the discussion. Without challenging the notion of a hierarchy of laws the Puritan, by invoking the idea of regeneration, could secure a law to guide the conscience in matters of indifferency more directly derived from God than anything to which the magistrate could lay claim. This new law was, of course, the second covenant announced in the Gospel; a law, so it was held, that explicitly freed believing Christians from external ceremonial conformity:

The state of religion under the Gospel is far differing from what it was under the Law; then was the state of rigour, childhood, bondage and works, to all which force was not unbefitting; now is the state of grace, manhood, freedom and faith, to all which belongs willingness and reason not force; the Law was then written in the tables of stone, and to be performed according to the letter willingly or unwillingly; the Gospel, our new covenant, upon the heart of every believer, to be interpreted only by the sense of charity and inward persuasion.[24]

The effect of the second covenant was clear. It gave the believer a direct, subjective access and responsibility to the will of God in indifferent as well as necessary things. It provided the believer with the one thing that could free him from the claims and control of the civil magistrate in indifferent things, namely, superior moral knowledge. Since God had chosen to speak in the 'new man', guiding his conscience by immediate communications, any external constraint upon the actions that conscience might prompt was illegitimate; quite clearly it was not 'within the province of... civil magistrates, to impose their own interpretations on us as laws or as binding on conscience'. The magistrate's claim to authority and his defenders' claim to knowledge were thus at once dissolved. Such knowledge, set beside the inward certainties of the true believer, is 'fallible' and any authority that relies on it, if it grieves the conscience of the believer, is accordingly 'sinful'.[25] The inwardness of the new law is irreducible: 'The testimony of the Spirit alone is that by which true knowledge of God hath been, is and can only be revealed.'

The lesson of all this was obvious and invariably drawn:

The civil magistrate [has] no power to restrain or constrain his subjects in things indifferent, as in eating of meats, wearing this or that garment, using this or that gesture, but...they are bound to try and examine his commands, and satisfy their own reason, conscience and judgment before the Lord, and...they shall sin if they follow the magistrate's command, not being fully persuaded in their own soul and conscience that his commands are according to God.[26]

And invariably at this point discussion spilled over into a complementary argument about the nature and consequences of Christian liberty. For the new covenant, meticulously described by Puritans as a new law, was plainly a law of liberty.

To the regenerate man belief and practice were inseparable and freedom to frame practice according to his belief was the 'great privilege' of the Gospel; there could thus be 'no place left for the magistrate or his force' in any question of religion. No more could there be any doubt as to the extent of the liberty claimed by the elect under the new covenant. It could only be a liberty in things indifferent. Bagshaw made this point as effectively as any of his predecessors:

> Our religion is styled the perfect law of liberty, which liberty I understand not wherein it consists if in things necessary we are already determined by God, and in things indifferent we may still be tied up to human ordinances and outside rites at the pleasure of our Magistrate.[27]

It was precisely this difficulty of Bagshaw's that the Anglican account of Christian liberty undertook to resolve. Christian liberty, like the substance of faith and worship, is an inward phenomenon. It is a freedom from certain false and onerous beliefs. Among these is the belief that any particular use of an indifferent thing is of *any* relevance to salvation. Accordingly, it makes no difference to the liberty of a Christian what use of indifferencies is imposed:

> The liberty of a Christian to any indifferent thing consisteth in this: that his judgment be thoroughly persuaded of the indifferency of it; it is the determination of the judgment in the opinion of the thing, not the use of it, that taketh away Christian liberty.[28]

Anglicans before Locke had used this argument without being altogether happy with it. Cogent as it could be made to look, it had one critical inadequacy which Sanderson and Taylor at least had already perceived. It failed to dispose of the problem of error. Hence it could not properly meet the sixth and final Puritan objection, the argument from scandal. Here, the epistemological basis of the whole dispute was finally laid bare.

It was an agreed position of Protestant theology that for the 'weak' the perceptions of an erroneous conscience are binding. St Paul's concession to the weak brother—a concession that made him in effect the stronger party in any moral dispute—was not challenged. Aquinas had concluded from the statements of the Apostle that since conscience, even when in error, binds, and since one could therefore sin both in following and in ignoring an erroneous conscience, the only safe course was to subordinate conscience to other, more skilled authorities.[29] But Protestants had repudiated these Thomist guides and reasserted the competence of individual consciences. And now the combination of

Aquinas' rule, 'if everything were known no action could be without moral significance, but without this full knowledge there must be a degree of indifference about many things', with the Protestant recognition of conscience as an agent of knowledge, led even Sanderson to admit a loop-hole in his elaborate theory of obligation. A man whose conscience was informed by 'invincible' error could not be required by a magistrate to behave in ways he thought sinful without being forced to sin indeed:

But now on the other side, if the things so mis-judged to be unlawful, be in any way necessary; either in respect of their own nature or by the injunction of authority; then the person is by that his Error brought into such a strait between two sins as he can by no possible means avoid both so long as he persisteth in that error. For both if he do the thing, he goeth against the persuasion of conscience; and if he do it not either he ommiteth a necessary duty or else disobeyeth a lawful Authority.[30]

On this position Anglican theology could not improve. Sanderson's own solution was simply evasive: 'Out of this snare...there is no way of escape but one, which is to rectify his judgment.' For, as Taylor had pointed out, the weak and errant Christian is not aware that his judgment needs to be rectified. Nor can he be shown his error since, *ex hypothesi*, it is established 'invincibly' in his conscience. Taylor was led to conclude that an invincibly erroneous conscience must be obeyed even in defiance of the known command of a lawful superior.[31]

The Puritan writers seized on this weakness, of course. The New Testament, they pointed out, forbids Christians to scandalize the weak: 'let no man lay a stumbling-block in his brother's way'.[32] But indifferent things when imposed are just such stumbling-blocks and occasions of scandal. There is no divine necessity, no certain knowledge, about them. Yet weaker brothers who mistakenly, but conscientiously, suppose a necessity in them are by the imposition forced into a necessity of sinning. Since subjective conviction is enough to create sin the only way in which sin can be avoided is by preventing occasions for error—that is, by allowing a freedom of action in those things which, for lack of objective knowledge, are called indifferent.

To meet this argument the Anglican casuists redefined their terms. Sin, they now argued, lies in taking offence or in the results of taking offence, not in giving it when the occasion of the offence

is indifferent. As Hammond triumphantly concluded (again antici-
pating Locke), Christ himself was a stumbling-block. To give
offence, then, is not necessarily to sin; but 'no man is offended or
scandalized, but he that falls into some sin'. A weak brother
imitating an action that is lawful or indifferent in itself but against
his own conscience certainly sins; but the example he follows is
innocent. It is in his own conscience that the reform is needed.
Given a sober concern for the truly weak there is thus nothing in
this argument to prevent the imposition of ceremonies.[33]

The assumption in Hammond's account of the problem of
scandal is, however, that error is vincible, that indifferency is an
objectively demonstrable condition, and that anyone who sees the
use of an indifferent thing as unlawful can be shown to be mistaken. But in the Puritan discussion of error (and in that of Taylor
and Sanderson, too) error is not treated as a measure of perversity
but as an indication of ignorance. It is because of this ignorance
that invincible error is possible; and it is the fact of objective
ignorance that obliges men to follow their own consciences in
these cases. Few Anglicans were willing to recognize just how far
their handling of the problem of indifferency embroiled them in
this question of the accessibility of moral knowledge. On the
other side there were always writers ready enough to remind
them.

Thus Richard Sibbes could ask: 'How shall we know whether
we have the Spirit of Christ or no?', and then answer himself: 'It is
a working thing...it will work in him that hath it...it transforms, making the dark light...it convinces.'[34] It was hardly help-
ful to call such conviction error unless one could find some means
of validating the knowledge that led one to do so. In this respect
the orthodox Anglican appeal to theories of law was no more than
a formal and delaying device. In the hands of relentless investiga-
tors such as Lord Brooke or Roger Williams the elaborate theory
of law had already been dissolved into a denial of the competence
of any man to determine indifferency for any other. Echoing the
Thomist position Brooke makes indifferency altogether a measure
of ignorance: 'There is no one thing, no one act in all the world,
that I may do or not do, *ad placitum*, at my pleasure, all circumstances considered.' For, he explains, 'all indifference comes only
from the darkness of our understanding...nothing is indifferent
in re, in se'. But for Brooke our own understanding, defective as it

is, is the only light we have and the best we can hope to have: 'It lies not in the power of all other men living to determine what seems indifferent to one man's understanding, since he may perhaps not see what they all see, and *e contrario*.' 'Understanding and truth', however, 'can be but one'; in the face of uncertainty and error the individual can be bound only to do 'what is best, or at least on exactest search seems best', to his own reason. A man's reason is the 'candle of God which he hath lighted in man'.[35]

Sceptical of any objective access to truth but confident of some kind of fortuitous consensus of subjective perceptions when guided by reason, Brooke was willing to contemplate that potential anarchy at which Anglican rationalism baulked: 'who shall tell us what is *recta ratio*?' he asks, and answers, '*recta ratio*'. In vain for Locke to complain: 'every man's *recta ratio* is but the traverses of his own steps'. For writers like Brooke, men are committed to a search among indifferent things in which, just because there are no guides to truth outside the individual intellect, they must always be free to follow 'the dictates of right reason'; 'and if right reason have not or cannot determine me, to which side soever I incline and rest, I sin'. Therefore, of course, 'no power on earth ought to force my practice more than my judgment'; 'what is lawful and necessary to one that sees it so' may be equally unlawful or indifferent to any or every other. The truth cannot be known.[36]

Few writers pursued the epistemological implications of error as far as Brooke, who concluded, 'Things are all of one nature, variegated only in our apprehensions.' But these implications were seldom far below the surface of any argument in which the idea of error and the Protestant conceptions of conscience and of 'Scripture as the sole interpreter of itself to the conscience' were brought together. A hundred years before Bagshaw reopened the debate in Oxford, the members of St John's College, Cambridge, had seen that the want of knowledge was the ground on which a liberty in the use of vestments could best be urged. So had the authors of the *Humble Supplication* in 1609. In 1644 Goodwin had again observed 'the grand imprudence of men running the hazard of fighting against God, in suppressing any way, doctrine or practice, concerning which they know not whether it be from God or no'. Nor could the more sensitive Anglicans fail to see where the common Protestant concession to a man's duty to follow his belief 'according to his light' properly led:

In this world we believe in part, and prophesy in part, and this imperfection shall never be done away with till we be translated to a more glorious state: either then we must throw our chances and get truth by accident or predestination, or else must lie safe in a mutual toleration and private liberty of persuasion, unless some other anchor be thought upon where we may fasten our floating vessels and ride safely.[37]

What was needed on either side of the debate to provide this 'other anchor' was not yet more elaborate codification of laws, nor yet more painstaking scriptural exegesis, but a thorough reconstitution of knowledge. If it could be shown that what Anglicans called error was indeed erroneous and that the higher laws they invoked had some substantial existence, then the surrender of personal moral responsibility for which they called could perhaps be justified. But if these had to remain matters of doubt, interpretation and supposition, if conscience and inner persuasion were the only means of 'knowing' higher commands that the individual could be sure of, then the qualms of conscience could not be so easily set aside. As the Baptist, John Murton, argued: 'If these learned men could free us from the Lord's wrath, or if they might answer for us and we be free; it were safe for us to submit ourselves and captivate our judgments and practice to them.' Till then we must remain our own moral agents. And therefore men would 'not escape the ditch by being led blindfold by the magistrate'.[38] Couched, thus, the Puritan case was irreducible. Locke was to cap his own version of the conventional argument from law by quoting the scriptural injunction to obedience: 'Be subject not only for wrath but for conscience sake.' But Milton had already answered him with the critical, destructive, question: 'How for conscience sake—against conscience?'[39]

The debate on the Great Question thus concealed a greater question which for almost a century Puritans had been asking the defenders of imposition to confront. By forcing men to contemplate the diversity of human beliefs, values and practices, by forcing successive generations to wrestle with the most knotty problems of knowledge and moral perception, the debate on indifferency came to call in question the viability of an entire, old, respected and official ideology. It took a long time for anyone trained up in that ideology to see these deeper implications of the debate and to open his eyes to the possibility of a wholly new system of thought built on wholly new criteria of knowledge. Locke was to be the first to accept the challenge and move through this debate to the necessary fundamental intellectual innovations.

Those who chose to take the side of authority in this debate had, then, to deploy a set of arguments that by 1660 had become traditional. Locke did so. But he was also to be led by the traditional weaknesses of those arguments to investigations more radical and more consequential than any of the defenders of authority had ever before attempted. The question that arises is therefore this: Who was John Locke in 1660? Why was he disposed to enter the debate as he did and how was he peculiarly qualified to see and to explore the loop-holes in the debate and so to emerge finally as one of the world's great reconstituters of ideology?

THE DUTIES OF INTELLECT: ORDER, PEACE AND METHOD

We know very little of John Locke before his arrival in Oxford. The evidence about his early life in Somerset is ample but inconclusive. I see no reason, however, to assert as does Aaron, that Locke's 'fundamental attitude to life was determined for him once and for all in that simple home at Belluton'—nor that that simple home was the sort of place where he was likely to have 'learnt the meaning of political liberty'.[40] Rather, the character of Locke's home was set by the harsh and uncompromising presbyterianism of the men who briefly ruled England in the late 1640s. Locke's father and his father's patron were both active members of that rural counter-élite that won control of almost every county in those years. The ministers and elders of the Bath and Wrington Presbyterian 'classes' included many close friends and relations of the young Locke: Samuel Crook, the minister who had baptized him, his uncle Peter Locke of Chew Magna and his cousin Edmund Keene of Wrington, the elder Samuel Tilly, John Burges of Stanton Drew, and the family's patron and landlord, Alexander Popham. Another cousin, Richard Locke of Bristol, claimed to have lost two ships and to have been ruined by his efforts on behalf of Parliament. Peter Locke was one of the 'factious party' at Chew Magna which had the Anglican vicar of that village violently evicted and installed the elder Henry Stubbe in his place.

The correspondence between Locke and his father has none of the urbane sophistication of his letters to friends in Oxford; the tone is one of an austere piety.[41]

All this tempts one to suggest that it was the determined Calvinism of his earliest environment rather than any more academic source that inspired the highly voluntaristic treatment of law that we find in Locke's first political writings. But the information about his life and interests before 1655 will permit no more than the most tentative of suggestions.

What we discover after 1655 is a man deeply insecure, minutely methodical and thoroughly academic. Locke had become an academic intellectual. He had grown to be a man who had, as he himself wrote, 'an Academic goblin' as the 'particular Genius that ruled and directed his course of life'.[42] And the immediate responsibility of the academic man in the 1660s was to seek out and expound the principles of order. This was the distinctive professional commitment of the seventeenth-century 'homo academicus', as Leibniz was to put it.

In 1660 Locke was wholly caught up in this profession and its commitments. His most probable destiny was holy orders. As a Student of Christ Church without sufficient independent means he was faced with the pressures of two complementary traditions: occupationally, to pursue ecclesiastical preferment; intellectually, to handle, elucidate and maintain the categories of the Schools. Both functions in this clerical career were governed by the maxim of Aquinas, 'sapientis est ordinare'. The priest was to expound the pattern of moral obligation which was God's plan for man; the scholar was to expound the complementary pattern in nature. For eight years Locke had been educated toward this end. His book-lists for this time reveal a man who, with whatever doubts and reservations, is entirely immersed in the orthodox literature of the education he had received—formal disquisitions on the scholastic liberal sciences, oratory, logic and theology; polite moralizing theogonies; the works of Sanderson, Seneca and Cicero.[43]

The idea that the peculiar duty of the intellectual was to set forth the secrets of order was a commonplace of the age. To Kenelm Digby, a contemporary author whose work Locke was reading before 1660, it was that duty which dignified intellectual activity above every other:

Looking into this matter; the first consideration we meet withal is, that our understanding is in her own nature an *orderer*; and that her proper work is to rank and put things in order... And that in every kind we see that he is master and architect... who can best, or most, or farther than his fellows, set things in order.[44]

The theme of order was no less compelling to Locke himself. The elaborate concern we find in his Latin *Tract* to define a *perfecta regula*, the argumentative weight of such terms as *bene compositus ordo*, make sense only when we recognize the force of his commitment to the pursuit of order in general.

That commitment is reflected most clearly in the concern he shows everywhere in his early works and notebooks for two means always intimately connected with the end of order: peace and methodical intellectual procedure. The centrality of order to all serious intellectual inquiry was axiomatic for his generation. His personal experience of the world from his tenth to his thirtieth year gave him a vested interest in peace and in the orderly social relationships associated with peace. His education convinced him of the necessity of method.

Among Locke's earliest writings are four tailor-made poems. One of these, written for his patron Alexander Popham, is unpublished. The others were printed in the official volumes presented by the university to Cromwell and Charles II. These three men had little in common save their authority. But the theme of Locke's verses is the same on each occasion. He hails each man in turn as the harbinger and guarantor of peace. Two of the poems are built on a pun on Cromwell's name—*oliva pacis*. While the majority of Locke's colleagues chose to celebrate victory in their contributions, Locke insists on peace. The Restoration poem is the most explicit; the return of Charles means simply that anarchy will at last give way to peace, and therefore to order:

> As in the world's Creation, when this frame
> Had neither parts, distinction, nor a name
> But all confus'd did in the Chaos jarre
> Th' embleme and product of intestine warre,
> Light first appears...
> Beauty and Order follow, and display
> This stately fabrick guided by that ray.
> So now in this our new creation when
> This isle begins to be a world again,

> You first dawn on our Chaos, with designe
> To give us Order...
> Till you upon us rose and made it day
> We in disorder all and darkness lay.[45]

The weight of Locke's words and synonyms is intrusive—light, beauty, order, peace, the Restoration on the one hand; darkness, disorder, chaos, war, the immediate past on the other. The place of analogy in seventeenth-century argument has often been demonstrated and cannot be too much stressed. Locke's own analogies are at once completely traditional and of the widest moral dimensions. Doubtless, he wrote his poems to order but the selection of idea and image are his own and cannot be ignored. A medieval intellectual system lurks in his thought. It is the key to the otherwise enigmatic or merely flowery use in political argument of such aesthetic terms as *decor* and *venustas*, and to the frequent association of *libertas* and *tranquillitas*, order and beauty. As Tillyard said of a similar pattern of thought, 'the arrangement is "comely" not just because it is pretty or seemly but because it harmonises with a universal order'.[46]

Locke sought peace in several ways. His first instinct was not to seek a political alternative to disorder but to take refuge from it in personal relationships. And these relationships were themselves to be closely ordered, governed by an elaborate formal civility. They were to be purged of that crude spontaneity one might expect to find among Somerset farmers—and which Locke had learnt by 1660 to regard as comic. If his letters display a capacity for friendship, they display a greater concern to define his friendships formally, to maintain a calm, contrived and graceful personal world as an asylum from the 'tempests and overflows' of the world at large. The circle of Locke's friends in Oxford was a community modelled consciously on the polite elegance of its literature. The ideal was the dispassionate conversation of Barclay's *Argenis*. The common style was the elevated wit of the *Letters* of Balzac. The common idiom was that of 'the School of Compliments', the high language and conceits elaborated in the courtesy literature, which, alongside orthodox academic works of logic and casuistry, seems to have been Locke's main reading before 1660.[47] The hallmark of the 'School of Compliments' was, notoriously, the propensity to surrender content to form, to let conceits and stylistic patterns dominate meaning. Locke had mixed feelings about so mannered an existence; but there were moods and times in which he found it powerfully attractive.

The pattern of personal withdrawal can be found again in his growing inclination in these years to embrace the philosophy of Seneca. In an early letter from Pensford he self-consciously describes his chosen role: 'Methinks I find myself hard and half iron already and can turn a churlish insensible outside to the world.' Writing to his father in June 1659 he claimed that 'all these tossings have served but to rock me into a pleasant slumber whilst others dream (for our life is nothing else) of nothing but fire, sword and ruin'.[48] His intellectual concerns at the time of the Restoration—if they are accurately reflected in his notebooks—were almost entirely within the sphere of private moral philosophy. Of the four great branches of philosophy recognized in his own classification of 1661, *theologia, politia, physica, prudentia*, it was the last that engrossed his attention. He defined the main ends of prudence as *felicitas* and *tranquillitas*. And he listed as the principal 'media ad hos fines', on the one hand *sui cognitio*, on the other *in passiones suas imperium*. Locke was later criticized for being too excellent a 'master of taciturnity and passion'; it seems he had been his own teacher in this respect. In 1660, at least, he had subordinated political and social concerns to private friendships, to introspection and to safely academic pursuits: 'The world itself and all its frippery are scarce worth one furious thought; he that pays down any part of his quiet and content for it hath a hard bargain.'

By 1665 this withdrawal had degenerated into the modish cynicism often thought typical of the Restoration period. Osborne's satirical *Advice to a Son* features frequently in his notes and correspondence, as does *Grobrianus: the School of Slovenrie*. One of his pupils, John Scudamore, now published a satire on military and political virtues, *Homer à la Mode*. In his collections of poetry, Crashawe and works like Herbert's *Christ's Resurrection* are replaced by such jingles as: 'And I wish in Heaven his soul may dwell | That first devised the leather Botell.'

Perhaps there are traces of posturing in these attitudes. His wish to retreat from the world may have excelled his ability to do so. His expressed concern for method, on the other hand, was fully matched by his talents. His first published work, after all, was the *Nouvelle méthode de dresser les recueils*—a new method of arranging information.

In 1660 the evidence of Locke's interest in method is to be found in his commonplace books. The purpose of these books, appropriately headed *Adversaria* and *Lemmata*, was itself to organize. The volumes that have survived make it clear that between 1655 and 1669 Locke maintained parallel series of notebooks dealing respectively with ethical and medical themes. The framework for this material lies in the tabulation of concepts and categories on the opening pages of the *Adversaria 1661*. Here we find the first of a series of elaborate classificatory schemes that punctuate Locke's manuscripts. This is in fact the most comprehensive and ambitious of them, filling five pages of a quarto volume. The purpose of the tables is to lay out in systematic form the whole content of human thought and knowledge; to divide this knowledge into appropriate categories; and so to establish relations between branches of knowledge and identify problems for investigation.[49]

The major divisions of Locke's scheme have already been mentioned. They are the four fundamental sciences—the nature of the spiritual universe and its laws, the foundations of civil society and their forms and sanctions, the nature of the physical universe or 'the science of bodies', and the moral end of the individual and the means towards it. The precision and completeness with which the minor categories of this system are set out invite comparison with such encyclopedic exercises as the *Janua Linguarum* of J. A. Comenius (1631) and the *Ars Signorum* of Dalgarno (1661), although Locke's purpose is if anything more obviously heuristic. The complement of his tables is the string of detailed descriptions of theological and ritual systems, monetary values, weights and measures and comparative social customs that appear in his papers. The information is organized, carefully and exactly, in accordance with his general apparatus of classification.[50]

The young Locke, then, was a consciously and elaborately methodical thinker. And the end to be achieved by methodical thinking was the systematic comprehension of the universe, of its relation to men and of the relation of men to each other. In his *Logicae Artis Compendium*, a book Locke read before 1660, Robert Sanderson had not only explained the general principles on which knowledge should be ordered and analysed, he had also established for several generations of English scholars the broad and compelling intellectual purpose of ordering, tabulating, and similar methodical procedures. For Sanderson method and order are synonymous in their relation to the pursuit of knowledge; and the pursuit of knowledge is itself an 'ascent' towards a 'universal conclusion', which is the understanding of the divine order in all its precision and splendour. The indispensable means of this ascent is a methodical style of work.[51]

Whatever inconsistencies there may be between the political ideas of the young and the mature Locke, there are two themes that run unchanged through his entire career. One is the insistence on disciplined procedure, the enthusiasm for measuring, tabulating, arranging, comparing that spreads through all his work. The other is his assumption of the paramount interest and importance of theological questions and of the relatedness of all other sciences to theology. It is around theological knowledge that his diverse pursuits can be seen to cluster. It is the quest for such knowledge that gives purpose and cohesion to his successive writings and positions. For him there was, as he wrote in *Of the Conduct of the Understanding*,

one science (as they are now distinguished) incomparably above all the rest...I mean theology, which containing the knowledge of God and his creatures, our duty to him and to our fellow creatures, and a view of our present and future state, is the comprehension of all other knowledge, directed to its true end; the honour and veneration of the creator and the happiness of mankind.[52]

As an echo of Sanderson across a span of forty years this statement is remarkable. It suggests one more way in which Locke may properly be called a man not of the Great Revolution but of the Restoration.

Yet in 1660 there is a certain ambivalence if not in his thought at least in his behaviour. The organizing of his thought around theological problems and problems of knowledge derived from orthodox theology cannot be doubted. Nor can his concern for method, order and peace. Yet he did not, as a man of his background and interests would naturally have done in that age, enter the Church. Though he managed to 'keep [his] repute in Christ Church', and though he ended his 'funeral' speech as Censor in 1664 with the conventional exhortation to those seeking virtue, 'duo sunt praecipue loca mature semper frequentanda: aula ubi disputare templum ubi orare discant', he would not himself take orders.

On the contrary, as his biographers have all pointed out, he went to some lengths to avoid entering upon an ecclesiastical career. Oxford was for him the centre of civilization in 1660. The activities, studies and relationships he valued most were all concentrated there. The country was uncultivated and barbaric by comparison. And yet he would not take orders as a condition of staying in Oxford. Of the fifty-five places for Senior Students in Christ Church only five could at that time be held by men not in or reading for orders. And yet Locke despite his insecurity and his willingness to conform in so many respects held out against this pressure.[53]

His reasons seem to have been intellectual rather than material ones. As John Strachey wrote when Locke consulted him in 1663: 'Your Genius and Studies do now cross your present interest, and you must necessarily declare yourself for one.' In the event he declared against his present interest, offering no reason for doing so except that, by taking orders, 'I unavoidably lose all my former studies'. In 1666 we find him explaining again that it was this commitment to broader intellectual pursuits that 'made me a long time refuse very advantageous offers (of preferment) of several considerable friends here'. Yet we know of only two things that Locke was studying in these years: natural law and medicine. The former interest was in no way incompatible with a clerical career. It was clearly the pursuit of medicine and chemical science in general that he was unwilling to abandon.[54]

This interest can be traced back to at least 1655 and it culminated in his decision to make medicine the basis of a career outside the university in 1667. Four things should be noted about Locke's medical studies if we are to appreciate their place in his general intellectual and political development. First of all, medicine was an autonomous profession which had intellectual affinities with both moral and natural science; it provided a bridge to what was at that time the most rapidly and excitingly expanding of all fields of knowledge—the broad field of 'physic'. A revolution in chemical science was being effected in Oxford and medical activity gave Locke access to it; the influence of the major innovators, Van Helmont, Willis, Boyle, is evident throughout his notebooks. Secondly, the study of chemistry and the application of it to medical practice was for Locke's generation a fundamentally religious pursuit. The motives of the Oxford scientists were at bottom religious motives. Science and theology were complementary pursuits for them—this is implied in Locke's tabulations of the spheres of knowledge, of course. Willis's house in Oxford was a centre of Anglican worship as well as of chemical experiment throughout the Interregnum; the religious purpose that led Boyle to the study of nature, 'the wonderful elaboratory of God', is well known.[55]

Thirdly, to many of Locke's generation the scientific study of nature, although thought to be a complement to theological inquiry, was believed to hold out a surer prospect of reaching the common goal—demonstrable knowledge of the fundamental principles of universal order. It held out a hope of knowledge from which the irreducible element of trust in all religious knowledge could be eliminated. It offered the sort of certainty which seventeenth-century intellectuals had come to need and which old modes of knowledge, it was increasingly clear, could not provide. Thus John Pearson, whose *Exposition of the Creed* (Oxford, 1659) Locke read on the eve of the Restoration, distinguishes between the two orders of knowledge and adds that the naturalist's 'propositions and conclusions are not said to be credible but scientifical', whereas 'the faith of a Christian is an assent unto truths credible'. The attractions of 'scientifical' demonstration in any epistemological argument were compelling to a generation which had known nothing but dissent over truths credible. And, finally, there is a striking parallelism in the development of Locke's medical and political ideas between 1660 and 1667. Stewart has noted the 'fit' of Locke's medical and ethical writings after 1667, the common empiricism of the *Essay Concerning Toleration* and the *De Arte Medica*.[56] Dewhurst's study of Locke's medical papers for the years immediately before and after 1660 has led him to conclude that 'during the early period Locke was a thoroughgoing iatro-chemist' in the old tradition of the renaissance—in other words, that his medical thought, like his political thought, was caught up in a highly elaborated, formal, deductive system of ideas of which the ultimate purpose was moral.[57] How far he allowed his medical and ethical ideas to act directly on one another we cannot say. Certainly, as he adapted to the scientific revolution his mind was increasingly opened to the possibility of a revolution in epistemology. The impression of coherence, orderliness and sweeping scope in his thought is once again confirmed.

Meanwhile, in 1660 he was enmeshed in tradition; his teaching practice, the form and terms of his Latin writings, the categories used to organize knowledge in his commonplace books, all reveal a man entirely at home in the old conventions of scholastic thought and argument. Only occasional letters suggest that he already had doubts about the usefulness of those conventions, or betray a man who, despite most of the evidence he has left us about himself, was more concerned with meaning than with form, with 'clearing a truth' than with preserving an ideology.

We may conclude, then, that Locke was not a philosopher in the modern sense in 1660. The evidence suggests, rather, that he was not sure what he was. Conscious of himself as an intellectual with an intellectual's responsibilities, he was casting around to discover and establish his own particular intellectual identity. He had acquired a strong sense of the political, moral and scientific importance of order. And this made him sensitive to the uniquely disorderly issue of indifferent things. In turn, his efforts to handle that issue brought him face to face with the urgent question of the epistemological status of natural law. Natural law is not an issue debated in the *Tracts*. But it emerges from the *Tracts* as an imperative problem. Reliable knowledge about natural law, scientifical knowledge in effect, had to be obtained if the argument made in the tracts, or any similar traditional moral argument, was to stand up. Because Locke was a serious, sceptical and academic man, engaged on a very broad front in the pursuit of knowledge and unwilling, once involved with a problem, to be put off by the need to ask new or awkward questions, he accepted that challenge. Thus nurtured, the seeds of doubt visible in 1660 turned the young conservative into a great radical philosopher.

For Henry Stubbe, the 'whole question' of the Restoration was 'toleration or no toleration and not monarchy and the Stuartian interest'. For Locke, equally, it was not a question of particular rulers, nor of 'liberal' versus 'authoritarian' values, but on every level of experience a question of order or no order. His own experience, the question in dispute, and the immediate political situation converged to equate order with an uncompromising intellectual, moral and political conservatism. He could hardly have known in advance that the nature of the Great Question would make his attempt to reassert a conservative position in 1660 the pivot for his own subsequent development as a liberal.

NOTES

1 Wood, 1891, I, pp. 369, 408; *Register of the Visitors.*

2 Bagshaw, 1664; Wood, 1903, III, p. 4, and 1891, I, p. 269. Cranston, 1957, pp. 57–73; R. S. Jones, *Ancients and Moderns*, pp. 147 ff.

3 B.M. Add. MSS 32553, fols. 8–18—this correspondence of Stubbe and Hobbes remains a curiously neglected source; cf. Owen, 1826, VII, p. 279.

4 Wood, 1891, I, pp. 229 and 336, B.M. Add. MSS 32553, fol. 33; and cf. MS Locke c. 18, fol. 191, a letter from Strachey to Locke a fortnight after the episode reported by Wood in which Strachey gently mocks his friend as 'a young Master of Arts with all his formality on', to be told in reply by Locke, 'I must be excused if not arrived to that pitch as to look down with contempt on the formalities of a M.A.'

5 Wood, 1891, I, p. 369; Reynolds, 1826, I, p. 91 and v, p. 135.

6 English *Tract*, p. 25.

7 MS Locke c. 24, fol. 175.

8 Fell, 1659, p. 10; it is interesting to compare the arguments used to persuade Cromwell to take the Crown as reported in Whitlock, 1660, pp. 10, 55; *Register of the Visitors*, pp. 2, 17; Morley was himself a leader of the movement to secure a 'comprehensive' national church, cf. Bosher, 1951, pp. 105 ff.

9 Walton, 1678; Wood, 1891, I, p. 369, claims that both of the students of Christ Church expelled on 8 August 1660, William Sagery and Henry Stubbe, were men of violent habits; *Register of the Visitors*, p. 42; cf. the curious story in the *Register* of Benjamin Berry, one of the four chaplains of Christ Church, who was not expelled despite the fact that 'he hath not yet read the Common Prayers in the Church'.

10 Bosher, 1951, pp. 189–90; Wood, 1891, I, p. 327; Wood 276. A. 347 in the Bodleian Library is a copy of Hood's edict.

11 Wood, 1891, I, pp. 348 ff.; Wood argues that Fell's efforts were *both* tyrannical and *futile*. Elsewhere (p. 371) he suggests that the Presbyterians and Independents gave as good as they got—at least until the middle of 1661. With reference to rites and ceremonies he says that 'they endeavoured to make those things ridiculous', and generally had the better of the controversy, 'until the Act of Conformity came out'.

12 Stillingfleet, 1660, p. 38.

13 The problem of the use of indifferent things is handled in four stages in the New Testament. First the idea of indifferency itself is introduced; *then* the notion of conscience appears: thirdly, in I Corin-

thians, these two ideas (one an *ad hoc* concession to the political need to carry the Gospel to the Gentiles, the other the core of Paul's own distinctive pneumatist ethics) are, on the initiative of the Corinthians, brought into explosive contact with one another. Finally 'superior' sanctions are sought to contain the subversion of all order which the conjunction of conscience and indifferency implied. The Protestant Reformation repeated the same pattern of argument; cf. Pierce, 1955; Spicq, 1938; McNeill, 1954; Sykes, 1956.

14 Hooker, v, lxxi, 4.

15 Brooke, 1641, pp. 22–30, seizes the nature of the dilemma and anticipates Locke's mature position by insisting that the only substantial feature of any dispute over indifferent things is what each party *considers* indifferent. Like Locke after 1667 he demands toleration on the grounds of ignorance. Burges, 1631, *passim*.

16 Sanderson, 1660, iv, xx; Hooker, iii, x, 7; Parry, 1660, pp. 5–7.

17 Sanderson, 1660, vi, iii; Morton, 1619, ch. 11.

18 Morton, 1619, ch. 11; Sanderson, 1660, vi, iii; Powel, 1608, p. 52.

19 Woodhouse, 1938, pp. 39, 221–2; Milton, 1659, pp. 21–2, 33–6; Bradshawe, 1660, iii, p. 10; Owen, 1826, xix, p. 398.

20 Burgess, 1660, pp. 32–5; MS Locke c. 20, fol. 179, suggests that Samuel Tilly was possibly an intermediary between Locke and Burgess and that he may have shown the latter the manuscript of Locke's English *Tract* in the winter of 1660.

21 Hammond, 1644, iv; Burges, 1631, ch. iv; English *Tract*, p. 16; Latin *Tract*, pp. 14–15.

22 Sanderson, 1660, vi, xxii; Taylor, 1660, ii, ch. i, 10, v.

23 Hammond, 1644, i; Sanderson, 1660, iv, xx and v, xxii; Hooker, v, lxxi, 4; English *Tract*, p. 23; Latin *Tract*, p. 12.

24 Milton, 1659, p. 25, and cf. pp. 7, 16, 55; Ames, 1643, p. 108; Vane, 1655, p. 385; Williams, 1644, pp. 9, 49, 100, 130 and 219–22.

25 Walwyn, 1644: 'To compell me against my conscience is to compell me against what I believe to be true, and so against my faith: now whatsoever is not of faith is sin'; cf. Sibbes, 1639, pp. 78, 90, 112, 155–6 and 648; Busher, 1614, pp. 15–16.

26 Williams, 1644, p. 286.

27 Bagshaw, 1660 (*a*), p. 4; Robinson, 1643, p. 40.

28 Sanderson, 1657, Preface, and cf. Latin *Tract*, pp. 16–17; Stillingfleet, 1660, p. 57.

29 I Corinthians viii. 9–13; Aquinas, 1 *a*, II *ac*, qu. 9, art. 6; Pierce, 1955, p. 81.

30 Sanderson, 1657, iv; in short, 'men's judgments may make that which is good in its own nature become evil to them in the use'.

31 Taylor, 1660, i, iii; Morton, 1619, p. 153.

32 Romans xiv. 13; Bradshawe, 1660, vii; Jeanes, 1659, p. 18; 1660
passim.
33 Hammond, 1644, ii, i–xvii; Morton, 1619, v, ix; Locke, Latin *Tract*,
pp. 8–11.
34 Sibbes, 1639, p. 63.
35 Brooke, 1640, pp. 4 and 127 ff.; 1641, pp. 22–30.
36 Brooke, 1641, pp. 13, 22 ff.
37 Taylor, 1847, vii, p. 19; Hoopes, 1950; Strype, 1821, i, p. 390;
Jordan, 1932, ii, p. 237; Goodwin, 1644, p. 1.
38 Morton, 1662, p. 34.
39 Milton, 1659, pp. 30 and 55–8; Bradshawe, 1660, vii, 2.
40 Aaron, 1937, p. 3.
41 Shaw, 1900, ii, appx. 3; MS Locke, c. 14, fol. 165 and c. 24, fol. 173;
Bristol Deposition Books, pp. 409–18; Wood, 1903; B.M. Add. MSS
28273—the notebook of Locke's father.
42 MS Locke c. 24, fol. 231.
43 See particularly the notebook endorsed *Lemmata* (MS Locke e. 6)
and the account book (MS Locke f. 11) which lists both Locke's
own reading as a student and the books he bought for his pupils
when he started teaching in Christ Church at the end of 1660. The
book *Lemmata* is arranged as a commonplace book, its sources are
listed on the fly leaf (the latest publication date is 1654), and those
most quoted are the *Prolusiones Academicae* of the Jesuit Famiano
Strada—formal disquisitions on the scholastic liberal sciences,
oratory, logic, etc.; Du Bartas, *Divine Weeks and Works*, the best
known of the polite, moralizing theogonies of the early seventeenth
century; and the *Epistulae Morales* of Seneca. Typical entries in this
book are those under the heads *Eloquentia, Lingua, Rhetoricae finis,
Oratio perfecta et bona qualis*. The list in the account book (MS Locke
f. 11) adds several textbooks, Sanderson's *Logic*, Smith's *Logic*,
Trevis's *Logic*, classical texts, and works of Anglican theology
(Hammond's *Fundamentals*, Allestree's *Duty of Man*, etc.). Two
works only in these lists suggest any interests outside the framework of a thoroughly orthodox ecclesiastical training, the *Methodus*
of Bodin and the *Astronomy* of Gassendi.
44 Meyer, 1952, pp. 155–8; Digby, 1658, ii, viii.
45 *Britannia Rediviva*, 1660; *Musarum Oxoniensum*, 1654. The Christ
Church contributions to the 1654 volume were headed by that of
Owen and we may perhaps consider all the Students who followed him
as among the 'creatures' of the Dean, in Stubbe's phrase. Bagshaw
contributed as Praelector in Metaphysics. Locke's tutor, Thomas
Cole, also wrote, as did his friends Ward, Godolphin and Hodges.
The latter was, with Locke, among the twenty-four university poets

who wrote in both 1654 and 1660. The panegyrists of 1660 included most of Locke's closest friends: Hodges, Uvedale, Towerson, Nurse, Percivall and Hoskins, also Wood's 'young pragmatic', Robert South. For other political poems by Locke cf. MS Locke c. 32, fols. 7–10.

46 Tillyard, 1950, p. 13; cf. Bethell, 1951; Lovejoy, 1936; and MS Locke f. 31, fol. 18.

47 Cranston, 1957, ch. IV, has explored Locke's early social circle in detail. The picture he finds is one of constant insecurity and anxiety overlaid with an elaborate formal 'civility': cf. MS Locke c. 11, fols. 229, 233, c. 24, fols. 276, 280, 281. His letters adhere to set Balzacian form—the exploration of all the literary possibilities of a chosen conceit at whatever expense to meaning; cf. MS Locke c. 10, fol. 17, c. 16, fol. 129, c. 24, fol. 49, and Abrams, 1961.

48 MS Locke c. 24, fols. 14, 173, 182.

49 Bodleian Library, MS Film 77, pp. 1–3: the volume contains several attempts to formalize the categories of knowledge; on p. 24 there is *Adversaria Philosophia* and on p. 290, *Sapientia*; apart from such comprehensive efforts there are many classifications of particular branches of knowledge, e.g. p. 156; and cf. MSS Locke c. 27 and c. 28.

50 MSS Locke e. 4 and f. 18–21 (the medical notebooks); cf. Howell, 1956; Abrams, 1961.

51 Sanderson, 1615.

52 Locke, *Of the Conduct of the Understanding*, XXIII.

53 Von Leyden, 1954, p. 238; MS Locke c. 17, fol. 162, and cf. Fox Bourne, 1871, I, pp. 67 ff.; Cranston, 1957, pp. 77, 95–8; MS Locke c. 16, fol. 188, c. 18, fols. 214, 217v and c. 24, fols. 9–13, 49, 221–2, 289.

54 MS Locke c. 24, fols. 214, 221.

55 Boyle, 1662; Allen, 1946; Westfall, 1959; Pagel, 1934 and 1935.

56 Pearson, 1659, p. 10; Brown, 1897, p. 5; Stillingfleet, 1662.

57 Private communication; and cf. Dewhurst, 1962, pp. 30–1.

THE POLITICS OF CONSERVATISM:
THE BESIEGED CITY

The political philosophy of the *Tracts on Government* is best described in the words John Stuart Mill applied to the positive philosophy of Comte, as the politics of the besieged city.

In the Latin *Tract* Locke retails a curious story which had gripped his imagination and which I think distils his understanding of politics in 1660. It is the story of a Chinese city blockaded for many months by Tartars and driven at last to surrender:

The gates were thrown open to the hostile army and all the inhabitants gave themselves up to the will of the triumphant victors. They delivered into their enemy's hands their persons, their wives, their families, their liberty, their goods and, in short, all things both sacred and profane. But when they were ordered to cut off the plait of hair which it was a national custom among them to wear they took up arms again and fought desperately until every one of them was killed.

The two distinctively Lockeian themes here are the concern with the partiality of men for their own arbitrary and trivial habits and prejudices, and the image of the polity in a state of siege.

The sense of partiality is ubiquitous. Hitherto information about distant societies had been used to demonstrate the fundamental similarity of men. Political arguments had been built on the theme of universal corruption or universal equality. Hobbes makes reference to the American Indians for this sort of purpose. But Locke is impressed by differences rather than similarities. His political theory rests on the assumption that differences must be taken as given, that 'our Beauty' is quite simply 'others' Deformity', and that between societies there are no common criteria in terms of which differences can be resolved, 'esteem putting all the difference of value'. He can find no basis for disciplining men's partiality for their own opinions; rather, 'we are all Quakers': 'Men live upon trust and their knowledge is nothing but opinion moulded up between custom and interest, the two great luminaries of the world, the only lights they walk by.' Men's judgments are at once irreducibly divergent and all equally insubstantial. This is the source of the problem of politics, and of the need for a transcendent solution:

That which I look to is that hand that governs all things, that manages our chaos and will bring out of it what will be best for us and what we ought to acquiesce in. I have long since learned not to rely on men, these bubbles however swollen and glittering, soft and inviting are not fit to be leaned on and whoever shall make them his support shall find them nothing but a little gilded air.[1]

And the problem is aggravated by the fact that civil society is permanently besieged. Locke's deepest assumptions about the natural inclinations and proclivities of men find expression in his claim that most men are incapable of civilized and collective life. He speaks, therefore, of society as being threatened from *outside* when referring to human beings who were technically subject to the same government as himself. It is not mutiny that threatens the ship of state but the forces of nature outside it. This, the most familiar of all political analogies, is Locke's commonest metaphor; and his use of it is charged with feeling: 'A ship methinks is no improper name for this island, for surely it hath no foundation.' In 1660, to his horror, he saw the ship 'putting forth into a new storm':

Nor will the largeness of the governor's power appear dangerous or more than necessary if we consider that as occasion requires it is employed upon the multitude that are as impatient of restraint as the sea, and whose tempests and overflows cannot be too well provided against.[2]

The image of the state as a ship permits much elaboration. Locke develops his theme with consistency and enthusiasm; magistrates are the crew of the ship, the 'people' are the passengers and, distinct from the people, outside the ship, the 'multitude' is the storm-tossed sea on which the ship must sail. The people are obliged to submit to the 'steering' of the magistrate and to allow him 'sole guiding' of the ship if they are to be safe from the wanton violence of the waves, the non-people, the multitude. 'Would it be thought dangerous or inconvenient', he asks, 'that anyone should be allowed to make banks and fences against the waves, for fear he should too much encroach upon and straighten the ocean?' A surrender to rigorous authority is the condition of survival for the people. The role of the magistrate is to protect them. And it is this duty that obliges him to steer the ship with a firm and strong hand

> who would rather be content to steer the vessel with a gentle than a stiff hand would the winds and waves permit him; he increases his forces and violence only with the increase of the storm and tumult; the tossings and several turns of the ship are from without and not begotten in the steerage or at the helm.[3]

Changing his image he offers another threefold distinction to illumine his sense of the nature of politics. The political order is composed of 'gods', who are magistrates, 'men' who are the responsible subjects, and 'beasts', or the multitude. Though these analogies are completely conventional Locke clearly believes that he is here offering a fundamental analysis of the whole nature of politics, and probing 'the spring and wheels that give it motion'. Government exists to provide bulwarks for civil society against the multitude, that multitude, 'always craving, never satisfied', over whom 'there can be nothing set...which they will not always be reaching at and endeavouring to pull down'. This is the nightmare that gives force to the conclusion on which he so frequently insists—that absolute authority is the 'unalterable' condition, the 'foundation' of all 'order, society and government in the world'.

Locke's politics spring spontaneously from these general conceptions. His idea of partiality, his acute sense of human self-liking, his understanding of reason as the creature of prejudice are focused politically in the idea of the multitude, cynically disabused descriptions of which open both *Tracts*:

> The generality of men conducted either by chance or advantage take to themselves their opinions as they do their wives, which when once they have espoused, they think themselves concerned to maintain, though for no other reason but because they are theirs.

> quotusquisque nam pene est qui in hac re sibi temperare potest, qui sedato animo huiusmodi disputationibus se patitur interesse, nec credat suam rem serio agi summi viribus ne dicam vi et armis propugnandam.[4]

And the same insights lead him further, to his insistence that human partiality generates not simply diversity, dissidence and folly but malice. It is not just that the multitude is wanton and weak; the great threat to government and order lies in the fact that the multitude is led by men who are purposefully destructive, who know what they are about and feel no shame. Locke, like Comte, rests his case for absolute government on a conspiracy theory of politics. He reserves a special venom and contempt for those who maliciously 'inflame' the people, the sinister leaders of the mob. For these leaders are deserters from the ranks of the 'people', 'knowing men' who ought to know better, men not beasts but men of ill will, not simply men with different convictions from Locke's own. He has no understanding of or sympathy with Bagshaw's enthusiasm for 'variety'. Rather, he inveighs against the malevolence of the leaders of the many, and his censure is most harsh when those leaders are men of his own type—intellectuals, writers and churchmen. The fault of the 'generality' is but their folly and partiality, their 'zealous mistakes'. The fault of their leaders, 'crafty men', is more ominous:

[Their] cunning and malice have taken occasion to pervert the doctrine of peace and charity into a perpetual foundation of war and contention; all those flames that have made such havoc and desolation in Europe and have not been quenched but with the blood of so many millions, have been at first kindled with coals from the altar, and too much blown with the breath of those that attend the altar who forgetting their calling...have proved the trumpeters of strife and sounded a charge with a 'curse ye Meros'.[5]

Elsewhere, their 'native ugliness' is held up to the 'contempt of the world'; they are inspired only by 'ambition and revenge'; they deceive the people with 'secret contrivances'; in their 'private studies' they have 'conjured up...war, cruelty, rapine, confusion'; their object is to 'fire and inspirit' the multitude and so, amid 'violence and cruelty', to 'despoil us'.

Joined to the pessimistic view of human nature which made him see the state as ringed round with malignant and irresponsible enemies, we find a political teleology. The state, for Locke, is justified by its ends. The image of the ship, of course, implied an end, a direction. And for Locke this direction exists independently of the intentions of the pilot. The job of the latter was not just to keep the ship of state afloat, but to keep it on its proper course and bring it to its proper destination. The ship was to be steered, 'not on to the rocks but into harbour', 'oh, for a pilot that would steer the tossed ship of this state to the haven of happiness'. Men must accept the decisions of the pilot because only he can keep the ship afloat. But the pilot himself is bound by the end or 'final cause' of magistracy.[6]

This end, in turn, is nothing but order, *bene compositus ordo*. Partiality makes the state necessary; the pursuit of order justifies it. If men must be brought to see that their safety and tranquillity lie in surrendering their own opinions and allowing the ship to be steered by its pilot, the magistrate must equally understand that if he steers off course, if he rules in defiance of the end of government, he sins.

The source of these attitudes betrays Locke's intellectual conservatism. The image of the state as a ship was standard ecclesiastical usage, a platitude of the age: 'I have learnt it out of the pulpit whence I hear it every Sunday.' Its currency and its use for the purposes to which Locke puts it both lie beyond the seventeenth century in the traditional political theory of the Schools. They derive from Cicero, from Aristotle, and from Plato. It was Socrates who first asked the question that Locke echoes; to whom would you entrust a boat, to a trained pilot or to anyone who comes along, *quemvis a plebe*? Whatever use Locke may have made in the *Tracts* of the sociological arguments for strong government devised by seventeenth-century materialists, his commitment is ultimately to this older idealist tradition. For him, as for his predecessors, the end towards which the state must progress is a moral equilibrium, order, defined by the absence of human partiality.[7]

So much for the core of Locke's politics in 1660. He has a sceptical and anti-rationalist view of human nature; a besieged-city conception of political values; a conspiracy theory of political life; and a classical, teleological idea of the state. Into this framework he drew materials from virtually every available contemporary source of any standing. He made use of every political and social theory of any acknowledged weight to sustain his case against the free use of indifferent things. So far as sources can be perceived in his writing, he seems to have been quite remarkably eclectic in his conservatism.

This is apparent in the political categories entered in the *Adversaria 1661*. Locke here recognizes two 'foundations' of government each of which he discusses in the Latin tract, *ius paternum* and *consensus populi*. In the *Adversaria*, as in the *Tracts*, he treats these as equally viable hypotheses as to the origin of government and as the only two which either need to be taken seriously or have any general intellectual standing. He uses both without giving any impression that he felt at all constrained to settle for either. In addition to the question of how government is established, there is the separate issue of its legislative form. Here again Locke is eclectic. Although in this case he indicates a personal preference—for undiluted monarchy—he accepts the propriety and legitimacy of quite different forms. And in the *Adversaria 1661* he identifies four possible 'fundamental constitutions' of states: monarchy, aristocracy, democracy and a 'mixed' form. Any of these systems can sustain a state. Nowhere in his writings does he seem to regard it as his business to weigh their respective merits.[8]

In the *Tracts* in particular he is at pains to give the impression that it is irrelevant to his argument which theory of the origin of government and which view of the proper form of sovereignty one adopts: 'verum de his nihil statuo'...he insists. His use of social contract arguments in the English *Tract* is presented, elaborately, as a concession to a hypothesis one may take up or ignore at will; 'if you choose to take such and such a view you must still come to the conclusion that...', is the form of argument he favours.

Most commentators—Gough is an exception—have taken Locke's mode of argument at face value. But recent studies of Locke's later writings have suggested that face value is something one cannot safely attribute to any work by Locke. In the *Two Treatises* we find him using what he knew from his own earlier studies to be the thoroughly unsatisfactory concept of natural law as though it were quite unproblematic. Cox claims to have discovered a persistent strategy on Locke's part of insinuating radical positions into arguments which, in their form, terms and design, would seem to be acceptable to those in political or ecclesiastical authority. A principal tactic of this strategy was to associate such positions with the views of eminently respectable authorities such as Hooker and the Bible. In the light of such doubts about Locke's methods of political argument, we must surely ask whether his open-handed treatment of the fundamental questions of political theory and his seemingly simple relationship to the orthodox Anglican tradition are all that they appear, especially when we find that in 1661 he consciously regarded the means to fame or power as 'the governing of passion by rhetoric'.[9]

Locke mentions Hooker on two occasions in the *Tracts*. He refers to Sanderson once and deletes a second reference. He does not mention Hobbes at all. Yet the weight of commentary plainly implies that the reverse order would more nearly reflect the true intellectual importance of each of these sources for Locke's early thought. The only other writer explicitly mentioned is Bishop Maxwell, whose anti-presbyterian essay, *The Burden of Issachar*, is cited as authority for a particularly extreme observation in the English *Tract*.[10]

Ostensibly Locke discusses Hooker in the English *Tract* only because Bagshaw had made a point against that 'eminent champion of truth'. Locke declares that he has read no more than the Preface to *The Laws of Ecclesiastical Polity*. But he takes the opportunity, in enlarging on his inability to 'make good' Hooker's arguments, to identify his own case with that of his 'learned and reverend' predecessor. We are invited to suppose that his argument against Bagshaw is a humble reiteration of a case made by Hooker. In fact Locke's argument is distinctly more radical than that of his source. According to Bagshaw Hooker's argument accepted that a meaningful distinction could be made between civil and religious indifferent things. But Locke's gloss assumes that while Bagshaw foolishly upholds such a distinction Hooker, like Locke, denies it. Locke's whole argument turns on this denial. And Hooker is made to appear to back such an argument—which, as quoted by Bagshaw, he does not.[11]

The appeal to Hooker in the Latin *Tract* is of more fundamental importance. Locke's whole case turns on his ability to derive obligations from a universal, demonstrable system of law. When he first takes up the analysis of law, he at once refers to Hooker and quotes the famous definition of law from Book I of *The Laws of Ecclesiastical Polity*: 'That which doth assign unto each thing the kind, that which doth moderate the force and power, that which doth appoint the form and measure of working, the same we term a law.' Here again the impression intended would seem to be that Locke's exposition will follow that of Hooker, that his system of law, like Hooker's, will be functional and teleological.

The passage from which Hooker's definition comes leaves no doubt that what demonstrates the existence of a law for him, and is the true hallmark of law, is regularity of working in relation to some 'fore-conceived end'. But this is not the case for Locke. For him it is neither the mode of operation nor the end which in the first instance distinguishes a law. It is its derivation from the will of a superior authority.[12]

Now Hooker explicitly rejects this voluntaristic conception of law in the section of his book immediately following that from which Locke quotes. He insists that law is to be judged teleologically. Any principle that directs 'unto goodness of operation' is a law since law is defined by its end. His position is quite at odds with the theory of 'the learned' in which law merely articulates an essentially unjudgeable order 'set down' by God. He discusses that theory—the theory that the 'name of law' applies 'unto that only rule of working which superior authority imposeth'—and repudiates it. Locke, on the other hand, despite his bow to Hooker, adopts just such a theory.[13]

The question arises of how far Locke knew that his use of Hooker was misleading. By prefacing his treatment of law with the passage from Hooker he distracts attention from the voluntarism of his own position. Such a position had many disadvantages which Locke may well have wished to avoid; the notorious champions of voluntarism in the immediate past had been the Presbyterians on the one side, Hobbes on the other; the position involved a degree of authoritarianism not altogether pleasant to contemplate; and it directed attention to epistemological questions hardly raised by the calm rationalism of Hooker. I am inclined to think Locke knew what he was doing; particularly as Sanderson's general definition of law, which is very close to the one Locke actually uses, is coupled with the quotation from Hooker in the manuscript of the Latin *Tract*, and then carefully deleted.[14]

In Oxford at least, Sanderson's standing as a moral philosopher was probably higher than Hooker's in 1660. Locke's debt to Sanderson is clear; his debt to Hooker is questionable. Why, then, cancel a quotation from Sanderson and appeal instead to Hooker on a matter of such critical importance as the nature of law? Because, I think, he felt that only a voluntaristic position could support the degree of political authority he needed but was not yet ready to plunge into the epistemological abyss that opened up when one faced the problem of demonstrating just what God had willed. It is that abyss which Hooker's view of law so neatly avoids.[15]

In Hooker's system obligation derives not from the supposed superiority of law-makers, but from the self-evident purpose of law—the need to pursue and realize order. Locke, too, was attracted by this position. He would have liked to treat laws rather than law-makers as the sufficient basis of obligation.[16] Thus, where Hobbes and Sanderson make the *ius gladii* the crux of sovereignty Locke follows Hooker in making it the *ius legislativa*. And in the Latin *Tract* he tries to show that the question of what is and is not a law can be settled without reference to the idea of power. But Hooker's remarkable Christian confidence had enabled him to set aside the problem of the ulterior sanction of laws without qualms. As Baker points out, Hooker was the last English author who took the 'axiom of knowledge' for granted, who could write as though the 'great rationalistic assumption' of Christianity, the assumption of sure access to the nature and purposes of God, had never been challenged. In Locke's generation the axiom of knowledge was still asserted, but the confidence had evaporated. Locke *had* to discuss law in terms of will. But for him, as for most latter-day Christian conservatives, Hooker's majestic refusal to reason beyond the fact of law remained an ideal, however unattainable. Hooker, after all, had not been unaware of the dangers beneath the surface: 'They that seek a reason of all things do utterly overthrow reason.' Sixty years and innumerable 'disputations' had made the dilemma that much more acute for Locke.[17]

But Locke may have had a second, less reputable reason for deleting his reference to Sanderson. His interest in Sanderson's arguments may have been outweighed by a temperamental sympathy with Hooker, but there can be no doubt that the immediate influence on the form and terminology of the Latin *Tract* was that of Sanderson. To direct attention to the author of the *De Obligatione Conscientiae* was to reveal an intellectual debt of striking proportions. As it is, Sanderson is used throughout the *Tract* and the debt is nowhere acknowledged.

Locke mentions Sanderson in the English work in the passage where he refers to Hooker and for the same reason—because Bagshaw had discussed him. He makes no distinction between the two authors, though he says that he read Sanderson's lectures, albeit with 'haste and inadvertency' at 'their first appearance in public'. He had clearly studied them more closely by the time he wrote the Latin *Tract*. Passage after passage reveals a borrowing not just of ideas and categories but even of turns of phrase. In his conception of divine worship, for example, Locke follows

Sanderson in detail. The way he expounds the nature of obligation is Sanderson's way. The formula he adopts to deal with the origin of government is Sanderson's formula. His distinction between the liberty of the will and the liberty of the judgment is Sanderson's distinction. One could reasonably argue, indeed, that the *Tract* is little more than a paraphrase of lectures v, vi and vii of Sanderson's book.[18]

But there are ways in which the similarity is more apparent than real. Most of the terms of Locke's argument come from Sanderson. But in the critical passages of Locke's case the borrowing is formal, not substantial. Where Locke is in closest agreement with Sanderson, where the suggestion of plagiarism is strongest, as in the account of divine worship, Sanderson is himself speaking for the whole body of Anglican moral theology. Elsewhere the apparently indiscriminate borrowing of categories and forms of argument often conceals a subtle but consequential shift of emphasis and meaning. This is especially true of Locke's account of law.

For Locke, as for Sanderson, the defining characteristic of law is its derivation from a competent will, an 'efficient' cause. But Locke is in fact *more* rigorous in asserting this position than Sanderson. Despite his voluntaristic definition of law the latter actually envisages three distinct ways in which law entails obligation. There is the 'efficient' cause, the will that makes a law; there is the 'material' cause, the matter about which the law is made; and there is the 'final' cause, the purpose for which the law is made. Each of these may be more or less just and the obligation to obey will be modified accordingly. For Locke the efficient cause is really all that matters.

The final cause of law, he argues, is inscrutable so far as subjects are concerned. Governors certainly sin if their laws are not tailored to the final cause of government, but since only God can judge this question it is of no practical political importance. Locke thus avoids having to follow Sanderson through the ungainly investigation of *salus populi suprema lex* views of the final cause of government which dissipates the argument of the last two lectures of the *De Obligatione Conscientiae*. He can do so because he is more voluntaristic than Sanderson. All that matters for him is that inferior law-makers should be properly authorized to exercise their wills by the will of the paramount law-maker, God.

In the same way Locke contrives to minimize the importance of the material cause of obligation. The propriety of the subject-matter of any law is, he argues, determined in advance by the moral status of the will of the legislator. Thus, although the hierarchy of laws postulated by Locke is identical to that postulated by Sanderson so far as the subject-matter of each type of law is concerned, Locke can reasonably claim that his classification represents an essentially new system. Sanderson names his laws indifferently from their efficient and material causes. The laws recognized by Locke are identified exclusively in terms of their authors, the wills that create them, their efficient causes. Even Hobbes, who promised a classification of laws derived from the authors of each type in *De Cive*, never went as far as Locke towards developing such an analysis.

And there is no sign of Sanderson's tendency to allow that final or material factors could seriously qualify the obligation of laws made by a properly authorized law-maker. The rule that 'where the matter is lawful the standard of obedience is not the intention of the law-maker, which cannot be known, but his will which creates obligation' would itself suffice to justify the imposition of indifferent things. But Locke goes further and rules, as a true voluntaristic system requires, that even where the matter of an injunction is unlawful the subject has only a partial escape from obligation: 'The subject is bound to passive obedience under any decree of the magistrate whatever, whether just or unjust... though indeed if the matter be unlawful the magistrate sins in commanding it.'[19]

In short, all that Locke leaves open to question is the competence of the efficient cause of law. *Everything is made to turn on the moral authority of the magistrate's will.* And since in his account of law lower legislators obtain their authority from the acts of will of higher legislators, the pivot of his argument turns out to be the problem of the origin or foundation of government. His claim that he is *not* concerned with that problem, though it is made in both *Tracts*, is perforce naïve or disingenuous. An exploration of the source of human legislative authority was integral to his theory of obligation. He could afford to talk casually or hypothetically about the origins of government only if he could be sure that *any* view of those origins would demonstrate the effective authorization of a legislative will. Now it is Locke's repeated claim that this is indeed the case and that therefore, to quote one of the many passages in which he makes this point, he does not need:

to meddle with that question whether the magistrate's crown drops down on his head immediately from heaven or be placed there by the hands of his subjects, it being sufficient to my purpose that the supreme magistrate of every nation what way soever created, must necessarily have an absolute and arbitrary power over all the indifferent actions of his people.[20]

But in order to make good his claim he is carefully selective about the theories of the origins of government that he chooses to discuss. He picks the purest of all available versions of the *ius paternum* theory to represent all patriarchal arguments, and the most thoroughgoing statement of social contract theory to serve for all contract arguments. Yet he sensibly shows signs of dissatisfaction with both of these theories in their pure form. To this extent he weakens his own argument. But by the same token he emancipates himself from the influence of both Filmer and Hobbes.

From 1660 to 1672 Locke regularly treats patriarchal theory as one of the two possible fundamentals of political theory. Gough and De Marchi both find a patriarchalist influence which they trace to Filmer in the *Tracts*.[21] Many of the analogies he invokes to give meaning to his conception of the nature of political authority are drawn from the relationship of father and child. It is at least possible that he had made some study of Filmer before 1660. There are two references to *The Anarchy of a Limited or Mixed Monarchy* in a notebook dating from 1659 and in one of these Locke reproduces Filmer's account of absolute monarchy and notes, 'huiusmodi monarchia optime defenditur'.[22] He writes in the *Tracts* as though he supposed that one could argue directly from the idea of a *ius paternum*, an immediate grant of power by God to the heads of families, to a legitimation of the will of the magistrate.

But a half sentence in the Latin *Tract* makes it clear that he was not happy with this supposition. Having presented patriarchal theory as a received view of the sources of civil power he goes on to raise a difficulty which, if developed, would effectively nullify it: 'ex paterno iure ius ad imperium...haud facile constabit.'[23] It was just the authority for transforming fathers into legislators that patriarchal theory in his view failed to provide. He was to return to this difficulty, of course, in the first of the *Two Treatises*. Meanwhile we may wonder whether his endorsement of patriarchal politics in the *Tracts* was much more than a concession to contemporary axioms and assumptions. As he recognizes in the Latin *Tract*, he had no need to argue further with anyone who would accept a patriarchalist theory of the origins of government—those who thought magistrates were born to rule would in any case endorse his case for the imposition of indifferent things. This being so, he did not need to explore the problem which he seems already to have perceived in the patriarchal argument. Patriarchalists could be left to satisfy themselves that the magistrate was adequately authorized to make law.

The only substantial account of the authorization of magistrates that Locke offers in the *Tracts* is thus to be found in his restatement of arguments from the second fundamental he chose to recognize, *consensus populi*. And here the question arises of the influence of Hobbes.

It has been argued that the ideas of Hobbes are more clearly visible in the *Tracts* of 1660 than in any of Locke's other works. Thus, Gough and Cranston, pointing to a series of verbal parallels in passages of the English *Tract* and passages of *Leviathan*, ascribe to Locke's early political theory a 'definitely Hobbesian' character. Cranston cites Locke's description of the condition of men without government, claiming that it is 'unmistakably cribbed' from Hobbes's longer and less abstract account. Where Hobbes envisaged

no place for industry because the fruit thereof is uncertain, and consequently no culture of the earth, no navigation nor use of commodities that may be imported by sea, no commodious building, no instruments of moving and removing such things as require much force, no knowledge of the face of the earth; no account of time, no arts, no letters, no society, and, which is worst of all, continual fear and danger of violent death, and the life of man solitary, poor, nasty, brutish and short;

Locke imagines 'no peace, no security, no enjoyment, enmity with all men and safe possession of nothing, and those stingin swarms of misery which attend anarchy and rebellion'.

It would have been strange if Locke had not echoed Hobbesian attitudes in some degree in 1660. It is not just, as Laslett says, that 'Hobbist notions were in the air'. The notorious champion of Hobbes, the translator of *Leviathan*, Henry Stubbe, was Locke's neighbour in Somerset, his fellow pupil at Westminster, his contemporary at Christ Church, his correspondent, and the object of his professed admiration as a political author. Quite apart from which, the logic of Locke's case against Bagshaw itself impelled Locke to argue from consent as the source of government to absolute authority as its essential character. Of such arguments Hobbes was the acknowledged master.[24]

However, I find the business of spotting verbal parallels inconclusive. In particular, the Hobbesian account of the condition of masterless men was itself something of a platitude of the age by 1660. It was certainly not Hobbes's exclusive property. Before *Leviathan* was published, Sanderson, in a work we know Locke read, had described life without government in terms that are close to Hobbes but closer still to the young Locke:

nihil inter homines tutum erit, nihil ab injuriis, perjuriis, fraudibus, rapinibus, caedibus, perduellionibus, immune; exulent necesse est e terra, sine quibus conservari non possunt Respublicae et hominum societates, Religio, Justitia, Aequitas, Fides, Pax.[25]

Very similar formulations can be found in many other authors of the 1640s. Thus, Anthony Ascham writes: 'Without Government, no laws, no propriety and distinction or severance of rights; and what then ensues but miserable confusions and shoreless excesses by encroachments upon one another.' Dudley Digges, a monarchist author writing in 1644, similarly anticipates both Locke and Hobbes in standing consent theories on their heads to produce an absolute state: 'What the supreme power...does is truly the act of all and none can have just quarrel of what they themselves do.' For Digges, as for Locke, the 'transferring every particular man's power into the hands of one', the 'making his will the will of them all', is an unavoidable condition of political society— 'necessity enforces it'. Like Locke and like Hobbes he has many grim accounts of the pre-political condition of man, that 'unhappy condition amidst fears and jealousies, wherein each single person...doubted lest the hand of every man might be upon him'.[26]

Hobbes gave such views their definitive articulation. But the ideas involved are those of an older authoritarian tradition forced, before Hobbes, to come to terms with the theory of consent. Locke, like Digges and Ascham, felt himself obliged to argue with those who believed that consent should be the basis of government. Like them he was therefore led to embrace the form of argument which Hobbes was to develop more cogently than any other writer. I can find no evidence to suggest more than a fortuitous proximity of this sort, however.

And there are important differences. Locke agrees with Hobbes that primitive human liberties must be alienated for political society to be created. And he agrees that as a result of the way those liberties are alienated the commands of magistrates are in effect the subjects' own decisions made by proxy. But Hobbes insists that the alienation of private freedom that makes society must also be an alienation of judgment—so that, 'that which shall be commanded is no less the [individual's] judgment than the judgment of the magistrate'. Locke follows the Anglican orthodoxy in reserving the freedom of judgment to the individual and thus holding that freedom of conscience is possible even while we obey the magistrate in all our actions. Hobbes eliminates the freedom of conscience as well as that of action. Even Henry Stubbe was moved to object that this was to 'deify the magistrate'.[27]

Again, for Hobbes it was the rigorous ethic of self-preservation that made the alienation of man's primitive freedom a compelling obligation. For Locke, as for Digges, it was the older, ideal conception of scholastic metaphysics, 'order'. Men must surrender their freedom, not to preserve themselves but to preserve order. The obligation is couched in the language of Hobbes but its force is quite different. Digges explained the 'necessity' of absolute authority in 1644 in just the terms Locke was to use in 1660: 'Because without this the essence and being of a State were destroyed, which is Order. For if this ceases, first and last be confounded and the city is dissolved into a multitude and that which should be one body, becomes so many independent men.' Locke's argument has the same circularity; unlike that of Hobbes it is essentially pre-sociological.[28] In so far as he commits himself it is to that third way of establishing government envisaged by Sanderson—in which sovereignty is willed by God as the condition of order, particular sovereigns are selected by consent.[29]

Locke, then, voices an established constitutionalist and conservative position. In those characteristic respects in which Hobbes himself departed from that convention Locke tends not to follow him. He makes no use of the dynamic mechanism of the ethic of self-preservation. His meagre references to natural law suggest the notion of a body of quite orthodox principles of morality. He makes no use of the idea so essential to Hobbes of natural law as a set of prudential constraints that can be rationally deduced from the character of the human predicament. The one doubt he expresses about the theory of consent in the Latin *Tract* suggests that at a very critical point he was not prepared to be as ruthless as Hobbes in deriving obligations from compact. He does not see, he says, how a right 'of life and death' can be delivered to the magistrate by the surrender of man's primitive liberty. This is a point on which Hobbes himself is ambiguous. But Hobbes chose to allow mutually exclusive rights and leave the resolution to force; the magistrate has the right to condemn to death; and the condemned man has the right to escape—if he can. Neither right invalidates the other. And it is right that the stronger party should prevail. Locke, as we have seen, turns his face against such a position. His overriding concern is to embrace every political situation in a network of unambiguous law. Where the theory of consent fails to do this he is unhappy with it.

On the other hand, Hobbes, despite his pessimism, builds his system of politics on an assumption of human rationality. His natural laws bind only when they are found out by reason; and unless his natural laws bind Leviathan cannot be created. He has to suppose that natural law will in practice be found out, naturally, by reason. Locke's pessimism rests by contrast on a profound anti-rationalism. For him reason is irretrievably the creature of interest and prejudice. Law, on the other hand, exists independently of the malignant and prejudiced determinations of human reasoning. It expresses both the more substantial rationality of God and a will of incontrovertible authority. Ultimately it is the will of God commanding order, not the rationalized instinct of self-preservation, that Locke invokes.

In short, Locke's position is neither a direct reflexion of any single source nor a mere piecing together of sources. It is a synthesis of sources in a distinctive pattern which is already Locke's own. He uses the formulas of Sanderson (and of the old constitutionalist tradition) to explain the origin of power. But in the last resort he opts for the argument from consent and not, as Sanderson did, *ius paternum*. And the act of consent and contract he describes is not the restricted constitution-making grant usual in that tradition but the self-alienating surrender demanded by Hobbes. Yet he is too committed to the ideal of the autonomy of law to accept the whole of Hobbes's account of the pre-conditions and consequences of compact. Conversely, he knows that law is not autonomous and constantly refers back to the authority of law-makers. The only developed account of the authorization of human law-makers that he offers is that of Hobbes. But he ignores Hobbes's laws of nature and concomitant sociology of politics, and thus the necessity of obedience, which he asserts cannot be simply inferred from the conditions of existence, as it was by Hobbes. It is not obvious that order necessitates obedience in the way that Hobbes's natural laws do—as Bagshaw was quick to point out.

At this point he follows Hooker and Sanderson in appealing to the central conception of the active and consequential will of God. Locke's argument raises no problems if he is right about what God has willed. But unlike Hooker and Sanderson, Locke was not prepared to state with the traditional bland authority just what God had willed and how we knew it. He pays lip service to the traditional idea of the two complementary modes of knowledge but in the event he has no account of natural law and only a doubtful account of revelation. Yet, far more than those of Sanderson, his arguments and his system of law depend upon the actuality of an articulate and competent will at every level. Thus in effect his arguments can only dissolve on the edge of speculation about the content and accessibility of the will that sustains the whole system. His line of thought is curiously exposed—vulnerable to doubts and criticisms which could hardly fail to destroy the age-old ideology which in 1660 he embraced so wholeheartedly.

To explore these doubts and criticisms, or to achieve the solid demonstrations of moral knowledge which the political conclusions of the *Tracts* required, Locke had to become a philosopher. What is impressive is that he did so with so little change in his fundamental moral-political assumptions. Over twenty years later he could formulate the central dilemma of arguments about moral obligation more clearly; but his distinctively voluntaristic approach to the problem remains unaltered:

To establish morality, therefore upon its proper basis, and such foundations as may carry an obligation with them, we must first prove a law, which always supposes a law-maker, one that has a superiority and right to ordain, and also a power to reward and punish... the next thing then to show is that there are certain rules, certain dictates, which it is his will all men should conform their actions to, and that this will of his is sufficiently promulgated and made known to mankind.[30]

The importance of will rather than content in this approach to law led Locke whenever he was in doubt to appeal to revelation rather than reason. After 1660 he turned his attention to natural law as an academic exercise more or less required by his need for a demonstrable law-maker. But in the tracts themselves, as in his later writings, his distinctive approach led him to take the safer course. He seems deliberately to avoid arguments that suggest the possibility of rational access to divine law—he deletes a critical passage on natural law which has this tendency from the English *Tract*. He does not want to debate the problem of how the divine will is known any more than he wishes to debate the origins of government. His position is that, whatever the origins of government, sufficient is known about the divine will to demonstrate the ineluctable necessity of extreme civil obligations.

This position was tolerable so long as Locke was talking only to Christians from whom he could reasonably expect certain basic acts of faith. But for a writer as aware of radical religious diversity as Locke was, even in 1660, as conscious of the Turks, Chinese and Indians, such a shelving of the problem of knowledge could not be finally satisfactory. Locke argues that the divine will is sufficiently known for the necessity of political order to be beyond dispute. At the same time he argues that the ignorance, diversity and partiality of men is such that magistrates are the necessary agents of order. He thus argues partly from demonstrable ignorance, partly from presumed knowledge. It was almost inevitable that he should next try to establish that the minimum of knowledge essential for his argument was in fact available.

Locke in 1660 belongs, then, in the classical, pre-Lockeian, tradition of political thought. The *Tracts* are a last statement of an old world-view. Both the problem involved and the categories used are backward-looking. The man himself had been trained in archaic skills and assumptions, the archaicism of which had not yet been quite acknowledged. Yet, within the traditional framework, Locke's position in 1660 is an extreme one. If we follow Gierke's famous analysis of medieval theories of law it is clear at once that Locke stands well towards the nominalist pole of the scholastic continuum. The tracts may be read as but one more contribution to that 'deep reaching question of scholastic controversy... whether the essence of law is will or reason?' Influenced by Aquinas, and more recently by Hooker, the central English tradition had asserted a compromise between these views—but a compromise that inclined to the 'realist' view that the constitutive element of law was *iudicium rationis quod sit aliquid iustum*. Locke, without repudiating the compromise, gives extraordinary weight to the view of the opposite party, the nominalist view, that 'law becomes law merely through the will that this or that shall pass for law and be binding'. He is kept within the traditional framework by his nagging, countervailing concern that what passes for law shall also be just. But if we are to appreciate his later development and his unique contribution to the reconstituting of ideology in the eighteenth century we must start by seeing that at the outset of his career he both stands within the arch of the traditional scholastic compromise and has taken a position on the nominalist wing of that compromise. Such a position was to prove an apt base for radical intellectual innovation.[31]

NOTES

1 MS Locke c. 24, fols. 173–5; Latin *Tract*, p. 5.

2 English *Tract*, p. 22; MS Locke c. 24, fol. 14.

3 English *Tract*, p. 23; Latin *Tract*, p. 9.

4 English *Tract*, *The Preface to the Reader*, p. 1; Latin *Tract*, p. 1.

5 English *Tract*, pp. 24–5; cf. Hooker, 'Preface', pp. 97–8, 106–9.

6 Latin *Tract*, p. 6; MS Locke c. 24, fols. 14, 172, 175; cf. Sanderson, 1660, v, xxvi.

7 English *Tract*, *The Preface to the Reader*, pp. 1–3; MS Locke c. 24, fol. 14; cf. Fell, 1659, and, for an account of the similar usage in classical writings, Plato, 1941, 488a–489a; Bamborough, 1956; Finley, 1962.

8 Bodleian Library, MS Film 77, pp. 1–3.

9 He was notoriously a master of this art: cf. Dr Fell's opinion that 'there is not in the world such a master of taciturnity and passion' (Public Record Office, 30/24/47/22). For Locke's strategy of argument see Cox, 1960, chs. 1–11, and, for an early example of it, English *Tract*, p. 22.

10 Maxwell, 1644, and English *Tract*, p. 22; Cranston, 1957, p. 62, but also Von Leyden, 1954, who does recognize the preponderant influence of Sanderson, pp. 27, 30–3.

11 Compare Bagshaw, 1660 (*a*), p. 14, and Hooker, v, lxxvi, 4.

12 Latin *Tract*, p. 7; a similar position is taken by Sanderson, 1660, v, ii; by contrast Hooker I, x, 7 dismisses the obligations created out of mere will as not qualifying as law.

13 Hooker, I, iii, 1; Latin *Tract*, p. 6; Von Leyden, 1954, pp. 42–3; cf. the interesting deletion from the MS of the English *Tract*, p. 18, of a passage on the law of nature in which Locke had come close to accepting the rationalist fallacy of Hooker (and Grotius) that the law of nature can be known from the general consent of men. In his *Essays on the Law of Nature* Locke formally denied this proposition.

14 Latin *Tract*, p. 6.

15 Hooker, I, vii, and x, 8.

16 Consider the verbal difficulties he runs into in his efforts to avoid referring law to any sanction other than law itself—'if a law be lawful...', etc., Latin *Tract*, p. 8; and the more important case on p. 12 where he eschews the example of Sanderson and Hobbes, who made the *ius gladii* the essence of sovereignty, and instead follows Hooker in making it the *ius legislativa*; cf. Sanderson's *Preface* to Ussher, 1661, sect. xv.

17 Hooker, I, vi; Baker, 1952, *passim*; this study repays attention—it is Baker's view that it was the 'axiom of knowledge' that sustained the medieval world-view by short-circuiting radical epistemological inquiry, and that the demolition of the axiom was thus the mainspring of a general 'decay of Christian humanism'. At the very least this argument serves as a perfect paradigm for the intellectual biography of John Locke.

18 The following comparisons are instructive: Latin *Tract*, pp. 3–4, and Sanderson, 1660, VI, xxvi—on the nature of worship; Latin *Tract*, pp. 6, 16–17, and Sanderson, 1660, v, iv–vi and VI, ii—on the nature of obligation; Latin *Tract*, p. 12, and Sanderson, 1660, VII, xv—on the origins of government; Latin *Tract*, p. 17, and Sanderson, 1660, VI, iv—on the nature of liberty.

19 Latin *Tract*, p. 6.

20 English *Tract, The Preface to the Reader*, p. 5; Latin *Tract*, pp. 12–14.

21 Bodleian Library, MS Film 77; MS Locke c. 28, fol. 41; Gough, 1950, p. 180; De Marchi, 1953, who maintains quite bluntly that a decade of civil chaos had led Locke 'a subire più direttamente la suggestione del pensiero "autoritari" dello Hobbes, del Filmer e del Bodin'.

22 MS Locke d. 10—the notebook headed *Lemmata Ethica*: for a discussion of the Filmer references see Laslett, 1960, pp. 33, 131, 137.

23 Latin *Tract*, pp. 11–12.

24 Gough, 1950, p. 180; Cranston, 1956, pp. 47 ff., and 1957, ch. IV;

Laslett, 1960, p. 21 is more judicious: 'The two men were closer then than at any other time, but beyond this point we should not go.' Stubbe, incidentally, was in trouble at Oxford as early as March 1658 for his notorious sympathies with Hobbes, cf. Abrams, 1961, p. 240.

25 Sanderson, 1660 (but the lectures were delivered in 1648), II, and cf. Milton, 1649, sect. x, 1651.

26 Ascham, 1649, p. 9; Digges, 1644, p. 2; all the works in this and the last note had been read by Locke before 1667, probably before 1660.

27 Hobbes, *De Corpore*, II, vi; *Leviathan*, II, xvii; Latin *Tract*, p. 12; English *Tract*, pp. 2–3; and cf. English *Tract*, p. 33, where Locke removes from his text the only unequivocally contractarian statement to be found in either *Tract*; Latin *Tract*, p. 17.

28 Digges, 1644, pp. 2, 28, 31; Digges is also at one with Locke in arguing from the general premise, 'states are framed upon a sinister opinion of men'.

29 Sanderson, 1660, VII, xv; Latin *Tract*, p. 12, *but* Sanderson ends up placing his trust in *ius paternum* (sect. xvi).

30 MS Locke c. 28, fol. 152; this is the conclusion of a paper headed Of Ethick in General: for a discussion of this document see Von Leyden, 1954, pp. 69–75.

31 Gierke, 1922, pp. 172–3; for an equally conservative handling of the great question of indifferent things from the rationalist point of view see Stillingfleet, 1660, ch. 2, who argues directly from the 'Principles of the Law of Nature'; cf. Hall, 1649, and Parry, 1660, who likewise refuse to 'shut reason out of doors' by denying the immediate availability of the law of nature. Stillingfleet and Parry spent the rest of their lives in the embrace of the 'axiom of knowledge': only Locke escaped.

IV

CONTINUITIES: THE 'TRACTS' AND LOCKE'S LATER WORKS

What is the relationship between the *Tracts on Government* and Locke's later writings? The discontinuities are very evident. In 1660 he says: 'The supreme magistrate of every nation what way soever created must necessarily have an absolute and arbitrary power over all the indifferent actions of his people.' And seven years later: 'I say all practical principles, or opinions...and the actions following from them, with all other things indifferent, have a title also to toleration.'[1]

Dramatic and permanent change might well have sprung from the circumstances of his life after 1660—from his political experience of the effects of intolerance; from his unsatisfactory struggle with the theory of natural law; from his growing commitment, confirmed by his scientific inquiries, to empiricism; and from his escape from the academic conventions of Oxford to the more pragmatic circle of Shaftesbury. Yet the discontinuities in Locke's thought are easily exaggerated. And underlying and containing the changes are important continuities; ways in which his mature liberalism as well as his psychological and epistemological ideas remain rooted in the assumptions of 1660.

What did Locke do when he had finished the *Tracts*? His official duty was to teach philosophy in Christ Church. Much of his energy and interest went into the practice of medicine, however. And the influences on him here were those of Helmont, Boyle and Willis; and increasingly of Sydenham. He was actively, albeit modestly, engaged in the business of stripping away the old mystical superstructure of chemistry and making it a science of observation and measurement. His early and decided commitment to an empirical philosophy of nature perhaps explains his rowdy behaviour at the lectures of the Rosicrucian Peter Stahl: 'While every man besides...were writing, he [Locke] would be prating and troublesome.' We may speculate as to how far his new philosophy of science spilled over into his ideas on moral and political questions. Certainly, by the time he wrote the manuscript of the fragment *De Arte Medica* he had reached a position thoroughly subversive of the stand he had taken in the *Tracts*:

True knowledge grew first in the world by experience and rational observations; but proud man, not content with the knowledge he was capable of, and which was useful to him, would needs penetrate into the hidden causes of things, lay down principles and establish maxims to himself about the operations of nature, and thus vainly expect that nature, or in truth God, should proceed according to those laws which his maxims had prescribed to him.[2]

And the stand taken in the *Tracts on Government* was, as we have seen, vulnerable to subversion. It was a very distinctive variation on an orthodox theme. Locke's next step was to try to make good its weaknesses.

The moral philosophy of the medieval world-view was made up of several sets of multiple-choice theories. Knowledge sprang from revelation, or principles of reason, or sense-perception and rational inference. Government sprang from patriarchal authority instituted by God, or from the consent of men to live together in peace and mutual security. Obligation derived from the content of what was commanded, or from the purpose of the command, or from the will that issued it. Natural law embodied the will of God but also the principles of human nature. What held this elaborate structure of antinomies together was the axiom of knowledge— the assumption that all the presumed means of knowledge were equally competent and would give access to fundamental moral truths.[3]

In the *Tracts* Locke formally maintains the axiom of knowledge but in order to settle the Great Question he adopts a position which lays stress on will rather than matter or purpose as the source of obligation, and on consent rather than patriarchalism as the basis of government; a position which gave cardinal importance to natural law, but at the same time virtually discounted reason. To understand Locke's development after 1660 we must first consider the relationship of three main tenets of this early position. First, natural law exists and is the essential bridge between religion and government, between moral and civil obligation. This is asserted in the *Tracts*, reaffirmed at length in the sixth of the *Essays on the Law of Nature*.[4] Second, reason is not a source of knowledge. The question is begged in the *Tracts* but examination of it in the second of the natural law writings leads unequivocally to this conclusion.[5] And, finally, we are not bound by anything except what we know to be the will of a law-maker. This is explicit in the *Tracts on Government* and in all Locke's later writings.[6]

Now, assuming that there is such a thing as natural law and that without it neither divine positive nor human positive law would be of any effect, the problem that arises is this: how can men know what natural law requires and how can they know that it obliges them (i.e. that it embodies a law-making will)?

Locke was not a man to shirk his intellectual responsibilities. Required to teach philosophy between 1662 and 1664 he addressed himself to precisely this problem. In this respect the continuity of the *Tracts* and the *Essays on the Law of Nature* is manifest. But so is the failure of the *Essays* to resolve the difficulties which the *Tracts* had raised. As he explored the hidden assumptions of his earlier argument, they dissolved in his hands. Thus, he concluded first that, revelation apart, there is only one true source of knowledge. As one could have predicted from his correspondence as early as the 1650s this is not tradition or reason: 'Nothing indeed', he now concludes, 'is achieved by reason, that powerful faculty of arguing, unless there is first something posited and taken for granted.' All that is left is sense-perception. Natural law is either known 'from those things which we perceive through our senses', or it is not known at all.[7] But even if sense-perception followed by ratiocination could find out natural law (which Locke, perforce, asserts it can), does such knowledge carry an obligation? We must discover not only the content of natural law but the authoritative will from which it derives. Can sense-perception do this? Locke does not give a direct answer. But the answer implicit in the natural law writings of 1662–4 is, no. Instead, he shows that once men have inferred the existence of a purposeful deity from their sense-perceptions of the universe, they can easily go on to infer that natural law is the expression of divine purpose.[8]

But this is to run away from the problem. The empirical status of these critical inferences is nowhere examined. It is not surprising that Locke admitted at the end of his term of office that he had been worsted by his pupils in their disputations on natural law. He had argued himself into a crisis. He asserts the possibility of a demonstrative science of ethics, but in the meanwhile he takes refuge in faith. And this was to raise a still more dangerous set of questions—questions about the epistemological standing of belief. Here Locke shied away.[9] Meant as a way of clarifying and consolidating the philosophy implicit in the *Tracts* (by transferring the discussion to a more fundamental level) his study of natural law ended by exposing it still more clearly as a flimsy and hazardous metaphysic. What was Locke to do? Retrospectively we can see that he did three things. He abandoned the discussion of natural law: recognizing, as another Oxford writer on indifferency had done in 1660, that the 'punctilles of the law' were a subject wherein 'the more a man flutters the more he is entangled', he never again attempted a close analysis of the nature and implications of law, natural or positive.[10] Instead, he shifted his attention to a yet more fundamental level, taking up the problem of the nature of knowledge, and more specifically of how sense-perception can establish moral knowledge. And, thirdly, he acknowledged the extent of human ignorance and its social implications.

Not all the stages in these three developments are visible. But at least one critical moment is known to us. Some time before the summer of 1671 Locke tells us that he and 'five or six friends, meeting in my chamber' had discussed a subject which Tyrell, who was one of the number, described as 'the principles of morality and revealed religion'—the problem with which Locke had come face to face in 1664. Von Leyden goes further and presumes, 'that the discussion among Locke's friends was at first about the law of nature as the basis of morality and its relation to natural and revealed religion'. If so, this group, like Locke in 1664, 'found themselves quickly at a stand by the difficulties that arose on every side'. The next step is plainly recorded:

After we had a while puzzled ourselves, without coming any nearer a resolution of those doubts which perplexed us, it came into my thoughts that we took a wrong course; and that before we set ourselves upon enquiries of that nature it was necessary to examine our own abilities, and see what objects our understandings were or were not fitted to deal with. This I proposed to the company who all readily assented; and thereupon it was agreed that this should be our first enquiry.

The problem of ignorance had been formally confronted. Around this major innovation Locke's mature philosophy now began to unfold.[11]

87

Here we may usefully trace this unfolding (and to the very end
the continued if shadowy presence of the thought world of the
Tracts) in three main directions.

LAW: OBLIGATION, CONSENT AND KNOWLEDGE

After 1667, as before, Locke's interest in law was always twofold:
to show how law could be known and how it obliged. And whenever it is the problem of obligation that most concerns him the
voluntaristic theory enunciated in the *Tracts* reappears.[12] We find it
in the *Essays on the Law of Nature*: 'Since nothing else is required to
impose an obligation but the authority and rightful power of the
one who commands and the disclosure of his will, no one can
doubt that the law of nature is binding on men.' And we find it
again in the *Two Treatises* where the discovery and articulation of
a legislative will is made a necessary condition of legitimate
government. But now of course Locke substitutes a tangible civil
law stemming from a public will for the obscure law of nature
stemming mysteriously from the will of God which he had invoked
before. Yet here, as in the *Tracts*, the problem of sovereignty is
seen as one of discovering a *ius legislativa*—hence, a superior will.[13]

Voluntarism is reasserted, too, in the brief discussion of law in
the *Essay Concerning Human Understanding*: 'Good or evil', Locke
there rules, 'are drawn on us by the will and power of the law-
maker.' And if he has little to say here about the law of nature it is
surely because he now knew he could find no way of equipping it
with those substantial sanctions that are the 'true nature of all
law' and follow from the immanence in law of a known legislative
will. He restricts his discussion to such laws as carry effective
obligations, making the difference between them and potential
laws such as the law of nature quite clear. The connexion of effective laws with a legislative will is manifest: 'Without a notion of a
law-maker it is impossible to have a notion of a law and an obligation to observe it.' But as for the law of nature:

Because we cannot come to a certain knowledge of those rules of our
actions without first making known a law-giver with power and will to
reward and punish, and secondly without showing how he has declared
his will and law, I must only at present suppose this rule.

It fails to draw any obligation on us and therefore, in the *Essay*, it fails as a law.[14]

By 1695 Locke was willing to drop even the supposition of a law of nature for purposes of obligation. His objection to the rationalist account of natural law in *The Reasonableness of Christianity* is simply that it postulates a law 'of no authority'. However 'excellent in themselves', the laws of nature can never 'make a morality', never 'rise to the force of a law'. Whatever hopes he may have had of discovering natural law, Locke did not change his immediate doctrine of obligation after 1660. Rather, it was more clearly articulated as his hopes faded:

> It is plain that human reason unassisted failed men in its great and proper business of morality. It never from unquestionable principles, by clear deductions, made out an entire body of the law of nature. What will [reason] do to give the world a complete morality that may be to mankind the unquestionable rule of life and manners? What would this amount to, towards being a steady rule, a certain transcript of a law we are under? Mankind might hearken to it, or reject it, as they pleased; or as it suited their interest, passions, principles or humours. They were under no obligation.

The moral propositions of Christian revelation, by comparison, do oblige because the very manner of their promulgation reveals a will of unchallengeable authority:

> Such a law of morality Jesus Christ hath given us in the New Testament by revelation. Here morality has a sure standard that revelation vouches and reason cannot gainsay nor question; but both together witness to come from God the great law-maker.

The idea of two bodies of law differently promulgated which he employed in 1660 has given way to the recognition that, because one is promulgated (if at all) in a manner too obscure to give men access to the will behind it, it cannot in practice qualify as law.[15]

But this was to elaborate and clarify his first position rather than to depart radically from it. Locke ends where he started— with no consequential idea of the law of nature as a distinct moral norm because such an idea cannot be squared with the voluntarism that was from first to last essential for his theory of obligation.

Yet he continues, as he had done from the start, to assert the possibility of an alternative, rationalist, notion of law; to make reservation after reservation in favour of a possible law of nature.

Why does this ambivalence persist? He was torn, I think, between his sense of intellectual integrity and a traditional impulse springing from his education to achieve a rational and consensual account of society and politics. The latter motive lies behind his persistent claim that a natural law basis for obligation exists in principle. But the former, the nagging awareness of just how much reason could 'gainsay or question', always brought him up against the central epistemological dilemma: 'It is true there is a law of nature; but who is there that ever did, or undertook to give it us all entire, as a law?' From this dilemma he could only escape by surrendering his ideal position, the rationalist argument, to a more effective operational one, the argument from will.

Thus in John Locke the old intellectual order produced its gravedigger. Seeking to reaffirm the axioms and verities of the traditional ideology in which he had been trained, he found himself continually laying bare the substructure of assertion, ignorance and bad logic on which that ideology had been built.

But he did so despite himself. When it is the problem of how law is known that concerns him, the rationalist theme of the *Tracts* reappears. After 1680 he invokes the idea of self-evidence to infer the possibility of a quasi-mathematical demonstration of morality, a Euclidean morality in which obligation would be implicit in the process of knowing. The contention that morality can be modelled on mathematics first emerges from his efforts to save a rationalist view of natural law in the seventh of the *Essays on the Law of Nature*. Even in *The Reasonableness of Christianity* the intellectual feasibility of an ethical system deduced by 'clear and evident demonstrations' from 'principles of reason, self-evident in themselves', is not denied. But nowhere, after 1660, does Locke accept this possibility as a substitute for obligation.[16]

What we find instead is a growing stress on the *ends* for which obligation exists. In the *Tracts* he justified political authority almost entirely in terms of the 'efficient' cause of obligation, the legislative will. Its 'final' cause, the purpose for which government is first set up, constrained the magistrate only in heaven. After 1667 the balance of these arguments changes; will remains the source of obligation, but the use of power is more strictly limited: 'What was the end of erecting government', he now argues, 'ought alone to be the measure of its proceeding.'[17]

Here is a real innovation. How was Locke led to it?

The force of Locke's arguments in 1660 sprang from his use of a consent theory of the origins of government. But he did not then directly acknowledge the importance of this theory in his system of thought. He had, in discussing power in the English *Tract*, reached the point of saying 'it being the consent of parties and not an immediate grant from God that confers it'—but he had then removed the admission from his text. With each later work he embraced the same theory less equivocally, less hypothetically, with greater frankness and conviction. And from this change a more general reorienting and clarifying of his thought seems to flow. He argues with growing cogency in successive works that consent itself imposes a voluntaristic restraint on the magistrate. Will remains the basis and essence of the state. But the politically effective and consequential will is now human. In various acts men turn their natural rights into effective power—in the form of a common and collective legislative will, 'the essence and union of the society consisting in having one will'. And this 'public will' both gives the actual legislator his authority and sets clear limits to it.[18] Locke is not consistent about the powers of action that follow from this arrangement. In the *Two Treatises* he envisages circumstances in which men may act against the magistrate; but in the *Letters Concerning Toleration*, although the criteria for judging magistrates are those of the public good, the end of government, the only legitimate judge is once again God.[19]

This inconsistency is not surprising. Indeed it is difficult to find an internally consistent account of the relationship of popular consent to magisterial authority anywhere in Locke's writings. The germs of his later view of the role of consent can perhaps be seen in 1660 in the doubts he expressed about the foundations of government in the Latin *Tract*. But it is the doubts themselves that are most characteristic of the man. He always remained a doubter—torn, as he admitted in his last major work, between arguments he wanted to embrace and a respect for logical difficulties that made such embraces impossible. In the end he remained intellectually entangled in the tradition in which he had been educated. His increasingly straightforward use of consent arguments simplified and emphasized his preference for the voluntaristic end of the traditional see-saw on obligation. Conversely, his voluntarism, which I take to be the fundamental instinct of his thought, combined with his new axiom of ignorance to incline him towards arguments from consent. But although his works did much to free his contemporaries from the old dualistic tradition, he himself remained within its frame of reference. And he exploited its ambivalent argumentative resources whenever he needed to— hence the impression of quite remarkable inconsistency his mature works have left on many modern readers.[20]

His own ambivalence can be resolved somewhat if we introduce a distinction between objective and subjective knowledge. By implication this distinction is central to all Locke's thought, especially his political thought, from 1667 onwards. It emerged directly from his discovery of ignorance in 1664–70. Objectively, 'there is a law of nature and that plain and intelligible to a rational creature'. But subjectively, 'the true ground of morality can only be the will and law of God'; the law of nature obliges those who think themselves obliged by it but to anyone else each man's natural law is 'but a saying of his'. For political purposes it was always the contradiction between subjective and objective knowledge that presented the real problem for Locke. Certainly, men might recognize their objective moral duties rationally by 'a rational apprehension of what is right'. Meanwhile, 'for the bulk of mankind...hearing plain commands is the sure and only course to bring them to obedience and practice'.[21]

We have already noted the importance of this sense of conflict between the objective and subjective situation of man for the writings of 1660. It remained of central importance as a key to the structure of Locke's later works as well. In particular, it lay behind the two major innovations in his treatment of law after 1667—his acceptance of a consent theory of government, and his gradual dismantling of the cornerstone of the *Tracts*, the axiom of knowledge. So long as Locke felt himself secure in the possession of objective knowledge he was prepared to advocate authoritarian government. But knowledge had been asserted, not demonstrated, in the *Tracts* and the more Locke tried to improve on this position the more sharp and formal his distinctions between actual and potential knowledge, between subjective and objective truths, became. And the more compelling, in turn, became the attractions of argument from consent. In no other way could a voluntaristic account of obligation be saved.

KNOWLEDGE: PARTIALITY, REASON AND TOLERATION

The same contrast between subjective and objective knowledge informs the development of Locke's general theory of man in society. And here again what we find is a mingling of change and continuity; a working out of insights already present in the *Tracts*; but with these insights now providing a basis for quite different political proposals. The dominant idea throughout is the idea of partiality.

'Our deformity is others' beauty', was a permanent postulate of Locke's thought. Much of the force and originality of the *Tracts* of 1660 lies in his fascinated contemplation of the diversity and arbitrariness of social custom in different societies. He invokes the incompatibility of such customs to demonstrate the thoroughly indifferent and conventional nature of the subject-matter of human law. And there is a continuous development of this sense of social diversity—and of a consequent anthropological relativism in his later writings, notebooks and correspondence. The *Tracts* focus attention on an often neglected dimension of Locke's understanding of the world.[22]

In the fifth of the *Essays on the Law of Nature* Locke adduces a chaos of instances of moral beliefs and practices in order to demolish the proposition that 'the law of nature can be known from the general consent of men'. He uses this evidence to conclude

that there is almost no vice, no infringement of natural law, no moral wrong which anyone who consults the history of the world and observes the affairs of men will not readily perceive to have been not only privately committed somewhere on earth, but also approved by public authority and custom. Nor has there been anything so shameful in its nature that it has not been either sanctified somewhere by religion, or put in the place of virtue and abundantly rewarded with praise.

The *Adversaria 1661*, is filled with meticulous comparative notes on the religious and social beliefs and practices of China, India, Turkey and Japan. In each of the later writings on toleration there are new stories of men's wilful, arbitrary attachments to opposed forms of ceremony and ritual. And again these stories are used to demonstrate the moral indifference of all forms. In *The Reasonableness of Christianity*, his strongest argument for accepting the

Christian revelation is that unless you assume that Christ is the Messiah you cannot make *any* effective distinction between the moral rules of different sects and nations. The 'law of opinion' recognized in the *Essay* merely gives formal expression to this relativism. It was an easy and straight passage from the admission in the English *Tract* that 'order and decency depend wholly on the opinions and fancies of men' to a conditional toleration of all opinions and fancies in 1667, and thence to acknowledging 'fashion' as a law for 'the greatest part' in the *Essay*. All that was involved was a gradual realization of something Locke had sensed from the first—that practical morality rested on ignorance and convention, not on truth:

> Whatever is pretended, this is visible, that these names, virtue and vice, in the particular instances of their application through the several nations and societies of men in the world, are constantly attributed only to such actions as in each country are in reputation or discredit.[23]

Locke's inference from this state of affairs in 1660 was that the magistrate might properly impose any standards of virtue and vice which he thought would realize the divine command that 'all things be done decently and in order'. He was led to this conclusion in part by his feeling for the fragility of political order, in part by his asserted confidence that the magistrate's rulings on matters of virtue and vice could claim a superior (albeit, derived) moral and epistemological status to those of his subjects.

It was this last element of the argument that vanished after 1667. It could not consist with Locke's intuitive and increasingly explicit belief that partiality was ubiquitous. His distinction between objective and subjective truth applied to societies as well as to individuals and to magistrates as well as to subjects. Above all it applied to indifferent things. Once Locke had admitted that the magistrate in imposing moral rules 'can have no other guide but his own persuasions', the ground for imposing on which he had built the *Tracts* began to crumble away. The only proper basis for imposing would be a demonstrable ability or a demonstrable authority to judge between subjective accounts of truth; but Locke always denied that any mere man could make such judgments. On the contrary:

> Whatsoever privilege or power you claim, upon supposing yours to be the true religion, is equally due to another, who supposes his to be the

true religion upon the same claim; and therefore that is no more to be allowed to you than to him. For whose is really the true religion, yours or his, being the matter in contest between you, your supposing can no more determine it on your side than his supposing on his.[24]

To say that the magistrate is required to impose the true religion is simply to say that he is required 'by using force to bring men to that religion which he judges the true'.[25] But, as Locke's account of the partiality of human knowledge had always implied, magistrates are no more qualified to make or impose such judgments than any one else; once the epistemological assumptions of the *Tracts* had been discredited by his own subsequent study of the law of nature and of the nature of knowledge he quickly came to see that 'the princes of the world are...as well infected with the depraved nature of man as the rest of their brethren'. Toleration could rest on this insight; authoritarianism could not:

> To you and me the Christian religion is the true...Now do you, or I, know this, (I do not ask with what assurance we believe it; for that, in the highest degree, not being knowledge, is not what we now enquire after). Can any magistrate demonstrate...not only all the articles of his church, but the fundamental ones of the Christian religion? For whatever is not capable of demonstration (as such remote matters of *fact* are not) is not, unless it be self-evident, capable to produce knowledge, how well grounded and great soever the assurance of faith may be wherewith it is received; but faith it is still and not knowledge; persuasion and not certainty.[26]

The vision of partiality became the centre of every account Locke offered of the human situation. More and more he insists that men and societies alike are 'partial to themselves', 'biased by their interests', 'favourable to [their] own parts'; that they pick up values and opinions uncritically because they are 'convenient' and then cling to them unreasonably because 'they are theirs'.[27] In all his major works Locke treats this unthinking, socially conditioned prejudice in favour of oneself as 'the great cause of ignorance and error' in the world: 'Everyone declares against blindness and yet who almost is not fond of that which dims his sight...? Such are usually the prejudices imbibed from education, party, reverence, fashion, interest, etc.'[28] Objective moral truths, which remain in principle accessible to reason, are in practice never discovered and 'the reason is not hard to be found in men's necessities, passions, vices and mistaken interests, which turn their thoughts another way'. Men see the world as it suits them to see it; what they call truth is but a convenient received opinion:

Who is there almost that has not opinions planted in him by education time out of mind...which must not be questioned, but are then looked on with reverence, as the standards of right and wrong, truth and false-hood; where perhaps these so sacred opinions were but the oracles of the nursery, or the tradition and grave talk of those who pretend to inform our childhood, who receive them from hand to hand without ever examining them? By these and perhaps other means opinions came to be settled and fixed in men's minds, which, whether true or false, there they remain in reputation as substantial material truths;...and if they happen to be false, *as in most men the greatest part must necessarily be*, they put a man quite out of the way in the whole course of his studies. Men take up prejudice to truth without being aware of it, and after-wards feed only on those things that suit with and increase the vicious humour.[29]

In sum, 'we are all short-sighted', 'from this defect no man is free'; rather, all 'see but in part, and know but in part, and there-fore it is no wonder we conclude not right from our partial views'.[30] Partiality remains the distinctive feature of the col-lective predicament of man. And unlike the *Tracts* of 1660 his later works recognize this state of affairs as the only thing that can be reliably said and empirically demonstrated about human knowledge.

By contrast, men are rational to the extent that they master partiality. Rationality implies access to the law of nature and the prospect of a spontaneous social harmony—of society without the state. But for the purposes of political argument it is the primitive ascendancy of the self-interested passions that matters. 'Were it not for the corruption and viciousness of degenerate man...', liberalism would have been easy.[31] As it was, Locke could not forget corruption and so built his philosophy on two cardinal propositions: the immediate fact of partiality and the ultimate fact of an accessible, rational, God-given order. The actual equality of men in ignorance and self-love had to be complemented by a potential rationality and a potentially accessible rational order if Locke was to maintain even a nominally Christian understanding of the universe. Thus in the later works as in the *Tracts* we invari-ably find these two ideas linked dialectically as thesis and antithesis of his argument. If men are by nature partial they are also by nature potentially rational.[32]

To the extent that Locke recognized this as a common human predicament we would expect social and political arguments turning on his early distinction between 'knowing men' and the bestial multitude to be dissolved and modified. And so they are. The contrast persists but the tone in which it is drawn and the inferences drawn from it change. There is still the contrast in *Of the Conduct of the Understanding* between the freedom of the assiduously cultivated rational faculty of the wise and the mental helplessness and prejudice of those of 'low and mean education...no more capable of reasoning than almost a perfect natural'; there is the contrast in *Two Treatises* between the existence of a law of nature, 'plain and intelligible to all rational creatures', and the bias and ignorance that prevent most men from seeing it; and in *The Reasonableness of Christianity* between those 'men of parts' who 'by meditation light on the right', and the 'greatest part' who 'cannot know and therefore must believe'.[33]

But after 1667 the gulf between rational and irrational man is narrowed and bridged by the linked notions of actual ignorance and possible rationality. All are by nature partial but some few manage to approach a modest rationality. And the way in which they do so is open, in theory, to all, even to 'very mean people' —for 'the original make of their minds is like that of other men'. Men are of 'equal natural parts' and if some achieve a rational understanding it is as a result of 'exercise', not of some intrinsic difference of type. The law of nature is available to all 'who will but consult it', however few actually do so. And on the strength of these egalitarian assumptions Locke can now 'clear even the meanest condition of life from a necessity of gross ignorance', and show 'that more might be brought to be rational creatures and Christians...if due care were taken of them'. Disillusioned about the School philosophies of his youth Locke became more, not less, committed to education, more, not less, convinced that, while all share a common partiality, all 'are born to be, if we please, rational creatures'.[34]

Now Locke was not obliged to make concessions to the idea of potential rationality simply because he lost confidence in his own ability to expound and demonstrate the will of God. He did so because he wanted to; because he remained committed to the ideals of the conservative, rationalist Christian world view in which he was educated. His own dualisms (and supposed inconsistencies) match those of the Thomist tradition. Within that tradition his arguments shift as his intellectual and political experience requires. As he became more and more doubtful about the objective availability of moral knowledge, the equal status and partial nature of every man's subjective knowledge destroyed for him the authority of all possible forms of moral discipline. Believing now in a discoverable but perennially undiscovered order, Locke found himself unable to offer any safe guide through the 'endless maze' of private perceptions: 'I think we may as rationally hope to see with other men's eyes as to know by other men's understandings.' As Fraser pointed out, 'the really moral purpose' of Locke's mature writings is to be found most plainly in that section of the *Essay* which deals with the proposition: 'Men must think and know for themselves.'[35]

TOLERATION: PARTIALITY, KNOWLEDGE AND CONSENT

The new epistemology, together with the new view of society, 'everyone is orthodox to himself', was bound to produce a new politics. The effect is first and most apparent in Locke's doctrine of toleration.

His general approach to this question hardly changed at all. His object in 1667 and 1690, as in 1659, was

to demonstrate... that men of different professions may quietly unite under the same government and unanimously carry the same civil interest and hand in hand march to the same end of peace and mutual society though they take different ways towards heaven.

To this end he measured all claims to toleration against two standards: the obligations deriving from general moral knowledge; and the objects for which civil society was presumed to exist.[36] But as a result of ulterior changes in his thinking the meaning and effect of these standards in 1667 and 1690 were quite different from what they had been in 1660. He never admitted a general right of conscience to determine practice. And he always maintained the right of magistrates to make laws about indifferent things. But by 1667 his experience of the social effects of intoler-

ance and his growing doubts about the nature of religious knowledge had led him to identify almost all questions of religious
practice (as well as belief) as essentially subjective, speculative
matters with which government had best have no concern.
Here again the axiomatic place of the distinction between objective and subjective certainty in Locke's thought is all-important in
shaping the development of his views.[37] Objectively there are indifferent things. But subjectively these things are invested with
good or evil. And among the multitude of subjective persuasions
it is impossible to tell which are true and which false. Viewed thus
the concept of indifferency is destroyed.[38] What Locke does after
1667 which he had not done before is to accept the equal validity
of both objective and subjective states of knowledge. Men have
diverse beliefs about the moral nature of indifferent things. Objectively it does not matter which, if any, of these beliefs is true. But
subjectively, to the men who hold the beliefs, it matters that their
own perceptions should be treated as true. For they have no other
means of knowledge. Given the recognition of objective ignorance,
all that matters morally about indifferent things is that each man
should do what he thinks is right. And all that matters politically
is the effect that this may have on the achievement of peace and
mutual society.

After 1667, as before, it was the social consequences of religion
that immediately concerned Locke in his writings on toleration. It
was not, as Bagshaw and other earlier writers had held, the truth of
different views that mattered in Locke's eyes, but the simple social
fact of belief in them. And here, after 1667, Locke's new view of the
moral and epistemological status of private perceptions made itself felt. In the indifferent things of religious worship, he now had
to rule, individuals should be left free; objectively it is true that
these things are all indifferent but it is no less true that 'in
religious worship nothing is indifferent':

For it being the using of those habits, gestures, etc., and no other which
I think acceptable to God in my worship of him however they may be
in their own nature indifferent, yet when I am worshipping my God in a
way I think he has prescribed...I cannot alter, add or omit any circumstance in that which I think the true way of worship.[39]

As in 1660, he sees worship as an essentially private transaction
between the worshipper and God. Any moral opinion about the

acts involved in worship he thus now classes as 'speculative'. Which is to say that its epistemological status is unchallengeable; and also that by the same token it can create no social obligations. More generally, therefore, 'religious worship, being an action or commerce passing only between God and myself...produces no action which disturbs the community'. This being so, Locke's new theory of knowledge now leads him to extend to the time, place and manner of worship (the actions disputed in the *Tracts*) a general toleration.[40]

His only abrupt doctrinal break from the position of 1660 was to include not only opinions about worship but the acts that followed from them in the class of speculative actions. To speculations he was willing to grant a complete toleration even in 1660. But his argument then had distinguished sharply between speculations and their consequences and had been that liberty of conscience applied only to the former—leaving the magistrate free to constrain actions. In 1667 he classed the actions of religious worship with speculative opinions because, he claimed, from the point of view of society worship was the same kind of phenomenon as speculation, having 'in its own nature no reference at all to my governor or my neighbour'. The very case cited in 1660 to demonstrate the reasonableness of imposing in all indifferent questions (since all are of the same kind) is now used for the opposite purpose: 'Wearing a cope or surplice in the church can no more alarm or threaten the peace of the state than wearing a cloak or coat in the market.' And he goes on to condemn the hypocrisy likely to be produced by an application of his own earlier doctrine in much the same words Bagshaw had used in 1660: 'A sweet religion, indeed', he now says, 'that obliges men to dissemble and tell lies.'[41]

In 1660 Locke had virtually denied the objective indifference of all forms of worship by invoking the order implicit in the establishment of society under the will of God. After 1667 he explicitly denied their subjective indifferency because he now saw society as existing not for order but for individuals; or, more accurately, for an order that could only be recognized in the realization of individual purposes. In other words, it was not only the epistemological status of worship that had changed for Locke by 1667. Worship now 'produces no action which disturbs the community', because the community itself now exists for different ends. The relation of the state to the divinely enjoined order became increasingly tenuous and obscure in his writings as that order in its turn became increasingly inscrutable. Conversely, he held more and more to the view that government is created 'only for the quiet and comfortable living of men in society', and that it is for this end that 'the magistrate is ordained and entrusted with his power'. If Locke's new epistemology suggested the moral propriety of toleration, it was his growing commitment to a secular, consent-based theory of government that impelled him to do the proper thing.[42]

The new position is most clearly worked out in the *Letters Concerning Toleration*, where he adheres unequivocally to a consent theory of government and to the view that the magistrate's power is given him 'only for the preservation of all his subjects and every particular person among them'. This does not mean that he grants an absolute right of conscience in any sort of indifferent matter. On the contrary he grants in the *Third Letter* (what he had ruled in the *Tracts*) 'that indifferent things and perhaps none but such are subjected to the legislative power'. What Locke does, rather, is to apply a simple pragmatic test to every case in which toleration is claimed—is toleration or imposition more likely to promote the ends for which society exists?[43]

His new political theory thus saved him from a major difficulty which his new epistemology ought to have raised. By referring all disputed cases to criteria of political convenience he escaped the necessity of attempting a moral-philosophical resolution of the discrepancy between objective and subjective accounts of the disputed acts. Thus, he allows indifferent things, other than the forms of worship, only a conditional toleration after 1667—not because they are a distinct category of act but because they respond differently to his yardstick of social effects. All opinions about indifferencies are of the same kind as speculations and have in principle a 'title' to toleration; but some crop into actions which, unlike the forms of worship, are destructive of the great purposes of society—the securing of everyone in the 'just possession of things belonging to this life'.[44]

In the same way, although he now proposes to tolerate the individual conscience in matters of worship, he nowhere makes any concession to that theory of the rights of conscience which he had opposed in the *Tracts*. Rather, he uses the same argument he had developed in 1660 to invalidate such a theory—to allow the claims of conscience because they are conscientious is to destroy society:

> There being nothing so indifferent which the consciences of some or other do not check at, a toleration of men in all that which they pretend out of conscience they cannot submit to will wholly take away all the civil laws and all the magistrate's powers, and so there will be no law nor government.[45]

But here again Locke's new sense of the ubiquitous subjectivity of all actual moral knowledge is brought into play. As the agent of innumerable morally equal and mutually incompatible private perceptions, the conscience cannot possibly be accorded a right to toleration without precipitating chaos: the rule is clear, ' no opinion hath a right to toleration on this account, that it is a matter of conscience'. But the same doubtful status of conscientious knowledge must also disqualify it as a 'measure by which the magistrate can or ought to frame his laws'. The magistrate exists to promote the welfare of the whole society; he must ignore the conscientious convictions of any one part (including himself) while tolerating the convictions of all. His only criterion of judgment is to be the common good of his subjects. Consequently, Locke will not now have an arbitrary magisterial imposition of indifferent things.[46] The new epistemology which grew from his efforts to resolve the major weakness of the *Tracts*, running together with the new theory of government that grew out of the preferences implicit in the *Tracts*, thus produced the modest and pragmatic liberalism that was to give Locke his lasting place in the English pantheon.

It is tempting to infer the influence of immediate political experience on the doctrine of toleration which Locke produced after 1667. In 1660 he had assumed an impartial magistrate; the tone of his welcome to Charles leaves no doubt about this; he expected the King to impose order but he also imagined that the content of that order would somehow be non-partisan; the Restoration settlement was to realize the objective divine command to order without itself being embroiled in subjective disputes over the status of indifferencies. In 1667 and still more in 1690 what concerned him was the experience of living under a conscientious magistrate—a magistrate who insisted on making the same error of confusing subjective and objective knowledge that Locke had previously condemned in subjects. Between 1667 and 1669 Locke was actively engaged with Ashley in efforts to persuade Charles to establish toleration by prerogative. Ashley's memorandum to the King in 1669 followed the line of argument of Locke's essay of 1667. The central theme of both was that the magistrate has no direct concern with debated issues of morality but only with preserving 'the peace, safety or security of his people'—and that, just because issues of morality were controversial, the best means to this end was to tolerate all such opinions and actions 'so far as they do not tend to the disturbance of the State or do not cause greater inconvenience than advantage to the community'. It was not their object to deny the magistrate a right to legislate, but only to convince him that the criteria to be applied by legislators were the pragmatic criteria of convenience Locke had belittled in 1660 and not the polemical moral-philosophical ones that engaged the enthusiasms of their subjects. One of the strongest criticisms Locke made of Samuel Parker's *Discourse of Ecclesiastical Polity* (1669) was that Parker appeared to 'suppose the magistrate's power to proceed from being in the right'.[47]

He now approves neither arbitrary impositions nor indiscriminate toleration. The limits of toleration are set (as indeed they were in 1660) by the objective ends for which political society is thought to exist. It is in his account of these ends that we find the truly consequential changes in Locke's thought. The ruling of 1667, 'the magistrate's business being only to preserve peace, those wrong opinions are to be restrained that have a tendency to disturb it', is a long way from the absolute and arbitrary power of 1660. Ignorance and his new conception of political ends have largely removed the element of arbitrariness.

Whatever the influence of political experience and of his contact with Ashley, it is clear that Locke found an important source of support for his new doctrine of conditional toleration in the consent theory of government. In the *Essay Concerning Toleration* he states, as he had done in the *Tracts*, the possible viability of two theories of political society, consent and patriarchalism. But the substance of his case proceeds directly from the former. In each successive work he makes more direct use of this view; and as he does so he gives greater weight to men's immediate social aims as an effective constraint on magistrates.[48]

Consent does not, in any of Locke's writings on toleration, carry a right for individuals to act against the magistrate when in their judgment he fails to preserve peace or promote security. The *Two Treatises* are more ambiguous. But in the *Essay Concerning Toleration* and in the *Letters* the position adopted in the *Tracts* is reasserted; the judgment of the magistrate's actions remains a prerogative of God; if he abuses his power 'he will meet with the severest doom at the Great Tribunal'. The language is the same as that of the *Tracts*: 'Nothing can be a greater provocation to the Surpreme preserver of men than that the magistrate should use his power...to the service of his pleasure, vanity or passion and employ it to the disquieting and oppression of his fellow men.'[49] But whereas in the *Tracts* men remain bound to a passive obedience whatever the magistrate may do, they now gain a right of passive disobedience. The concession follows from the fact that the magistrate is now logically and morally bound not only by his responsibility to God but equally by the origin of his power in the will and gift of his subjects. Locke stresses this commitment at every opportunity. Men (including magistrates) have no power over moral acts because they have no certain knowledge of moral truths, and 'no man can give another man power over that over which he has no power himself'. Here again his developed epistemology and his clarified political theory unite to make him a practical liberal. The very diversity of convictions among his subjects makes the governor's duty apparent: 'The public good is the rule and measure of all law-making.' And without much definition of this 'public good' Locke can treat the idea as a general dissuasive from religious persecution.[50]

Thus, in the *Essay Concerning Toleration*, he re-examines and refutes the principal argument of the *Tracts* against toleration: 'That the magistrate's great business being to preserve peace and quiet...he is obliged not to tolerate different religions in his country since...they may occasion disorder.' His refutation rests firmly on his new understanding of the relationship between individuals and government—his theory of popular consent without popular control. He makes two points against coercion: 'It brings that upon a man which, that he might be freed from is the only reason he is a member of the commonwealth, viz. violence,' and the magistrate in using force does in part cross what he pretends to do which is the safety of all; for the preservation as much as possible of the propriety, quiet and life of every individual being his duty he is obliged not to disturb nor destroy some for the safety of the rest.

In short, the magistrate remains the sole judge on earth of welfare, peace and safety, but the origins and ends of magistracy can be invoked as immaterial but objectively substantial sanctions on his conduct. After 1667 he still maintained that indifferent things were the proper and only matter of human legislation and that the magistrate must, in principle, have power over them. But it no longer followed that magistrates could decree whatever they pleased: 'If a thing be not useful to the commonwealth though it be ever so indifferent it may not be established by law.'[51]

It is remarkable what a short distance Locke had to travel to reach his mature doctrine of toleration. That doctrine may be described as having a three-tier structure, as proposing three courses of political action for three types of opinion or act. In each case the criterion by which any given act is to be judged is its liability to produce effects subversive of the ends of society. He offers an absolute toleration to 'speculative' acts, including the way in which one chooses to worship God. He offers a conditional toleration to 'practical' and moral activities so long as these do not become 'dangerous to the state'—a provision which it remains open for the magistrate to interpret and which allows Locke himself to rule that such inherently innocuous activities as the Quaker wearing of hats may be suppressed if they become symbols of an anti-social political solidarity. And he denies toleration to those activities and opinions that he considers overtly or intrinsically 'destructive' to government—including Roman Catholicism and atheism. He declares against any attempt to put down or impose opinions as such (since the end cannot be achieved); but he approves the suppression of efforts to propagate opinions dangerous to society. The liberalism of such a doctrine is almost entirely a function of two ulterior intellectual developments: a recognition of ignorance about the epistemological status of moral and religious beliefs which led him to class worship in the category of speculative acts; and the adoption of a thoroughly secular and pragmatic definition of civil society.

As political philosophy, indeed, Locke's case for toleration is rather less rigorous and persuasive than was his earlier case against it. It is little more than a set of common-sense prudential recommendations loosely derived from a cluster of half-explored metaphysical difficulties. The magistrate is required to realize certain ends because of the consent basis of government. But the only judge of his performance is God. The argument (which of course is very reminiscent of that 'third' theory of government postulated in the Latin *Tract*), implies a concurrence of the public will, which makes magistrates, and the divine will, which judges them. But this is nowhere made explicit or systematically accounted for. Again, the magistrate is required to leave certain acts alone because they are private transactions between the individual and God. But at some obscure point, which the magistrate may determine, these acts may be judged dangerous to the state and so suppressed. And ultimately it is the mere obscurity of this critical dividing line that forces Locke to come down on the side of toleration rather than imposition. Everything turns on the want of knowledge, on the impossibility of any individual ever transcending the subjectivity of his own convictions:

Princes indeed, are born superior to other men in power, but in nature equal. Neither the right nor the art of ruling does necessarily carry along with it the certain knowledge of other things, and least of all true religion...The one only narrow way which leads to heaven is not better known to the magistrate than to private persons, and therefore I cannot safely take him for my guide, who may probably be as ignorant of the way as myself, and who is certainly less concerned for my salvation than I myself am.[52]

The best that can be done is to remove this dark and disputed area from the sphere of civil society. Maintaining the same categories of analysis that he had used in 1660, this is what Locke now does. The fact of ignorance means that the business of the commonwealth, civil peace, will only be achieved when magistrates and citizens alike abandon all efforts to impose their own partial versions of the truth on one another. 'Truth', indeed, 'would do well enough if she were once left to shift for herself.'

Meanwhile, toleration follows from ignorance and partiality. In *The Reasonableness of Christianity* Locke brings the wheel of argument full circle:

The rules of morality were in different countries and sects different. And natural reason was nowhere like to cure them...Where was it that their obligation was thoroughly known and allowed, and they received as precepts of a law? That could not be, without a clear knowledge and acknowledgement of the law-maker, and the great rewards and punishments for those that would or would not obey him.[53]

In each direction the changes in Locke's thought after 1660 take the form of a decisive concession to the importance of human ignorance, human will and human intellect. Politically, he found the authority needed to sustain obligation in the public will of men in society. In this theory of knowledge—once the difficulties of the *Tracts* had been properly articulated—he found that there was no knowledge that could provide a basis for discriminating between private persuasions. Yet theologically he remained certain that an objective morality existed and was available to reason. The individual was thus authorized, socially and morally, to search for truth. Until it was found, the only basis for practical obligation remained a voluntaristic one. Locke's voluntarism, however, was maintained in the context of a perennial tension between ignorance and faith that can be felt in all his works. And it was in combining a voluntaristic system of obligation with an assertion of the individual's ability and duty to look for the rational basis of that system that Locke made his great contribution to that 'social and ethical reconstitution of the individual' that was the over-arching concern of the intellectuals of his generation.

Not that the reconstitution was fully achieved, of course. Karl Marx abandoned the text of *Capital* at the point where he reached the question critical for his whole social analysis: what is a class? There is a similar symbolic break in Locke's thought; the paper *Of Ethick in General* ends with a starting-point:

The next thing then to show is, that there are certain rules, certain dictates, which it is his will all men should conform their actions to, and that this will of his is sufficiently promulgated and made known to all mankind.[54]

Locke could find only one way of proceeding beyond this point, and it was not the way of knowledge. Seen thus, the problems raised in 1660 in the authoritarian and rationalistic *Tracts on Government* were resolved, so far as they could be resolved, thirty-five years later in the liberal, fideistic arguments of *The Reasonableness of Christianity*. The axiom of knowledge, inviolate for half a millennium, had been destroyed. Henceforth, for Locke as for Lord Brooke, 'understanding and truth can be but one'.

NOTES

1 English *Tract*, p. 35; *Essay Concerning Toleration*, 1667: there are four versions of this work: references are given here to the MS of the last to be written, MS Locke c. 28, fols. 21 ff.; for the other three cf. Cranston, 1957, p. 111.

2 Public Record Office, 30/24/472; Wood, 1813, I, p. 52; Dewhurst, 1962, p. 38.

3 Baker, 1952, pp. 4–6; McAdoo, 1949.

4 English *Tract*, p. 24; Latin *Tract*, pp. 9–10; Von Leyden, 1954, p. 189.

5 English *Tract*, pp. 1, 24, 33; Von Leyden, 1954, p. 125.

6 English *Tract*, pp. 1, 3; Latin *Tract*, pp. 2, 6, 9–10; Von Leyden, 1954, p. 187; *Reasonableness*, pp. 575–9.

7 Von Leyden, 1954, pp. 115–35; MS Locke c. 28, fols. 148–52.

8 Von Leyden, 1954, pp. 181–9.

9 *Reasonableness*, pp. 575–6; Von Leyden, 1954, pp. 237–9; MS Locke c. 28, fols. 148–52.

10 The most conspicuous failure to examine the nature of law is of course in the *Two Treatises*, especially in II, xi and xii: throughout this discussion of legislative power it is assumed that the nature of law is not problematic; and cf. *Essay*, II, xxviii, 7. But the exploration of law continued in his private journals and notebooks, cf. MS Locke f. 5 and Von Leyden, 1954, pp. 67–9; also Savage, 1660, p. 10.

11 *Essay, Epistle to the Reader*, p. 1; Aaron and Gibb, 1936, p. 39; Rand, 1931, p. 303; Von Leyden, 1954, pp. 60–2; Cranston, 1957, pp. 140–1.

12 Abrams, 1961, pp. 262–72; Von Leyden, 1954, pp. 56–9, 67, 71–8, holds that Locke's voluntarism weakened as he grew older. My position is that while Locke regularly asserts the *possibility* of a rationalist theory of law, he always rests his immediate arguments about obligation on the alternative theory—doing so, indeed, just because the law of nature does not in practice govern the state of nature: in other words I agree with Strauss, 1956, pp. 224–6, Wild, 1953, p. 131, and Cox, 1960, pp. 79–81, rather than with Von Leyden, 1954, pp. 51 ff., and Laslett, 1960, pp. 79–81. It is worth pointing out that one's view of the ultimate role of voluntaristic theories in Locke's philosophy depends very much on how much attention one pays to his last major work, *The Reasonableness of Christianity*: Von Leyden does not mention it at all; cf. Singh, 1961.

13 *Two Treatises*, II, sect. 134, and cf. 88–9, 96, 143, 145, 212.

14 *Essay*, II, xxviii; IV, x, 6; Aaron and Gibb, 1936, p. 39; MS Locke c. 28, fols. 148–52, Of Ethick in General.

15 *Reasonableness*, pp. 576–7; and cf. Latin *Tract*, pp. 7–9, and MS Locke, f. 24, fol. 277; Von Leyden, 1954, pp. 109–21.

16 Von Leyden, 1954, pp. 199–201; *Two Treatises*, II, sects. 6, 12, 19, 57, 61, 63, 124; MS Locke f. 5, fol. 79; *Essay*, I, ii, 13; Aaron and Gibb, 1936, p. 117; Singh, 1961, p. 107; Cox, 1960, pp. 80 ff.; English *Tract*, p. 33; Latin *Tract*, p. 13.

17 MS Locke c. 28, fol. 21, *Essay Concerning Toleration*; *Letter Concerning Toleration*, pp. 252–3; *Second Letter Concerning Toleration*, pp. 282, 307 ff., and above all *Two Treatises*, where this theme is as obtrusive as the analysis of law is discreet, II, sects. 59, 107, 220, 240; cf. Laslett, 1960, pp. 111–13.

18 *Two Treatises*, II, sects. 212 and 221–43; Cox, 1960, p. 135.

19 Compare: English *Tract*, pp. 19–20; Latin *Tract*, pp. 6–7; *Two Treatises*, II, sects. 131, 134, 137, 139, 222, 240: 'Who shall be judge whether the prince or legislative act contrary to their trust?... I reply: The people shall be judge,' and *Letter Concerning Toleration*, p. 278, 'Who shall be judge between them? I answer, God alone.'

20 Compare Singh, 1961, and Strauss, 1952, for an extreme divergence of interpretation, also Gough, 1950, pp. 4–8, who sensibly points out that for Locke the 'voluntarist' *or* 'rationalist' dilemma was an unreal one: the problem was to achieve a balance, not to take sides; cf. Von Leyden, 1954, pp. 150–1, and *Essay*, I, iv; *Examination of Malebranche*, IV, sect. 53; *Two Treatises*, II, sect. 12.

21 *Essay, Epistle to the Reader*, pp. 17–19, where in answer to Lowde who had complained that the Essay confused public opinion and morality, Locke formally articulates the distinction; cf. MS Locke c. 28, fols. 21 v, 29, *Essay Concerning Toleration*; *Letter Concerning Toleration*, pp. 27 ff.; *Third Letter for Toleration*, ch. II; *Reasonableness*, pp. 144–5, 579.

22 English *Tract*, p. 16: 'Order and decency...depend wholly on the opinions and phancys of man and 'tis as impossible to fix any certain rule of them as to hope to cast all men's minds...into one mould.'

23 Von Leyden, 1964, p. 167; Bodleian Library, MS Film 77, pp. 128–42, 152, 154, 156; MS Locke c. 28, fols. 22, 32, *Essay Concerning Toleration*; *Letter Concerning Toleration*, pp. 253, 259–60, 272; *Second Letter Concerning Toleration*, pp. 286, 296, 307; *Third Letter for Toleration*, pp. 331, 358–61; *Reasonableness*, p. 579; *Essay*, II, xxviii.

24 *Third Letter for Toleration*, p. 457; cf. Latin *Tract*, p. 17; MS Locke c. 28, fol. 21 v, *Essay Concerning Toleration*; *Letter Concerning Toleration*, p. 268.

25 *Third Letter for Toleration*, p. 321, but this does not deter Locke from saying that in ideal circumstances Christianity 'will prevail' against

other religions because it is the 'true' religion (p. 480); here the contrast of objective and subjective knowledge is very explicit—the more so as Locke goes on to say that such ideal circumstances are never *in fact* likely to obtain.

26 *Third Letter for Toleration*, pp. 320, 481, and cf. King, 1830, pp. 161–203, the passages in Locke's *Journal for 1677* on 'Knowledge' and 'Study'.

27 English *Tract, The Preface to the Reader* and pp. 10–11; *Two Treatises*, II, sects. 124–5; *Essay*, IV, xvi, 3.

28 *Conduct of the Understanding*, p. 396.

29 *Reasonableness*, p. 576; King, 1830, pp. 188–90; *Journal for 1677* (my italics); and cf. English *Tract, The Preface to the Reader*, and p. 5, for similar views.

30 *Of the Conduct of the Understanding*, p. 387.

31 *Two Treatises*, II, sects. 124–8; and cf. *Reasonableness*, p. 577.

32 *Essay*, I, iii, 12–13, iv, 8–9 and IV, iii, 19–20, iv, 7, x, 1, xix, 4; *Reasonableness*, p. 578; *Third Letter for Toleration*, pp. 487–9; and the constant allusion to the obligations of natural law even while admitting that these laws do not actually oblige in *Two Treatises*, II, sects. 12, 19, 57, 61, 63, 124, 136; *Of the Conduct of the Understanding*, pp. 388–9.

33 *Of the Conduct of the Understanding*, p. 393; *Two Treatises*, II, sect. 124; *Reasonableness*, pp. 578–9.

34 *Of the Conduct of the Understanding*, pp. 393–5; *Two Treatises*, II, sect. 6.

35 *Essay*, I, iv, 24: cf. *Reasonableness*, p. 579; Fraser, 1901, pp. 48, 113.

36 MS Locke c. 27, fol. 12, Letter to 'S. H.': cf. MS Locke c. 28, fols. 21v, 25, 32, *Essay Concerning Toleration*; *Letter Concerning Toleration*, pp. 260–1, 268; *Third Letter for Toleration*, pp. 349, 354.

37 *Third Letter for Toleration*, pp. 367, 378.

38 MS Locke c. 28, fol. 21v, *Essay Concerning Toleration*; *Letter Concerning Toleration*, p. 263.

39 MS Locke c. 28, fol. 21v, *Essay Concerning Toleration*; cf. *Third Letter for Toleration*, p. 324.

40 MS Locke c. 28, fol. 22, *Essay Concerning Toleration*; *Letter Concerning Toleration*, pp. 262–4.

41 *Letter Concerning Toleration*, p. 261; MS Locke c. 28, fol. 21v, *Essay Concerning Toleration*, and cf. Latin *Tract*, p. 12, Bagshaw, 1660 (*a*), p. 13.

42 MS Locke c. 28, fols. 21, 24, 26, *Essay Concerning Toleration*.

43 MS Locke c. 28, fol. 25, *Essay Concerning Toleration*; *Letter Concerning Toleration*, pp. 262, 268, 269; *Second Letter Concerning Toleration*, pp. 306–9.

44 MS Locke c. 28, fol. 25, *Essay Concerning Toleration* and *Letter Concerning Toleration*, p. 252. And note that this change of view does not involve any attention in the detail of his argument or of interpretation of Christian revelation. The observations he makes on controversial texts in *Paraphrase and Notes on the Epistles of St Paul* are altogether consistent with the discussion of these texts in the *Tracts*; compare English *Tract*, p. 7, and *Paraphrase*, p. 135; English *Tract*, p. 12, and *Paraphrase*, p. 172; Latin *Tract*, p. 8, and *Paraphrase*, p. 175; also Abrams, 1961, p. 298.

45 MS Locke c. 28, fol. 24, *Essay Concerning Toleration*, cf. English *Tract*, p. 33.

46 MS Locke c. 28, fols. 25, 32, *Essay Concerning Toleration*, cf. *Letter Concerning Toleration*, pp. 252–3, 269–72.

47 MS Locke c. 28, fol. 25, *Essay Concerning Toleration*; Parker, 1670, and for Locke's comments on this work, MS Locke c. 29, fols. 7–9, and Cranston, 1957, pp. 131–3; for Ashley's memorandum, Christie, 1871, II, appx. I.

48 MS Locke c. 28, fols. 21, 28, *Essay Concerning Toleration*; *Letter Concerning Toleration*, pp. 252–3; *Two Treatises*, II, sects. 134, 135, 137, 139; cf. Cox, 1960, p. 81.

49 MS Locke c. 28, fols. 25–6, *Essay Concerning Toleration*; *Letter Concerning Toleration*, p. 269; and cf. English *Tract*, pp. 18–20, Latin *Tract*, pp. 6–7, 17.

50 MS Locke c. 28, fols. 21, 26, *Essay Concerning Toleration*; *Letter Concerning Toleration*, pp. 252, 259.

51 MS Locke c. 28, fol. 24, *Essay Concerning Toleration*; *Letter Concerning Toleration*, pp. 262–3.

52 *Letter Concerning Toleration*, p. 260.

53 *Reasonableness*, p. 576.

54 MS Locke c. 28, fol. 152.

EDITORIAL PREFACE

NOTES ON THE TEXTS, TRANSLATION, FOOTNOTES AND REFERENCES

The manuscripts of the *Tracts on Government* are relatively clean. Locke's grammar is erratic, his spelling random, his use of abbreviations and signs inconsistent. Nevertheless the *Tracts* present no particularly perplexing editorial problems. The texts we have would seem to be final fair copies and neither the script nor the organization of either work presents any major problem of interpretation. For this reason I have not attempted an exact representation of the archaic conventions or minor additions and deletions within the MSS—such a version is available in Abrams, 1961.

The English *Tract*

I have tried to produce a reading version in twentieth-century English. Spelling, capitalization and, in some cases, punctuation have been modernized. Any changes of this sort which could be thought to affect the author's meaning have been indicated in the notes. Locke's abbreviations are standard ones: *ye, yt, wch, wt, agt*, for *the, that, which, what* and *against*; *ment* and *tion* word endings shortened to *mt* and *con*; *X* and *Xan* for *Christ* and *Christian*; *magis* and *quest* for *magistrate* and *question*; and so forth. All these have been expanded. Where single letters have been dropped in the MS and the omission is plainly accidental, as in concer[n]ing, p. 12, or presu[m]ption, p. 32—the missing letters have simply been supplied without comment. All other changes made to the actual appearance, form and content of the manuscript have been noted.

Locke's text is written on a facing-page system which allowed the author to add to or change his argument on the left-hand page without breaking into the main text on the right. He indicates additions of this sort by Greek symbols in the margin of each page. Here, I have reorganized the manuscript as a continuous text using two types of notation: editorial modifications, ambiguous or obscure readings, and all work on the structure of the text are taken up in numbered references at the end of the *Tract*; literary allusions and interpretive comment will be found at the foot of each page of the text. I have indicated Locke's own pagination to make cross-reference to the manuscript itself rather easier. The footnotes to the text are meant to serve a number of purposes. First, I have tried to illumine the nature of Locke's treatment of the text of his adversary, Edward Bagshaw. Short of reproducing the whole of Bagshaw's pamphlet, the best means of assessing Locke's thoroughness and impartiality as a textual critic seemed to be to adopt the system of constant cross-reference to and quotation from Bagshaw, 1660 (*a*), which I have in fact used. In a number of cases reference is also made to points of argument and interpretation in my Introduction. Striking similarities of mood between the *Tract* and Locke's contemporary correspondence are noted. I have tried to identify such literary and political references as Locke gives and to indicate the various types of argument and behaviour he discusses in the contemporary literature. Throughout I have tried to note points of contact with or divergence from the arguments of the Latin *Tract* and of Locke's later philosophical and political writings, especially the works on toleration. These notes do not, however, seek to identify possible sources of the *Tract* or to compare Locke's position systematically with the arguments of, say, Hooker, Sanderson or Hobbes. This is attempted in the notes to the Latin *Tract* where Locke's argument is the same but unencumbered with the detail of his polemic against Bagshaw. Literary parallels are explored here only when the arguments in question do not reappear in the Latin work. To this extent I have taken at face value Locke's claim that he was, in writing the English *Tract*, 'careful to sequester my thought both from books and the times'.

The Latin *Tract*

While eliminating archaisms, I have tried here to produce a text as close as possible to Locke's own Latin manuscript. The translation, similarly, is in the main literal and for this reason frequently inelegant. Where it was necessary to add substantially to the text in order to render Locke's meaning in tolerable English or to delete or alter letters or words, this has been indicated by square brackets; if the change is controversial or dubious, further explanation is given in a footnote. Locke's own deletions or alterations are also observed in the footnotes, as are some possible miscopyings from the earlier draft of the *Tract* in MS Locke e. 6.

In the main the notes to the Latin *Tract* are references to this earlier draft which I have called MS A; I have noted significant alterations of words, structure or meaning between the two texts and on one or two occasions have allowed the translation of difficult passages in MS B to be guided by the text of MS A. Most of Locke's abbreviations in the MS are the standard Latin printing abbreviations: ē, ēē, n:, sc:, naā, D, for *est, esse, enim, scilicet, natura, Dico* (etc.), and the signs ' and ⁻ for the suffixes *us* and *um*: these have all been expanded.

The translation has no pretensions to style except where I have tried in one or two places to keep the flavour of a passage of elaborately 'fine' writing on Locke's part (e.g. MS pp. 17–18). Here, as in the Latin text, I have supplied or modified punctuation as the sense seemed to require. The notes to the translation are intended to provide a basis for the comparison of Locke's thought with that of other seventeenth-century political thinkers, in particular with the thought of Hooker, Sanderson and Hobbes, and with some of the writers on indifferent things discussed in my Introduction. Occasionally I have noted points of contact with the arguments of Edward Bagshaw. I have tried to identify the various 'adversaries' whom Locke discusses, to give substance to some of his rather imprecise allusions and references, and to note consistencies or inconsistencies of thought between the argument of the *Tract* and those of Locke's later works. I have also taken the opportunity to explain some points of translation and to indicate parallels with the English *Tract*. It was necessary to set rather arbitrary limits to the number of literary references taken up in these notes; I have tried to make the notes full without overburdening the text; there is thus, for example, no discussion of the use made by Locke of Bodin's account of sovereignty as compared with his use of Bodin in later works.

Quotations in English from the lectures of Robert Sanderson are from the Codrington translation of the *De Obligatione Conscientiae* of 1660; quotations in Latin are from the original (Allestry) edition of 1659/60.

THE FIRST TRACT ON
GOVERNMENT

FIRST TRACT ON GOVERNMENT

*The Preface to the Reader**   MS Locke c. 28, fols. 1–2

Reader

This discourse which was written many months since, had not
been more than *written* now but had still lain concealed in a
secure privacy, had not *importunity* prevailed against my intentions,
and forced it into the public.† I shall not trouble thee with the
history or occasion of its original, though it be certain that thou
here receivest from me a present, which was not at first designed
thee.‡ This confession how little soever obliging, I the more
easily make since I am not very solicitous what entertainment it
shall receive, and if *truth* (which I only aim at) suffer not by this
edition, I am very secure as to everything else. To bespeak thy
impartial perusal, were to expect more from thee than books,
especially of this nature, usually meet with; and I should too
fondly promise myself the good hap to meet with that temper that
this age is scarcely blessed with; wherein *truth* is seldom allowed a
fair hearing, and the generality of men conducted either by *chance*
or *advantage* take to themselves their opinions as they do their
wives, which when they have once *espoused* them think themselves
concerned to maintain, though for no other reason but because
they are theirs, being as tender of the credit of one as of the other,
and if 'twere left to their own choice, 'tis not improbable that this
would be the more difficult divorce.

My design being only the clearing a *truth* in question, I shall be
very glad if I have said anything that may satisfy her impartial

* Notes marked thus and presented at the foot of each page will be mainly
editorial comments, points of interpretation and cross-references to the writings of
Locke or to other relevant literature. Numbered references are to the notes on
pp. 175–81: they deal with deletions and insertions and other difficulties of the
Locke MSS. Points of presentation are dealt with in the Editorial Preface (pp. 112–
114), which also contains a general statement of editorial procedure. Locke's marginal addenda could not easily be incorporated in the text and have been retained as
marginal notes.

† The 'forcing' of the English *Tract* into public is discussed above, chapter 1;
cf. the letters of Gabriel Towerson to Locke (MS Locke c. 22, fols. 5, 7), 'there may
be some necessity that your papers should see the light', etc.

‡ It will be observed that Locke opens his *Preface* to the *Two Treatises* in a very
similar unamiable tone.

followers, being otherwise very careless how little soever I gratify the interests, or fancies of others. However that I may not give any advantage to this partial humour I shall take the same way to prevent it that the gentleman whom I trace hath trod before me, and by concealing my name leave thee concerned for nothing but the arguments themselves.

And indeed besides the reasons that persuaded my author to conceal himself there be many other that more strongly oblige me to it. Amongst others I should be sure to incur the censure of many of my acquaintance. For having always professed myself an enemy to the scribbling of this age and often accused the *pens* of Englishmen of as much guilt as their *swords* judging that the issue of *blood* from whence such an inundation hath flowed had scarce been opened, or at least not so long unstopped had men been more sparing of their ink and that these Furies, War, Cruelty, Rapine, Confusion, etc., which have so wearied and wasted this poor [p. 1]* nation have been conjured up in private studies and from thence sent abroad to disturb the quiet we enjoyed.† This objection then will lie against me, that I now run upon the same guilt I condemned in others, disturbing the beginnings of our happy settlement by engaging in a quarrel, and bandying a question which it would be well if it were quite forgotten, and hath been but too *loudly* disputed already. But I hope I shall deserve no more blame than he that takes *arms* only to keep the peace and draws his sword in the same side with the magistrate, with a design to suppress, not begin a quarrel.

I could heartily wish that all *disputes* of this nature would cease, that men would rather be content to enjoy the *freedom* they have, than by such questions increase at once their own *suspicions* and *disquiets*, and the magistrate's *trouble*, such discourses, however cautiously proposed, with desire of *search* and *satisfaction* being understood usually rather to speak *discontents* than *doubts* and increase the one rather than remove the other. And however sincere the *author* may be, the *interested* and *prejudiced* reader not seldom greedily entertains them as the just *reproaches* of the State, and hence takes the boldness to censure the miscarriages of the magistrate and question the equity and obligation of

---

* Page references in this form are to pages of the Locke MSS.

† Locke's distaste for public controversy is discussed above, chapter II; he makes the point again, more emphatically, in the Latin *Tract*, p. 1.

all laws which have not the good luck to square with his *private judgment.**

I confess it cannot be thought, but that men should fly from *oppression*, but *disorder* will give them but an incommodious sanctuary. 'Tis not without reason that *tyranny* and *anarchy* are judged the smartest scourges can fall upon mankind, the plea of *authority* usually backing the one and of *liberty* inducing the other: and between these two it is, that human affairs are perpetually kept tumbling. Nor is it to be hoped that the prudence of man should provide against these, beyond any fear of their return, so long as men have either *ambitious thoughts* or *discontented minds*, or till the greatest part of men are well satisfied in their own *condition*; which is not to be looked for in this world. All the remedy that can be found is when the *prince* makes the good of the people the measure of his injunctions and the people without examining the reasons, pay a ready and entire obedience, and both these founded on a mutual confidence each of other, which is the greatest security and happiness of any people, and a *blessing*, if ever, to expect now, and to be found amongst those many miracles that have restored, and we hope will continue his *Majesty* to us, very pregnant assurances whereof we have received in that great tenderness and affection to his people which his *Majesty* beyond parallel hath shown in the transactions of the late and opening of the present Parliament.†   [p. 2]

As‡ for myself, there is no one can have a greater respect and veneration for authority than I. I no sooner perceived myself in the *world* but I found myself in a storm, which hath lasted almost hitherto, and therefore cannot but entertain the approaches of a calm with the greatest joy and satisfaction; and this methinks obliges me, both in *duty* and gratitude§ to be chary of such a blessing,

---

* The similarity of this and the preceding paragraph to the opening passages of the Latin *Tract*, pp. 1-2, is remarkable, not only in mood but in many particular phrases.

† See above, chapter 1; the 'miraculous' character of the Restoration is a common theme of the Anglican apologists at this time; it recurs in the Latin *Tract* and is the gist of virtually all the poems in the Oxford celebration to which Locke contributed; cf., too, Clarendon, *The Continuation of his Life*, 1, p. 314; if the 'present' Parliament is that which opened on 8 May 1661, as seems probable, Locke's reference is presumably to the King's gesture, 'I am sure, as I can be of anything that is to come, that you will all concur with me and that I shall concur with you in all things that you may advance the peace, plenty and prosperity of this nation'.

‡ This paragraph is printed by Lord King, *Life and Letters of John Locke* (1830), 1, p. 13.

§ King omits the next twelve words.

and what lies in me to endeavour its continuance, by disposing men's minds to obedience to that government which hath brought with it that quiet and settlement which our own *giddy folly* had put beyond the reach, not only of our *contrivance*, but *hopes*. And I would men would be persuaded to be so kind to their *religion*, their *country* and *themselves* as not to hazard again the substantial blessings of *peace* and *settlement* in an over-zealous contention about things, which they themselves confess to be little and at most are but indifferent.

Besides the submission I have for *authority* I have no less a love of *liberty* without which a *man* shall find himself less happy than a *beast. Slavery* being a condition that robs us of all the benefits of life, and embitters the greatest blessings, reason itself in slaves (which is the grand privilege of other men) increasing the weight of their chains and joining with their oppressions to torment them.* But† since I find that a *general freedom* is but a *general bondage*, that the popular assertors of public liberty are the greatest engrossers of it too and not unfitly called its *keepers* and[1] I know not whether experience (if it may be credited) would not give us some reason to think that were this part of *freedom* contended for here by our *author* generally indulged in *England* it would prove only a *liberty* for *contention, censure* and *persecution* and turn us loose to the *tyranny* of a *religious rage*; were every indifferent thing left *unlimited* nothing would be *lawful* and 'twould quickly be found that the *practice* of indifferent things not approved by dissenting parties, would then be judged as anti-Christian and unlawful as their injunction is now, and engage the heads and hands of the zealous partisans in the necessary duty of reformation, and it may well be feared by any that will but consider the *conscientious* disorders amongst us that‡ the several bands of *Saints* would not want their *Venners*§ to animate and lead them on in the *work of the Lord*:

* But Locke contrives to forget this later on, cf. pp. 22 f., where he is confronted by Bagshaw's application of the same principle to the victims of ceremonial 'chains'; and Latin *Tract*, p. 17, 'cur rationem cur religionem nobis largitus est deus. . . ?' etc.

† This sentence, as far as *persecution*, is printed by King, 1830, pp. 13–14.

‡ The remainder of this sentence is printed by King, 1830, p. 14.

§ The insurrection led by the Fifth Monarchist Venner on 6 January 1660/1 provided the instance for almost all arguments against toleration in the following year. It was as eagerly disowned by Independents and Baptists as it was denounced by Anglicans, cf. *The Humble Apology of some commonly called Anabaptists* (1661); *A Declaration from the. . .people of God called Quakers* (1661); *A Renunciation and Declaration of the Congregational Churches. . .against the late horrid Insurrection* (1661).

Summus utrimque
Inde furor vulgo, quod numina vicinorum
Odit uterque locus, quum solos credat habendos
Esse deos, quos ipse colit.*

And he must confess himself a stranger to England that thinks that *meats* and *habits*, that *places* and *times* of worship etc., would [p. 3] not be as sufficient occasion of hatred and quarrels amongst us, as *leeks* and *onions* and other *trifles* described in that satire by Juvenal was amongst them, and be distinctions able to keep us always at a distance, and eagerly ready for like violence and cruelty as often as the *teachers* should alarm the *consciences* of their zealous votaries and direct them against the adverse party.

I† have not therefore the same apprehensions of *liberty* that I find some have or can think the *benefits* of it to consist in a liberty for men at pleasure to adopt themselves children of God, and from thence assume a title to inheritance here and proclaim themselves heirs of the world; not a liberty for ambition to pull down well-framed constitutions, that out of its *ruins* they may build themselves fortunes; not a liberty to be Christians so as not to be subjects; nor such a liberty as is like to engage us in perpetual dissension and disorder. All the *freedom* I can wish my country or myself is to enjoy the *protection* of those *laws* which the prudence and providence of our ancestors established and the happy return of his Majesty² hath restored: a body of laws so well composed, that whilst this nation would be content only to be under them they were always sure to be above their neighbours, which forced from the world this constant acknowledgement, that we were not only the *happiest state* but the *purest church* of the latter age.‡

'Tis therefore in defence of the *authority* of these laws that against many reasons I am drawn to appear in public, the preservation whereof as the only security I can yet find of this nation's *settlement* I think myself concerned in, till I can find other reasons

---

* 'Each party is filled with fury against the other because each hates its neighbours' gods, believing that none can be holy but those it worships itself,' Juvenal, *Satire* xv, lines 35 f. This is a favourite source for arguments of this type, cf. Hammond, 1644, 1, Of Conscience, and a further reference by Locke below, and a virtual paraphrase of this passage, Latin *Tract*, p. 15, his fourth explanation of the use of the word 'superstition'.

† This paragraph, as far as 'his Majesty hath restored', is printed by King, 1830, pp. 14–15, in a slightly abbreviated form.

‡ Cf. Whitlock, 1660, and Fell, 1659, for elaborate statements of this theme, and above, chapter II.

than I have yet met with to show their non-obligation as long as unrepealed, and dispense with my *obedience*. After this I hope I need not assure thee that neither *vanity* nor any *pique* against the author put the pen into my hand, the concealment we both lie under having sufficiently provided against that suspicion.* I[3] dare say could his opinion have ever won upon me, it would have been in that handsome dress and those many ornaments his pen hath bestowed upon it with all the advantages it was capable of. But I cannot relinquish the contrary persuasion whilst truth (at least in my apprehension)† so strongly declares for it, and I believe he cannot take it ill that whilst he pleads so earnestly for *liberty in actions* I should be unwilling to have my *understanding*, the noblest part, imposed on, and will not be so forgetful of his own *principles* as to deny me the *liberty* of dissenting and if he will permit himself to peruse these *answers* with the same desire of satisfaction wherewith he professes himself to have proposed his doubts, and I assure

[p. 4] him I read them, it may be hoped he will be persuaded *if not to alter his judgment* yet at least not to think them blind who cannot see in his *spectacles* or cannot find themselves by his arguments freed from that obedience to the civil magistrate in all things indifferent, which obedience God in his infinite wisdom hath made necessary and *therefore* not *left free*.

I‡ have chose to draw a great part of my discourse from the *supposition* of the magistrate's power, derived from, or conveyed to him by, the consent of the people, as a way best suited to those patrons of liberty, and most likely to obviate their *objections*, the foundation of their *plea* being usually an opinion of their natural freedom, which they are apt to think too much entrenched upon by *impositions* in things indifferent. Not that I intend to meddle§ with that question whether the magistrate's crown drops down on his head immediately from *heaven* or be placed there by the *hands of his subjects*, it being sufficient to my purpose that the supreme

---

* But at least in Oxford this concealment was far from as perfect as Locke implies, cf. chapter II above.

† This sort of instinctive reservation was to be the intellectual undoing of the debate on indifferent things and the making of Locke as a philosopher of knowledge, cf. chapter III above.

‡ This paragraph reproduces word for word the letter of 11 December 1660 suffixed to the MS of the English *Tract*, MS Locke e. 7, fols. 35–6.

§ Whatever his first intention, it is clear that Locke found that the problem of indifferency *forced* him to meddle with the larger question, cf. chapter II above.

magistrate of every nation what way soever created, must necessarily have an *absolute* and *arbitrary power* over all the indifferent actions of his people. And if his *authority* must needs be of so large an extent in the lowest and narrowest way of its original (that can be supposed) when derived from the scanty allowance of the *people*, who are never forward to part with more of their liberty than needs must, I think it will clearly follow, that if he receive his commission immediately from *God* the people will have little reason thereupon to think it more confined than if he received it from them until they can produce the *charter* of their own liberty, or the *limitation* of the legislator's authority, from the same God that gave it.* Otherwise no doubt, those *indifferent things* that God hath⁴ not forbid or commanded, his *vicegerent* may, having no other rule to direct his commands than every single person hath for his actions, *viz*: *the law of God*; and it will be granted that the people have but a poor pretence to liberty in indifferent things in a condition wherein they have no liberty at all, but by the appointment of the Great Sovereign of heaven and earth are born subjects to the will and pleasure of another.†

But I shall not build upon this foundation, but allowing every man by nature as large a liberty as he himself can wish, shall yet make it appear that whilst there is society, government and order in the world, rulers still must have the power of all things indifferent which I hope (Reader) thou wilt find evident in the following pages whither I remit thee. [p. 5]

Only give me leave first to say that it would be a strange thing if anyone amongst us should question the obligation of those laws which are not ratified nor imposed on him but by his own consent in Parliament.‡

* In the Latin *Tract* Locke does deal with the question of the derivation of government and suggests an alternative theory of its 'original'; but his conclusions are those of this paragraph; cf. pp. 12–14.

† The letter ends here (MS Locke e. 7, fol. 36).

‡ This last sentence has the appearance of a late addendum in the MS; its implications for Locke's theory of consent are discussed by Gough, 1950, p. 181; but the meaning of the sentence is obscure in the absence of a more specific reference. On 13 May 1661, the day before the publisher Allestry asked Tilly for final additions to the 'Treatise you left in my hand' (MS Locke c. 3, fol. 21), the Commons agreed that all M.P.s should be compelled to take the sacrament according to the Liturgy. If it is this Locke has in mind his statement is an unremarkable one. But he may be thinking of the decision to repudiate and burn the Covenant four days later; or even of the introduction of the 'bill for uniformity of public prayers' on 29 June. In which case the implicit theory of consent is more interesting (cf. *Commons Journals*, VII, 254 ff., 285 ff.).

*Question: Whether the Civil Magistrate may lawfully impose and determine the use of indifferent things in reference to Religious Worship.**

MS Locke e. 7

In order to the clearer debating this question, besides the granting my author's two suppositions, *viz*: (i) that a Christian may be a magistrate, (ii) that there are some things indifferent,† it will not be amiss to premiss some few things about these matters of indifferency,[1] *viz*:

1. That were there no law there would be no moral good or evil, but man would be left to a most entire liberty in all his actions, and could meet with nothing which would not be purely indifferent, and consequently, that what doth not lie under the obligation of any law is still indifferent.‡

2. That nobody hath a natural original power and disposure of this liberty of man but only God himself, from whose authority all laws do fundamentally derive their obligation, as being either immediately enjoined by him, or framed by some authority derived from him.§

3. That wherever God hath made known his will either by the discoveries of reason, usually called the law of nature, or the revelations of his word, there nothing is left man but submission and obedience, and all things within the compass of this law are necessarily and indispensably good or evil.¶

4. That all things not comprehended in that law are perfectly indifferent and as to them man is naturally free, but yet so much master of his own liberty, that he may by compact convey it over to another and invest him with a power over his actions, there being no law of God forbidding a man to dispose of his liberty and

---

* Locke's heading is Bagshaw's sub-title, 1660(*a*); both authors thus confront the problem as one of law. Locke's problem was to diminish the scope of the laws invoked by Bagshaw; cf. the discussion of the *perfecta regula* in the Latin *Tract*.

† For these 'suppositions' cf. Bagshaw, pp. 1–2; both are in fact qualified by Bagshaw; thus, for him, a Christian may be a magistrate because otherwise 'a gap is opened to all confusion', but Christians must rule 'in the Lord'.

‡ These premises are printed by Gough, 1950, pp. 179 ff.; cf. Latin *Tract*, p. 6, and note that this position is maintained in Locke's later works, *Essay*, II, xxviii; MS Locke c. 28, fols. 146–52.

§ This is the major proposition of Locke's early political thought and it effectively removes him from the camp of Hobbes; cf. chapter III above, and Sanderson, *De Obligatione Conscientiae* (1660), IV, ix.

¶ This dual conception of obligation is developed by Locke in Latin *Tract*, p. 10, and cf. Sanderson, 1660, IV, xx.

obey another. But on the other side, there being a law of God enforcing fidelity and truth in all lawful contracts, it obliges him after such a resignation and agreement to submit.[*]

5. That[2] supposing man naturally owner of an entire liberty, and so much master of himself as to owe no subjection to any other but God alone (which is the freest condition we can fancy him in), it is yet the unalterable condition of society and government that every particular man must unavoidably part with this right[3] to his liberty and entrust the magistrate[(a)] with as full a power over all his actions as he himself hath, it being otherwise impossible that anyone should be subject to the commands of [p. 1] another who retains the free disposure of himself, and is master of an equal liberty.[†] Nor do men, as some fondly conceive, enjoy any greater share of this freedom in a pure commonwealth, if anywhere to be found,[4] than in an absolute monarchy, the same arbitrary power being there in the assembly (which acts like one person) as in a monarch, wherein each particular man hath no more power (bating[5] the inconsiderable addition of his single vote) of himself to make new or dispute old laws than in a monarchy; all he can do (which is no more than kings allow petitioners) is to persuade the majority which is the monarch.[‡]

Having laid down these things, which I think[6] my author will not deny me, I shall content myself with one only argument rising from thence, sufficient to persuade me that the magistrate may lawfully determine the use of indifferent things relating to religion, *viz*: because it is lawful for the magistrate to command whatever it

---

[(a)] *By magistrate I understand the supreme legislative power of any society not considering the form of government or number of persons wherein it is placed. Only give me leave to say that the indelible memory of our late miseries, and the happy return of our ancient freedom and felicity, are proofs sufficient to convince us where the supreme power of these nations is most advantageously placed, without the assistance of any other arguments.*

[*] Cf. Latin *Tract*, pp. 7–9.

[†] Cf. Latin *Tract*, p. 12, but also *Hooker*, I, x, 4, and *Two Treatises*, II, sect. 91, where this passage from Hooker is quoted.

[‡] Possibly Locke has in mind here not only Bagshaw but his own neighbour, correspondent and (after 1660, displaced) contemporary at Christ Church, Henry Stubbe, whose *Essay in Defence of the Good Old Cause* (1659) Locke seems to have criticized on similar lines in a private letter, cf. chapter 1 above and appendix II.

is lawful for any subject to do. For, 1. whether* you suppose him immediately commissioned by God and by him entrusted with the care of the society, it is impossible to set any other bounds to his commands than what God himself by a superior law (to which with other men he owes an equal obedience) hath already prescribed him, all other things having an equal indifferency being left to the free determination of his will to be enjoined or forbidden, as he shall think most conducing to the good and peace of his people whereof he alone is the sole judge, else could there be no law made which could not be disputed, and all magistracy would have only an opportunity to persuade, not an authority to command obedience. Or, 2.† if the supreme authority and power of making laws be conferred on the magistrate by the consent of the people (since⁷ 'tis pleaded nature gives no superiority of dominion, but all [p. 2] men seem equal till some one's eminent virtues, or any other advantages hath directed the choice of the people to advance him, or custom and the general agreement hath affixed the supremacy to a certain person, line or election) then it is evident that they have resigned up the liberty of their actions into his disposure, and so all his⁸ commands are but their own votes, and his edicts their own injunctions made by proxy which by mutual contract they are bound to obey,‡ whence it clearly follows, that whatever any man hath the liberty of doing himself, one may consent and compact that another should enjoin him. And here I cannot but wonder how indifferent things relating to religion should be excluded more than any other, which though they relate to the worship of God are still but indifferent and a man hath as free a disposure of his liberty in these as any other civil actions till some law of God can be produced, that so annexes this freedom to every single Christian that it puts it beyond his power to part with it; which how much those places urged by our author do, will be considered in

---

* 'If' would make the sentence easier; cf. the similar formulation in Latin *Tract*, pp. 12–14. † Cf. Latin *Tract*, p. 12.

‡ Cf. *Hooker*, Preface, v (2): 'A law is the deed of the whole body politic whereof if ye judge yourselves to be any part, then is the law even your deed also.' Below, p. 32. Locke claims that the *Preface* is all he had read of Hooker at this time. Hobbes of course uses the argument widely, thus, *De Corpore Politico* (1651), pt. II, vi (5): 'When a man hath once transferred his right of judging to another that which shall be commanded is no less his judgment than the judgment of that other.' Both Hooker and Hobbes use the idea in the context of an 'organic' theory of politics, referring explicitly to the 'body' of society; Locke, too, fuses the two ideas, see above, chapter III, and Latin *Tract*, p. 12.

their order. I shall in the way only take notice of his distinction of indifferent things[9] into such [*as** are purely so viz: time and place of* (p. 2)† *meeting for religious worship, and other things that are commonly supposed indifferent but by abuse have become occasions of superstition such as are bowing at the name of Jesus, the cross in baptism, surplice in preaching, kneeling at the sacrament, set forms of prayer and the like‡*]. But how time and place are more purely indifferent, how less liable to superstitious abuse, and how the magistrate comes by a power over them more than the other, the law of God determining neither, they all equally relating to religious worship, and being equally obnoxious to superstition, I cannot possibly see.

The author's first argument§ is [*that because 'tis agreed that a Christian magistrate cannot force his religion on a Jew or Mahomedan, therefore[10] much less can he abridge his fellow Christian in things of lesser moment*] i.e. indifferent, a conclusion no way following from that supposition, as will evidently appear by these following reasons.

1. From the end and intention of penalties[11] and force especially in matters of religion, which are designed only to work obedience, outward violence being never to be applied but when there is hopes it may bend the dissenter to a submission and compliance. But the understanding and assent (whereof God hath reserved the disposure to himself, and not so much as entrusted man with a liberty at pleasure to believe or reject) being not to be wrought [p. 3] upon by force a magistrate would in vain assault that part of man (p. 2) which owes no homage to his authority, or endeavour to establish his religion by those ways which would only increase an aversion and make enemies rather than proselytes. But in things of indifferency it is far otherwise, which depending freely upon the choice of the doer will be entertained or neglected proportionally as the

* Passages in this form are cited by Locke from Bagshaw, 1660 (*a*); Locke's italics.

† Notations in this form are Locke's own references given in the margin of the MS—primarily page references to Bagshaw's pamphlet and to biblical texts.

‡ The quotation is incomplete; Locke misses Bagshaw's final instance, 'pictures in Churches'. The distinction was meaningful for Bagshaw since for him the relevant source of authority and discrimination was subjective; Locke finds it meaningless because he is pursuing objective criteria: Bagshaw elaborates the distinction, implicitly at least to meet Locke's objection, in his *Second Part of the Great Question*, cf. chapter II above.

§ Bagshaw, 1660 (*a*), p. 2. Locke here takes up a rhetorical flourish in his adversary's case, not its substance. In fact Bagshaw argues this point not as a deduction in this form but as 'directly contrary to the nature of Christian religion'; cf. chapter II above.

law shall annex rewards or punishments to them, and the magistrate may expect to find those laws obeyed which demand not any performance above the power of the subject, so that though it be true that severity loses its end which is to remove the offence not the man (and is therefore not to be made use of) when it is employed to plant religion, which cannot be wrought into the hearts of men by any other power but that of its first Author, nor any other way than what he hath prescribed, yet it is able to reach the external and indifferent actions of men, and may[12] in them be applied with success enough. And though the magistrate ought not to torture poor creatures whom he hath no hopes to amend, and so to discredit and abuse punishments, the great instruments of government and remedies of disorders, as to set them upon impossibilities where they are sure to be ineffectual, yet this doth no way tie up his hands from prosecuting those faults which may be thereby amended. 'Twould be tyranny in a father to whip a child, because his apprehensions were less quick, or his sight not so clear, or the lineaments of his face perhaps not so like his own as the rest of his brethren, who yet with equity enough might chastise the disobedience of his actions, and take this way to reclaim his wilful disorders. To conclude, rigour which cannot work an internal persuasion may notwithstanding an outward conformity, all that is here required,* and may be[13] as necessary in the one as useless in the other.

2.[14] Upon supposition of the magistrate's power derived from the people† (which is a question I shall not here dispute but only by allowing this hypothesis to those patrons of freedom as the ground of all their pleas and arguments show that it will afford but a very weak foundation to their opinion and that placing the

---

* 'all that is here required': the Puritan answer was of course presented in terms of mortal sin. Thus, Leonard Busher, 1615, and Thomas Collier, 1644. For arguments parallel to those of Locke within this debate see Thomas Whitfield, 1649, p. 11, Sixth Answer: 'The magistrate may be a means to cause men to make an outward profession and yield an outward conformity...' etc. But Locke fails to answer Bagshaw's deepest point here (p. 3), the argument that 'a cheerfull worshipper' is of the essence of Christianity.

† This paragraph, which is inserted on the facing page of the MS, is not (as Locke's numeration implies) related to any proposition of Bagshaw's; Locke introduces the contract of government theory because it is indispensable to his own argument, cf. chapter 11 above and n. 14 below. A number of the deletions within the paragraph are too thorough to be sensibly deciphered, but the purpose of the paragraph remains clear—to underline the ostensibly hypothetical character of his use of the contract argument.

original of the magistrate's power as low as they can yet will it reach all indifferent things).

A second reason against my author's conclusion[15] will be from the extent of the power and authority of the magistrate which, being received from the resignation of the people, can pretend to a jurisdiction only over those actions whereof they themselves were the masters;* but religion is none of these which is not to be assumed or laid down at pleasure. God in this wherein he hath a[16] nearer communion with men retaining a more immediate dominion over their minds, which are brought to an assent to such truths proportionably as God either by the wise contrivance of his providence, or a more immediate operation of his spirit shall please to dispose or enlighten them and as Christ himself tells us, [p. 4] *he reveals to babes what he hides from the wise and prudent*, and therefore (*Math.* 1. these discoveries and a consequent belief being not in their own 25)† power, 'twould be as irrational for men to engage to be of the same religion or persuasion with their magistrate, as to promise to have the same looks or constitution. Indeed[17] education, custom and conversation have no small influence on the persuasions of men, and are usually by laws provided for, but these work not by violence, they insinuate only, not compel. But the liberty God hath naturally left us over our[18] exterior, indifferent actions must and ought in all societies be resigned freely into the hands of the magistrate, and it is impossible there should be any supreme legislative power which hath not the full and unlimited disposure of all indifferent things, since if supreme it cannot be bounded by any superior authority of man and in things of indifferency God hath left us to ourselves. It is as certain, then, that the magistrate hath an absolute command over all the actions of men whereof they themselves are free and undetermined agents, as that beyond this he hath no authority, and therefore though he cannot enforce

---

* This 'chief reason' is the closest Locke comes to an unqualified avowal of contractarian views; as it was presumably first written (without the inserted qualification) it seems an emphatic assertion of contract theory; it is of course still compatible with the compromise theory he suggests in the Latin *Tract*, p. 12, and which he may have derived from Edward Gee, 1658, or from Sanderson, 1660, VII, xv. Cf. Bagshaw's use of this view; since subjects, he argues, 'have left their natural and voluntarily parted with their civil they ought not to be entrenched upon in their spiritual freedom'. Locke uses a similar premise to achieve the opposite conclusion in his later writings; cf. MS Locke c. 28, fols. 21–2, *Essay Concerning Toleration*, 'no man can give another power over that over which he hath no power himself)', etc.

† The reference is given thus by Locke; it should be to Matt. xi. 25.

religion, which they never had the liberty to give up to another's injunctions, yet all things which they had a power to do or omit, they have made him the judge, when, where, and how far they ought to be done, and are obliged to obey.

The author's second reason is because* [*This imposing things indifferent is directly contrary to Gospel precepts*]. Indeed, were this proved the controversy were at an end and the question beyond doubt, but amongst those many places produced I find not one command directed to the magistrate to forbid his intermeddling in things indifferent, which were to be expected if his determinations were against God's commands. 'Tis strange that in imposing things indifferent he should sin against Gospel precepts, and yet in the whole Gospel not one precept be found that limits or directs his authority.† 'Tis strange that that doctrine that enjoins submission to a Nero, should be thought to free us from subjection to a Constantine, that that which doth advance the throne and establish the authority of a heathen and a tyrant should weaken and pull down that of a good man and a good Christian. Had that monster commanded the Christians either out of prudence or peevishness, either to distinguish or expose that sect, to have worn white or black garments in the time of worship,‡ to have assembled in this or that place,[19] how would his injunctions have[20] been unlawful, any more than for a Christian magistrate to prescribe either time or place or habit to a Mahomedan for his worship if his Alcaron hath left them undetermined; indeed in those[21] that are determined he ought not to be forced as being made by the doctrine of his religion no longer indifferent. Had the first Christians received such commands from Nero, who can think they would have scrupled at his orders and by disobedience in these indifferent [p. 5] things disturbed their own quiet and the progress of the Gospel? 'Tis true as my author says, p. 15,§ their writings are full of arguments for liberty but it was for that liberty which was then encroached on and far different from what is here in question;

* Bagshaw, 1660 (*a*), p. 3. † Cf. Latin *Tract*, p. 5.

‡ Locke's use of instances is surely inspired by the issues of controversy within Christ Church; cf. chapter II, and note that he deletes from this sentence a reference to 'pictures in Churches' (cf. n. 19); his avoidance of this issue is as consistent as Bagshaw's inclusion of it; cf. chapter II.

§ Bagshaw, 1660 (*a*), p. 15: 'Only this is certain, that all the writings of the Christians for the first 200 years are full of nothing else but such arguments as evince a liberty, more absolute and universal than I contend for.'

'twas for the substantials of their profession and not against the addition of ceremonies; their oppression was from those[22] from whom they feared the subversion of the very foundations of their religion and not too gaudy and curious a superstructure; they complained not of being burdened with too many habits, but of being stripped stark naked. They[23] would have taken any garments so they might have been permitted with them to have put on Christ Jesus too. But an exemption from the power of the magistrate[24] though an infidel neither the Gospel nor they ever pleaded for; and shall a Christian magistrate find his authority weakened by that doctrine which strengthens a heathen's; must he first renounce his own kingdom before he enters into Christ's, cannot he be a convert and a king at once, and must our author's first supposition be still in doubt whether a Christian may be a magistrate?

The texts produced* inform Christians in general of the liberty purchased them by our Saviour, and there appears not in one of them any precept to magistrates to forbid their imposing indifferent things. But whether that liberty be to be understood as[25] an exemption from the magistrate's injunctions in religious worship, the word being used indefinitely without application to things either religious or civil and so not to be limited by the fancy of every interpreter unless the scope of the place shall favour it, we shall see in their particular examination.

The first is that [*our Saviour doth in many places inveigh against the* (p. 3)
rigid and imposing pharisees for laying yokes upon others and therefore (*Math.* 23
invites all to come unto him for freedom, 'Take my yoke upon you', saith *Math.* 11
he, 'for it is easy and my burden is light']. To this may be replied: *Jo.* 8)

1. That though Christ inveighed against the[26] incroaching pharisees[27] when they joined their traditions to the law of God and pressed them as equally sacred and obliging, as *Math.* 15, which was clearly contrary to the command of God—*Deut.* 4. 2, *Deut.* 12, 32†—therefore it follows not that he forbade the lawful magistrate to[28] limit things indifferent. Christ might check those

---

* Matt. xxiii. 1–36; Matt. xi. 24–30; John viii. 36; Gal. v. 1; James i. 2. Bagshaw, 1660 (*a*), p. 3; Locke in fact practically ignores one of these texts, John viii. 36, as well as Bagshaw's commentary on it: 'If the son set you free then are you *free indeed*, where by freedom I do not only understand freedom from sin; but from all human impositions.' Cf. p. 7; Locke merely asserts the contrary.

† Matt. xv. 6; Bagshaw's text here (p. 3) is Matt. xi. 30; and cf. Hammond, 1644, v, Of Will-worship, for a similar use of these sources.

proud and meddling people who would be busy beyond their power, and though they took upon them to interpret the old[29] law had no authority to add to it, and yet leave the magistrate free in the exercise of his power, it being no argument that because Christ condemned the impositions of the pharisees on the Jewish Church to which God had set down an unalterable platform, and as our author confesses, p. 14,[*] *In the minutest circumstances had provided for uniformity of worship,* that therefore he prohibited the Christian magistrate to determine those things which now he had left indifferent, that so their uses might be suited to the several exigences of times and tempers of people to whom the unchangeable and necessary doctrine of the Gospel should be revealed.

But, 2., we may take notice that Christ[30] in this place[†] at the same time that he dislikes the pharisees' impositions he commands the multitude nevertheless to observe what they bid them, v. 3; and in the same breath that he reproves their[31] hypocritical rigour he commands the people obedience.[32]

And[‡] the reason he gives for it, v. 2., is because they sit in Moses' chair. Whereby is meant that either they expounded Moses' law and so all that came within the compass of that law though heavy burdens yet was to be submitted to by the people; or else they sat in Moses' chair, i.e. supplied his room and were the governors of the people, and then they are meant as the Sanhedrin who our author says, p. 5, were then not only the ecclesiastical but civil rulers of the Jews, and then Christ's discourse runs thus, that the Jews were to obey the pharisees,[33] as their civil governors to whose commands they were to pay a ready obedience though they were heavy and burdensome; and so this place will make against

---

* This is, however, not quite Bagshaw's argument (p. 14), which is designed to show that the Jewish leaders in reforming religion were not exercising normal magisterial powers but depended upon a direct divine precept 'from which rigour and restraint all Christians are absolved'; in other words, not that Christian magistrates are forbidden to meddle with religion, but that they are *free* not to do so: 'The Jews had, Christians want divine authority to impose.'

† Matt. xxiii. 3; Locke appears untroubled by the ambiguity of this text, and ignores the moral condemnation for the sake of the political injunction: '*All things therefore whatsoever they bid you, these do and observe; but do not ye after their works; for they say and do not.*' Locke's interest is only in the political problem of the moment—how to provide and secure the bases of civil peace.

‡ This paragraph, which is an insertion on the facing page of the MS, is a close paraphrase and commentary on the same text, *vv.* 4 and 5. But Bagshaw's point is hardly more than that the 'analogy' of the Jewish 'princes' is of no weight or relevance to Christian practice on either side.

our author. In which sense soever it be taken the people were to obey, and the pharisees reproved not so much for imposing burdens as not bearing their part with others[34] because they tied up others with strict rules of[35] duty, and contented themselves with broad phylacteries and other outside easy performances.

And if we will observe these and other places[*] where Christ speaks to and of the scribes and pharisees, he levels his reproof against their hypocrisies, their affected outside worship, neglecting [p. 6] the inward and substantial (which nobody defends) and their usurping a liberty to mingle their traditions with the law of God, obtruding them as of equal authority with the divine injunctions and so binding burdens upon men's consciences which could not but be extremely criminal in a worship which God himself had framed and that with so much caution against any innovation or addition, that he descended to the lowest actions and most trivial utensils, not leaving out the very snuffers and firepans of the sanctuary—but of this I shall have occasion to speak hereafter. Though[36] here we may observe concerning all those places relating to Christ and the pharisees:

1. That where the pharisees enjoin things as magistrates and make laws[37] as men, there Christ commands obedience though it were burdensome, as *Math.* 23.[†]

2. That where they urge their traditions as the laws of God, Christ denies the obligation of such traditions[38] as traditions and proves it by the opposition of some of those traditions to the law of God, *Math.* 15,[‡] but yet doth not even there deny washing of hands to be lawful because they commanded it, though it seems his disciples neglected it in their practice[39] that they might not seem to countenance irregular injunctions of pretended divine traditions, which were contrary to the law of God which prohibited all additions.

That those places, *Math.* 11,[§] *Joh.* 8. 36, are to be understood of a freedom from sin and the devil and not from laws, the freedom of Christ's subjects being of the same nature with the kingdom whereof they were subjects, that is, not of this world or of the outward but inward man, is clear not only from the general current of interpreters but the places themselves; for where Christ invites them to submit their necks to his yoke because it is easy he tells

---

[*] E.g. Mark xii. 38–40; Luke xi. 39–52.   [†] Matt. xxiii. 3.

[‡] Matt. xv. 1–6.   [§] Matt. xi. 28–30.

them what ease it is they must expect *viz*:[40] rest to their souls, v. 29
—the whole antecedent discourse being of the internal work of the
gospel upon the heart, of faith and repentance, and the happiness
of those to whom God revealed the gospel and not relating at all to
their outward privileges or in the last glancing at any exemption
from the dominion and rule of the magistrate.[*]

(*Gal.* 5. 1)   The next Scripture urged[†] is [*stand fast in the liberty wherewith
Christ hath made you free and be not again entangled with the yoke of
bondage*], and here I shall consent with the author, that this verse, as
also the greatest part of the Epistle is the doctrine of Christians'
enfranchisement from the ceremonial law.[‡] But how he will [*from
thence draw an unanswerable argument against the urging of any other
now*[§]] I cannot see. His words are [*Since that the Mosaical ceremonies
which had so much to plead for themselves, upon the account of their divine
original, and which even after they were fulfilled by our Saviour still
remained indifferent in their use and were so practised by Paul, yet when
once they were imposed and a necessity pleaded for their continuance, the
Apostle writes so sharply against them, exhorting the Galatians to stand
fast in their liberty, as part of our Saviour's purchase; if this I say was the
case with those old rites, then much less can any now impose an invented
form of worship, for which there cannot be pretended the least warrant that
ever God did authorise it*]. I confess they had[41] their *original* from
divine authority, but 'tis as true that they had their *end*, too,[42] from
the same divine appointment, and it was as sinful to urge them as
obliging after God had abolished them, as it was to neglect them
whilst he enjoined their observation; they were a law till Christ, not
after, types and promises of the Messiah's coming and kingdom,
but not to be rules of obedience under it; those shadows vanished
upon the rising of our Sun of Righteousness, and therefore,
though their use were indifferent afterwards and lawful and their
[p. 7]   practice allowed both by the permission[43] of the Apostles and their
example too when it would any way advantage the gospel, or be

* Cf. the similar discussion of the scope and limitations of Christian liberty in
the Latin *Tract*, p. 13.
† Bagshaw, 1660 (*a*), p. 3. Cf. Locke, *Paraphrase and Notes*, ix, for a late and identical treatment of this text.
‡ This is but a formal concession on Locke's part: the point was common ground
to all Christian churches including the Catholics and was derived from St Thomas's
own account of Christian liberty, Aquinas, 11, i, 108, 1–2. The Reformation problem,
of course, was to decide what, if anything, could properly fill the gap left by this
emancipation; cf. chapter 11.
§ Bagshaw, 1660 (*a*), p. 3; Locke here quotes continuously from Bagshaw's text.

any means of gaining converts or securing the peace of the church, but to allow their imposition and to acknowledge that law still in force which was to be abrogated by the coming of the Messiah was to contradict their own doctrine, and deny that Christ was come which was their great design to establish, so that the things were left but the law that[44] formerly made them necessary removed, and for a man to think himself under the obligation of the ceremonial law and at the same time entertain the doctrine of the Gospel, was as impossible as to be a Jew and a Christian at once which St Paul, ch. 1, makes inconsistent.* So that it is no wonder he should so vigorously oppose the doctrine of subjection to the ceremonial law, which would ruin and undermine the very foundations of that religion he was then building; and so smartly handle St Peter[45] his fellow Apostle when by his carriage he seemed to confirm it.† But I think it will not follow that because that law ceased which was inconsistent with the Gospel that therefore the Christian magistrate's authority doth too, that because a law repealed by God himself could not be urged as in force, therefore no other law can be enacted. Those injunctions were rejected because the law from which they were urged was inconsistent[46] with the Gospel and so will the magistrate's be also when they can be proved inconsistent too, which must be by some other argument than that of the ceremonial laws being antiquated.‡ In vain, therefore, shall anyone from hence plead for any other liberty than what the Apostle asserts, which was nothing but a freedom from the ceremonial law which after Christ was bondage, as is evident from the whole Epistle, and the Galatians and all Christians *shall stand fast enough in their liberty* if they preserve it from the encroachments and corrupt doctrines of false brethren, ch. 2, v. 4§ and not the injunctions of the lawful magistrate. It was the false brethren that were most dangerous to Christian liberty, and ensnared the consciences with a bondage to that as a necessary law and of divine authority and so obliging the consciences which

* Gal. i. 10–24. † Gal. ii. 11–21.

‡ Locke is not really meeting Bagshaw's argument, however; Bagshaw claimed that the imposition of ceremonies was not allowed; Locke replies that it is not forbidden; into the gap that remains between them he then fits his theory of 'super-induced' law; cf. chapter 1.

§ Gal. ii. 4; the 'false brethren' in question are those Jewish Christians who, continuing to think observation of the ceremonial law necessary to salvation, sought to impose circumcision on all Christians.

God himself had repealed and nulled by sending the Messiah; the magistrate is not at all touched at in the whole Epistle: who,[47] notwithstanding the ceremonial law hath lost its obligation as the law of God, may enforce his own laws as the laws of a man who is the steward and judge of the public good.

But the author goes on [*It seems altogether needless that the Jewish ceremonies should as to their necessity at least expire and be abrogated if others might succeed in their room, and be as strictly commanded as ever the former were**]. Who would not presently reply that it seems altogether needless that the Jewish tithes should as to their necessity at least expire and be abrogated if other might succeed in their room and be as strictly commanded as ever the former were.†

[p. 8] Things are then needless when God removes them not when our fancies dislike or perhaps our conveniences oppose them. The ceremonial law began then to be needless when God thought fit it should be abrogated, and when he shall either abolish magistracy or restrain its power from things of the Sanctuary it will then so far be needless too, till then it will better[48] become the temper of a Christian patiently to obey than to presumptuously complain and murmur that God hath not put human affairs into a posture suited to his humour or squared the economy of the world or frame of the Temple according to the model of his brain.‡

(*Jac.* I. 25) [*Our§ religion is styled the perfect law of liberty, which liberty I understand not wherein it consists if in things necessary we are already determined by God, and in things indifferent we may still be tied up to human ordinances and outside rites at the pleasure of our magistrate.*] A plea which if granted doth at one stroke dissolve all human laws or the greatest part of them, our liberty consisting in the free use of all indifferencies as well civil as ecclesiastical and the authority of the magistrate (as I have proved) extending itself as much to one as to the other, I know not why a rebellious subject may not under the patronage of this text cast off his allegiance as well as a dissenting Christian forbear conformity, Christianity being called a law of

---

* Bagshaw, 1660 (*a*), p. 3; this quotation follows directly upon his last in Bagshaw's text.

† Lev. xxxvii. 30–4.

‡ This last argument is somewhat gratuitous; Bagshaw defends toleration as integral to God's dispensation.

§ Bagshaw, 1660 (*a*), pp. 3–4; Locke omits a connecting clause, 'for this only returns us to our bondage again'; otherwise the quotation is again continuous; the argument that follows is echoed in Latin *Tract*, pp. 13–14.

liberty without any limitation to this or that sort of indifferent things.

[*To those Scriptures*[49] *which deny all imposition may be added all those* (p. 4) *texts which consequently do it, such as are 'do to others as you would have others do to you'. And who is there would have his conscience imposed upon?**] If private men's judgments were the moulds wherein laws were to be cast 'tis a question whether we should have any at all.† If this be the rule that must measure the equity and obligation of all edicts I doubt whether any can challenge an universal obedience, when it is impossible that any law should be by human prudence so contrived which whilst it minds the good of the whole will not be inconvenient to several of the members, and wherein many will not think themselves hardly and unequally dealt with. The magistrate in his constitutions regards the public concernment and not private opinions which, biased by their own interest, or misled by their ignorance and indiscretion, are like to make them but ill judges of reasons of state or the equity of laws; and when we find the greatest part of men usually complaining, we may easily conclude, that they think that precept of 'do as thou wouldst be done unto' but ill observed by their superiors. Were magistrates to gratify the desires of men in all things to which by a partial interpretation they would extend this rule, they would quickly stand in need of a power not to make laws but worlds, and provide enlargements not restraints for the liberty of their sub- [p. 9] jects. And hence rises one of those necessities of government‡— that since men were not like (being favourable judges in their own cause)§ to be well satisfied with the equity of others, and would be

---

* Continuous quoting here, too, from Bagshaw's text; the reference is now to Matt. i. 12; John. vi. 31.

† Cf. Latin *Tract*, p. 16, and the letter from Locke to Godolphin, MS c. 24, fol. 49: 'therefore we shall need some other rule to guide us besides every man's private morals'; this letter, which ends by seeking Godolphin's support for Locke's brother in taking up the Law, since 'this tottering condition it doth now appear in doth not at all deter me being confident that nothing can be able to crush it but the ruin of the whole nation', is of July 1659.

‡ Cf. Hooker, 1, x, 4: 'no man might take upon him to determine his own right... inasmuch as every man is towards himself and them whom he greatly affecteth partial...'; the argument is very similar.

§ Cf. Du Bartas, *Quadrains of Pibrac*, p. 265, in the edition of 1641—that read by Locke:

> Never give sentence in thy proper cause
> In our own cause we all err easily,
> Our interest our proper judgment draws
> And ever makes the balance hang awry.

ready to judge that others[50] made use of their liberty, to their prejudice with neglect of this rule of equity, it was requisite to settle a peace and society amongst men that they should mutually agree to give up the exercise of their native liberty* to the disposure and prudence of some select person or number of men who should make laws for them which should be the rule of their actions one towards another and the measure of their enjoyments; but this by the by.

'Tis true, [*who would have his conscience imposed upon?*] and 'tis as true, who would pay taxes? who would be poor? who almost would not be a prince? And yet these (as some think them) burdens, this inequality, is owing all to human laws and those just enough, the law of God or nature neither distinguishing their degrees nor bounding their possessions. I grant all agree that conscience is tenderly to be dealt with, and not to be imposed on, but if the determining any indifferent[51] outward action contrary to a man's persuasion, (conscience being nothing but an opinion of the truth of any practical position, which may concern any actions as well moral as religious, civil as ecclesiastical†) be imposing on conscience and so unlawful, I know not how a Quaker should be compelled by hat or leg to pay a due respect to the magistrate or an Anabaptist be forced to pay tithes, who if conscience be a sufficient plea for toleration (since we in charity ought to think them as sincere in their profession as others than whom they are found less wavering), have as much reason not to feel constraint as those who contend so much for or against a surplice, for not putting off the hat grounded upon a command of the Gospel, though misunderstood, is as much an act of religion and matter of conscience to those so persuaded as not wearing a surplice.‡ Imposing[52] on

* Cf. Antony Ascham, 1649, pp. 4 f.; Philip Nye, *The Lawfulness of the Oath of Supremacy*, p. 19; Dudley Digges, 1644, p. 8; Hobbes, *Leviathan*, II, xvii, 'when men agree amongst themselves, to submit to some man, or assembly of men, voluntarily...'

† Cf. chapter 1 and Aquinas, I, 79, 13; Sanderson, 1660 (*a*), I, xviii; Hobbes, *De Corpore*, 'Conscience being nothing but a man's settled judgment and opinion'; Taylor, *Ductor Dubitantium*, I, i; and Latin *Tract*, p. 8. Locke's position here approximates to that of Hobbes (see, too, *Leviathan*, II, xxix); in the Latin *Tract* his position is modified in the direction of Taylor's formula, 'conscience is the mind of man governed by a rule and measured by the proportions of good and evil, in order to practice'. In both cases a large body of more theologically oriented definitions is passed over; cf. Antony Cade, *A Sermon on the Nature of Conscience* (1620).

‡ Locke's instances regularly concentrate attention on the matter in dispute in Christ Church—a restriction not at all typical of the debate on indifferency in general.

conscience seems to me to be, the pressing of doctrines or laws upon the belief or practice of men as of divine original, as necessary to salvation and in themselves obliging the conscience, when indeed they are no other but the ordinances of men and the products of their authority; otherwise, if you take it in our author's sense every lawful command of the magistrate, since we are to obey them for conscience sake, would be an imposing on conscience and so according to his way of arguing unlawful.*

['*You that are strong bear with the infirmities of the weak*'—whereas (*Rom.* 15)†
this practice will be so far from easing the burdens of the weak, that if men are at all scrupulous, it only lays more load upon them.] What[53] was [p. 10] meant by imposing or burdening the conscience I showed but now. But this text relating to scandal, which the author makes one of his arguments will be there more fitly spoken to,‡ I shall here only say that *bear with the infirmities* signifies no more than *not despise*§ in the beginning of the foregoing chapter, and so is a rule to private Christians not to slight or undervalue those their brethren who being *weak in the faith*, i.e.: not so fully informed and satisfied of the extent of their Christian liberty, scruple at matters indifferent, and are ready, as they are there described, *to judge* those that allow and practise them; and this a magistrate may do whilst he makes laws for their observance, he may pity those whom he punishes, nor in his thoughts condemn them because not so strong in the faith as others. So that¶ *this kind of rigour* is not *utterly inconsistent* as our author would persuade us *with the rules of Christian charity*, prescribed in this place, [*which no Christian magistrate ought to think himself absolved from. Since though as a magistrate he hath a power in civil things; yet as a Christian he ought to have a care that in things of spiritual concernment he grieves not the minds of any, who are upon that relation not his subjects so much as his brethren.*] If outward indifferent things be things of spiritual concernment I wish our author would do us the courtesy to show us the bounds of each and tell us where civil things end[54] and spiritual begin. Is a courteous saluting, a friendly compellation, a decency of habit according to the fashion of the place, and indeed subjection to the civil magistrate, civil

---

* This is one of the 'objections' which Bagshaw attempts to answer in his *Second Part*, 1661, p. 13.
† Bagshaw, 1660 (*a*), p. 4, where the reference is given (incorrectly) as Rom. xiv.
‡ I.e. when he deals with the general problem of scandal below.
§ Rom. xiv. 1.
¶ Bagshaw, 1660 (*a*), p. 4; the quotation is continuous.

things, and these by many are made matters of conscience and there is no action so indifferent which a scrupulous conscience will not fetch in with some consequence from Scripture and make of spiritual concernment, and if nothing else will scandal at least shall reach him.* 'Tis true a Christian magistrate ought to deal tenderly with weak Christians, but must not so attend the infirmities and indulge the distempers of some few dissatisfied as to neglect the peace and safety of the whole. The Christian magistrate is a brother to his fellow Christians and so may pity and bear with them but he is also their magistrate[55] and must command and govern them, and if it be certain that to prescribe to the scrupulous be against this Scripture and be to lay load upon the weak, he will find it impossible not to offend, and burden a great part,[56] some being as conscientiously earnest for conformity as others for liberty, and a law for *toleration* would as much offend their consciences as of *limitation* others.† The magistrate he *confesseth may bound not abridge their liberty*, a sentence very difficult to be under-

[p. 11] stood and hard to be put into other words.‡

[*Decency and order when it is of constraint not of consent is nothing else*
(I *Cor.* 7. *but in the imposer tyranny, in the person imposed upon bondage, and makes*
23) *him to be what in things appertaining to religion we are forbidden to be ' the servants of men'.§*] Which text cannot without force be applied[57] to any other but a civil *bondage*. The Apostle in that chapter gives them a resolution of some doubts which it seems they had proposed to him concerning the several relations and conditions of

---

* There are echoes here of many passages in Hooker, and among the later Anglican orthodoxy, cf. Hammond, 1644, I, Of Conscience, 'scarce anything so vile but hath the favour to be mistaken for conscience...', etc.; the references are again to the particular situation in Oxford as much as to the general controversy, cf. chapter II and Henry Stubbe, *A Light Shining out of Darkness* (1659), sects. xli–xlii, where 'the habits now used in the Universities' as well as 'friendly compellations' and such 'courteous salutings' as 'that compliment, your servant', are forcefully challenged on conscientious grounds; by 'darkness' Stubbe meant Oxford.

† Cf. Latin *Tract*, p. 11, and MS Locke c. 28, fol. 21v, *Essay Concerning Toleration*.

‡ But Bagshaw, 1660 (*a*), p. 4, does attempt an expansion which is not as useless as Locke suggests: 'to keep it from running into licentiousness (which is moral evil) but not to shackle undermine and fetter it under pretence of *decency* and *order*'. Locke in effect merely restates the argument from decency and order as though it were something Bagshaw had not considered. For Bagshaw's own very positive alternative conception of 'order' cf. chapter I.

§ Locke is here paraphrasing slightly (Bagshaw, 1660 (*a*), p. 4) and seems to obscure his adversary's point—that it is possible for the powers allowed to the magistrate in the interest of order to become 'an order of constraint' unless some countervailing sanctions are introduced.

men, as the married and unmarried, the servant and the free and in general tells them,[58] v. 20, that conversion to Christianity did not dissolve any of those obligations they were tied in before but that the gospel continued them in the same condition and under the same civil obligations it found them. The married were not to leave their consorts, nor the servant freed from his master, but because they were such as Christ had purchased with his blood and free men of his kingdom he thinks them fitter to be free, and advises them if they could to gain their liberty and not debase themselves to slavery and that too for the same reasons he counsels virgins to continue single, that they might the more freely attend the business of religion and not be entangled in the avocations and concernments of the world. Nor can those words '*be ye not the servants of men*' be possibly understood of obedience to the injunctions of the magistrate in matters of religion or be any answer to their question, Christianity being scarce then known to the heathen magistrate, who was more likely to persecute the profession than prescribe forms of worship in a religion new and opposite to his own. Nor could *servant* in this sense relate (as our author would have it)* *to the master extending his rule over the conscience*, who, *if a heathen*, might possibly forbid [but] would never fashion the worship of a Christian, *if a Christian*,[59] the argument at best would be but against the master not against the magistrate in prescribing rules of worship.† Though it[60] is very improbable that the Corinthians should at the very first approaches of this religion be so inquisitive after the smallest things of discipline, whereof all sects in their beginnings are not very curious as we find the first Christians were not, or that Paul in answer to their demands should provide against an evil wherewith they were not threatened, for who can think that masters that could not but know their servants' privileges and freedom in the gospel to be equal with their own should take upon them presently so magisterially to chalk out a way of worship to their servants, when yet they were scarcely acquainted with the particulars of the doctrine itself, and it is known that masters and servants, all the converts did usually assemble with their fellow Christians and join in the same worship with the [p. 12]

---

* Bagshaw, 1660 (*a*), p. 4.

† This curiously feeble argument is in fact deleted in the MS, cf. n. 59, but the text as left by Locke makes very poor sense and it seemed best, therefore, to restore the passage.

church they were of; I shall not therefore fear to affirm the *Be you not the servants of men*, v. 23, is but repeating the advice he gave, v. 21, *if thou mayst be made free use it rather*.

The third argument is [*because it is contrary to Christian practice**]. To this I answer in general that precepts are the rule of our duty and not practice which is to be judged of by[61] them.† God hath made his commands the measure of our obedience and not the lives of his saints, who were men and might and did err, and therefore are to be tried by the law they were to approve themselves to. 'Be ye followers of me as I am of Christ' was St[62] Paul's rule.‡ Indeed the life of Christ is a perfect example of holiness but[63] yet there are many things in it above, and in the lives of all his followers many things besides and some *sit verbo venia* beneath our imitation. For who thinks he ought to imitate St Peter in that which St Paul opposed him in?§[64] Or in denying his master?¶ 'Tis by the command we are to learn where they walked right, I'm sure where we ought to tread in their steps.

(p. 5)   [*The first shall be that of our Saviour Christ who was of a most sweet and complying disposition, yet when his Christian liberty came once to be invaded he laid aside gentleness, and proved a stiff and peremptory assertor of it. To omit many passage of which his story is full, I shall mention but*

(Math. 15)‖ *one and that was his refusing to wash his hands before meat.*] What Christ did here I know not[65] how it could be said to be in defence of his *Christian liberty*. Indeed he came to promulge the great law of liberty to believers, to redeem men from the slavery of sin and Satan and subjection to the ceremonial law,** but he himself was made under the law, lived under it, and fulfilled it, and therefore it

---

  * Bagshaw, 1660 (*a*), pp. 4–5.

  † This type of proposition lies at the heart of Locke's thought in 1660 (cf. p. 21 and Latin *Tract*, pp. 13–16, also the letter, MS c. 24, fol. 49), and, as I believe, throughout his life. Against the trust of the Good Old Cause in good men Locke insists on good laws; he is concerned with the moral frame of reference, not with the dilemmas of individuals.

  ‡ I Cor. iv–xvi.

  § Gal. ii. 11–21. A familiar argument of seventeenth-century casuistry among Protestants; cf. Daille, *Traicté: De Usu Patrum*, a work which had great influence in shaping the thought of English divines such as Chillingworth (and see a note on this book in MS f. 14, 'an excellent treatise about the use of the fathers'). Sanderson, 1660, Praelect. iii, makes the same point in very similar terms, as do Owen, *Of Schisme* (1657), and Hammond, 1644, i, Of Conscience.

  ¶ Matt. xxvi. 70–5.

  ‖ Bagshaw, 1660 (*a*) p. 5, gives Matt. xxv, incorrectly.

  ** Cf. the identical treatment in Latin *Tract*, p. 13.

appears to me rather a vindication of his national Jewish liberty which was very much encroached on by the traditions of the pharisees, who though they *sat in Moses' chair** yet went beyond the bounds he had set them. God had delivered to the Jews an entire and complete platform of worship, prescribed and limited, too, all the circumstances and ceremonies of it, and so strictly tied them to that rule he had given that Moses himself was not permitted to deviate in the least from it, *Look that thou make them after the pattern that was showed thee in the mount*, Exod. *25. 40*. It could not then but be a horrid impiety and presumption for the pharisees not only to step into Moses' chair but also to ascend into Mount Sinai, and dare to mingle their wisdom with God's and take upon them to [p. 13] correct or perfect that frame which the great architect of heaven and earth had erected[66] for his sanctuary. This usurpation might well draw sharp rebukes from the meekest and most complying temper. Christ bore with the *infirmities* of the weak but not with the open *rebellion* of the haughty and obstinate; these were those who truly bound burdens on men's consciences by stamping a divine impression on their own counterfeit inventions and traditions and enjoined them under the penalties of God's displeasure and the curses of the law. But I think it will be no very good consequence[67] that because Christ opposed the usurpation of the pharisees, therefore a Christian may dispute the dominion of his magistrate;[68] that because the traditions of the Elders (which were such too as made the commandment of God of none effect, *Math.* 15. 6) were unlawful in a religion tied to a certain and set form which was to receive neither alteration nor addition, *you shall* (*Deutr.* 4. 2 *not add unto the word that I command you neither shall you diminish aught* Deutr. 12. *from it*, wherein God had left nothing arbitrary or indifferent, there- 32; *Prov.* fore all impositions are unlawful in a religion wherein almost all 30. 6) the outward actions are left undetermined and free; that because it was a part of the Jewish liberty not to be fettered with pharisaical traditions, therefore it is part of the Christian liberty not to submit to legal injunctions, and therefore it is no wonder that Christ should not prefer [*arguments from decency*†] before those from duty, not wash his hands when he could not do it without contracting guilt, nor pay obedience to that law which God had condemned and provided against by a repeated prohibition[69]—such traditions as they delivered to the people not as their own injunctions but

* Matt. xxiii. 2.   † Bagshaw, 1660 (*a*), p. 5.

as[70] part of the law of God, being properly additions to it and so consequently unlawful; but Christ, who here denied the obligation of forbidden traditions, did not thereby destroy either the indifferency of the action or the magistrate's power of enjoining it, and had Caesar commanded washing of hands at any time of the day I have no reason to think that Christ would have denied him this any more than tribute.

[*And*[71] *Christ leaves two unanswerable arguments which are of equal validity in things of the same nature as, first,*[72] *that this was not a plant of his father's planting and therefore it should be rooted up; from whence, I gather this rule, that when once human inventions become impositions and lay a necessity upon that which God hath left free, then may we lawfully reject them as plants of man's setting and not of God's owning.*[*]] In arguments drawn from examples the condition of the persons and nature of things ought well to agree, but in this case they are all far different. The Elders, though perhaps as our author says the Sanhedrin and so their rulers, yet did not impose these as lawmakers but pretended only to be the conveyors of the law of God by a tradition as sacred as any written precepts, whereas the magistrate urges his decrees in indifferent things as no otherwise binding than by virtue of his own authority as having the same original and obligation with all his other laws. The things there were prohibited traditions, for to urge anything as the law of God and a divine rule of his worship was clear against those positive commands of God in *Deuteronomy*, but here they are things free and indifferent so that what Christ here so sharply reproves was the hypocrisy of the *teachers* not the authority of *lawmakers*—their prohibited traditions not any impositions in indifferent things. From whence may be gathered this rule and no other; that when human inventions are pretended to be of divine original and imposed as such contrary to the positive commands of God and lay a dogmatical and divine necessity upon that which God hath left free (his deductions must stand so or else they will be besides the premises, and then he may infer that)[73] then we may

---

* Bagshaw, 1660 (*a*), p. 5; the reference is to Matt. xv. 13. The 'nature' of things (on which Locke concentrates his argument) is not the important question, of course; Bagshaw is really only concerned here to establish that ceremonial practice is 'left free' by God; his own theory of law will then produce the conclusion that the 'circumstances' of worship should be 'answerable to our inward impressions'. Locke constantly under-emphasizes this issue—though he confronts it directly and at length in the Latin *Tract*.

lawfully reject them as plants of man's setting and not of God's owning.*

[*The second argument our Saviour uses is that those things did not defile a man, from whence I infer that in the worship of God we are chiefly to look after the substance of things, and as for circumstances they are not worth our notice.*†] Which possibly is true of those that are left by the magistrate to our choice and not those which cannot be disregarded without disobedience to him and affront to his authority. [*They* (p. 6) *who press outward conformity in divine worship, endeavour to serve God the* [p. 14] *wrong way, and oftentimes do only force carnal and hypocritical men to present God a sacrifice which his soul abhors.*‡] The magistrate's laws make none *carnal and hypocrites* but find them so. He hath no commission to examine the hearts, but to take care of the actions of his subjects and though possibly he may increase their sin, whilst he endeavours to amend their lives, (an inconvenience which he must not hope to avoid since Christ's own sermons and edicts were not exempt from it, which as much increased the damnation of the obstinate made thereby the more odious in the sight of God, as they advanced the happiness and privileges of the obedient) yet the same God that abhors the sacrifice of the hypocritical compliant, would not approve the magistrate's neglect of duty, should he by too much forbearance indulge the growth of contention and disorder, where a restraint in things[74] indifferent might prevent it, the consequential miscarriages of others not at all lessening the obligation of his duty which is a care of the public quiet.§

[*Whilst to others that are more tender and scrupulous they make the*

* Cf. Latin *Tract*, p. 17; having granted Bagshaw's point that the pharisees were also magistrates the critical issue of the dispute becomes the discovery of the exact position of indifferency in the gospel; Locke's extension of the argument towards the discussion of magistracy as such is not strictly necessary.

† Bagshaw, 1660 (*a*), p. 5; the reference is to Matt. xv. 20. Locke paraphrases his opponent's argument quite considerably here. Thus Bagshaw has 'did not defile a man, i.e., as to his mind and conscience', being, 'more likely to offend nice stomachs than scrupulous consciences'; this gives rather more meaning to his subsequent point about 'substance' and relates closely to his next argument for conscientious integrity which Locke again ignores as he had done above (p. 11).

‡ Bagshaw, 1660 (*a*), p. 6, has only 'which he abhors'; and Locke passes over Bagshaw's supplementary point from Matt. xxiii. 26, 'O blind pharisee...', etc., that 'a most specious outside is consistent with inward filth and rottenness'. After 1667 Locke was to adopt this argument as his own; cf. MS Locke c. 28, fol. 30, *Essay Concerning Toleration*, and *Letter Concerning Toleration*, p. 261.

§ There is perhaps a tacit reply here, and in the next paragraph, to Bagshaw's discussion, p. 5, of the nature of Christian 'order' as an 'order of consent not of constraint' which Locke virtually ignored above.

sacrifice itself unpleasant, because they will not let it be what God would have it, a free will offering.*] The service of the inward man which God looks after and accepts may be a *free will offering*, a sincere and spiritual performance under what shape soever of outward indifferent circumstances, the heart may be lift up to heaven, whilst the body bows. And I know not[75] how any habit† can lie heavier on the spirits of any man and hinder its free motion towards God,

(*Acts* 16. 25)

than the stocks did Paul and Silas, or why anyone should pray less fervently, or doubt more of being heard in a church, and near an organ than Daniel in the den amidst the roaring of the lions.‡ All that God looks for in his worship now under the gospel is the sacrifice of a broken and a contrite heart, which may be willingly and acceptably[76] given to God in any place or posture, but he hath left it to the discretion of those who are entrusted with the care of the society to determine what shall be *order* and *decency*§ which depend wholly on the opinions and fancies of men, and 'tis as impossible to fix any certain rule to them as to hope to cast all men's minds and manners into one mould. He that will open his eyes upon any country or age but his own will presently see that they are ready to fight and venture their lives for that in some places which we should laugh at here. Our deformity is others' beauty, our rudeness others' civility, and there is nothing so uncouth and unhandsome to us which doth not somewhere or other find applause and approbation; and should the eastern and turbanned¶ nations embrace Christianity 'twould be as uncomely to them to be bare in the public worship of God as to us to be covered.[77] And this is so not only in different places but if we survey the several ages of the Church we shall find religion sometimes gay and glorious, beset with pomp and ceremony, some-

---

* Bagshaw, 1660 (*a*), p. 6; this follows directly on the passage last quoted.

† Locke here twice mentions surplices and then deletes the reference, cf. n. 75, suggesting again his restricted initial concern with the Christ Church issue, cf. chapter II—or his concern to avoid being too closely involved in it.

‡ Dan. vi. 16–22; cf. Hammond, 1644, III.

§ Cf. Powel, 1606, *Epistle Dedicatorie*, and chapter II; for Powel as for Taylor, *Ductor Dubitantium*, III, and Sanderson, 1660, VI, and for Locke here, the 'general command to order' leads immediately to a consideration of 'persons, places and times' as irredeemably delivered into the magistrate's hands.

¶ Turban-wearing, of course; cf. Latin *Tract*, p. 5, where Locke makes the same point almost in the same words; also, *Letter Concerning Toleration*, pp. 253, 259–60, 272; *Second Letter Concerning Toleration*, pp. 286, 296, 307; *Third Letter for Toleration*, pp. 351, 358–61; *Essay*, II, xxviii.

times plain and negligent, stripped of all show and outside, but [p. 15]
always decent and in order because suited to the present opinion of
the age;* esteem in this as well as many putting all the difference of
value, and why should not the magistrate's stamp and allowance
make the one current as well as the other, why should anyone complain his heart and affections (the only free will offering) were more
taken off from God than his friend, by the circumstantial determinations of the magistrate? What obedient son would less willingly (if it were so appointed him) meet his father in the church
than in the chamber, or find his piety slacken by consideration of
the place? Or what malefactor would complain of the injunction,
or pretend that he could not as fervently beg his life of his prince
in a cassock as in a cloak, were that the habit wherein he were
commanded to approach his presence? 'Tis true 'tis not unusual to
fright the weak and scrupulous with the terrible name of *superstition*,† to clap disgraceful appellations upon innocent actions to
deter men from them, a practice (as a learned man says well) not
unlike the cruelty of the barbarous heathens that covered the
Christians with those skins they had taken off from ravenous beasts
that under that disguise they might the better bait them. But
superstition if I understand it aright‡ is a false apprehension of
God, or of a false god, attended with a slavish fear of severity and
cruelty in him, which they hope to mitigate by a worship of their
own invention, and such sacrifices either of the lives of men or
beasts or tortures on themselves, as their fears persuaded them are
most like to expiate and satisfy the displeasure of the Deity. But
that superstition in this sense cannot be applied to the limitation of
indifferent things is clear; which are not understood to be designed
for atonement.§

* Cf. Stillingfleet, 1660, I, i, ii, for a contemporary work that also defends the
imposed use of indifferencies on grounds of the historical and cultural idiosyncrasies
of *communities*.

† Cf. Latin *Tract*, p. 14, where again Locke's main objection to the argument from
superstition seems to be the use of the term as a 'disgraceful appellation', 'tanquam
larvam'.

‡ Cf. Latin *Tract*, p. 14, for a more elaborate but similar definition; and Hammond,
1644, IV, Of Superstition; Hammond's 'second inconsequence', which corresponds to
Locke's conclusion in this paragraph and is reached by similar means, is 'that the use
of ceremonies or rites in the worship of God, if these be not distinctly prescribed by
Christ, should be called superstition'.

§ But the contrary argument was not that ceremonies were designed for atonement but that the 'weak' might think them to be so—as Bagshaw points out, 1660(a),
p. 12—that they were made 'significant'; cf. chapter 1.

But[78] our author here opposes free will offerings to commanded services and seems to make them inconsistent, which if true I know not how any Gospel duty can be acceptably performed and if [*in the worship of God to make the sacrifice such as God would have it a free will offering*]* it be necessary to follow no other rule but the various dictates of our own wills or fancies I hope hereafter we shall be secured from the fear of will-worship when whatsoever our own choice shall lead us to will be most acceptable because a *free will offering.*†

[*My second instance shall be the resolution of the Apostles in that famous and important query concerning the Jewish ceremonies, whether they were to be imposed or not. After a long dispute to find out the trust St Peter directly opposes those rites;*[79] *'why do ye', says he, 'tempt God by putting a yoke upon the necks of the disciples'—intimating that to put a yoke upon others, (and to impose in things indifferent is certainly a great one) from which either God had expressly freed us, by commanding the contrary or else tacitly freed us by not commanding them, this is nothing but to tempt God and to pretend to be more wise and holy than he.*‡] The case is almost the same here with that of the Galatians above, only the resolution was given there only by St Paul alone, here by a synod. The dispute here seems to be between some converted pharisees wedded to an opinion of their old ceremonies and the rest of the Church, and the answers given in the former case will serve here, only the author's [p. 16] deductions ought to be taken a little asunder[80] and considered.

St Peter might well oppose the *putting on this yoke on the necks of the disciples* not only because it so galled the Jews, but also being taken off and broken by God himself was not to be renewed; but this will not concern other things of indifferency. If we grant that things indifferent may be called yokes, it will follow from the metaphor that they are heavy perhaps but not unlawful, troublesome not criminal, and so are taxes and tributes and all penal laws,

* Bagshaw, 1660 (*a*), p. 6; a paraphrase rather than a quotation, however.

† The strongest objection to the Anglican case remained the charge of sanctioning hypocrisy. Neither Locke here nor Hammond, 1644, III, Of Will-worship, really meets this objection. Locke indeed does no more than emphasize the *hazards* of Bagshaw's view.

‡ Bagshaw, 1660 (*a*), p. 6; the argument on this 'instance' occupies two pages of Bagshaw's text; Acts xv is analysed in detail to show (*a*) that the Apostles had the power to impose indifferent things on the Church, and (*b*) that they ruled in favour of the exclusive imposition of things necessary, thus (*c*) precluding the *general* warrant and discretion left to the magistrate on Locke's interpretation. The biblical texts quoted in the following two pages are all from Acts xv.

which if yokes are not to be put upon the necks of Christians they may upon the same score plead for forbearance.* But who knows not that the stubborn necks of the people do often call for yokes and those strong and heavy without which it would be impossible they should be kept in order? But[81] the yoke here spoken of is of far another nature than the[82] imposition of indifferent things, the question was, as appears v. 1, whether the ceremonial law was still in force and obliged the converted Gentiles, whether circumcision were necessary to salvation. This the believing pharisees plead for, v. 5, but St Peter opposes and confutes, vv. 7, 8, 9, showing that God put no difference between the circumcised and uncircumcised but that they[83] equally believed and received the Holy Ghost; the synod therefore by a decree quits them from subjection to the ceremonial law, and only forbids them fornication (which was then generally in those countries esteemed a very trivial and almost indifferent thing and therefore might well be ranked amongst eating of things strangled which were thought to[84] carry as much guilt in them) and some other things which were necessary (not in their own nature) for the better uniting believers,[85] Jews and Gentiles, and to prevent scandal and offence between the strong and weak brethren. All the inference that can be drawn from hence is, that though the ceremonial law was a heavy yoke and is not now to be put upon the necks of Christians, yet the exigences of the Church and the condition of Christians may make the imposition of many things, (that are in their own nature indifferent) necessary.†

[*From which God hath either expressly*[86] *etc.*]—if God hath tacitly freed us from those things which he hath not expressly commanded I can acknowledge no book of statutes but the Bible, and acts of Parliament can have[87] no obligation. [*This is nothing else but to tempt etc.*]—'tis so if we interpose in matters forbidden or commanded by him already, in the rest the magistrate may use his authority without incurring this censure.

[*Again James decries those ceremonies upon this score, lest they should be*

* But Bagshaw's argument taking its stand on 'our inward impressions' holds that in respect of conscience, heavy is unlawful; the whole energy of Anglican counter-argument for more than a century had been directed to the elaboration of more 'objective' conceptions of law; cf. chapters I and II, and e.g. Hammond, 1644, I, Of Conscience, 'whatsoever undertakes to guide our actions...and hath not some law to authorize those actions, is not conscience whatsoever it is'.

† Cf. Latin *Tract*, pp. 9–10.

troublesome to the converted Gentiles.[*]] It could not but become their Christian prudence to open as easy a passage as they could to the conversion of the Gentiles, to remove all possible rubs out of their way and not cumber the progress of the yet infant Gospel with unnecessary ceremonies, but the magistrate when his already[88] converted people shall trouble themselves and him too about things indifferent and from thence grow into dangerous factions and tumults, may determine the business by injunctions or prohibitions without any prejudice to the doctrines of Christianity.[89] The magistrate indeed ought not to be troublesome by his injunctions to the people, but he alone is judge what is so and what not.[90]

[*Upon the hearing of those two*[91] *the result of the synod is very observable.*[92] *First from the style they use,* '*It seems good to the Holy Ghost and to us*', *so that whoever exercises the same imposing power had need be sure he hath the same divine authority for fear he only rashly assumes what was* (p. 7)† *never granted him.*] The magistrates now as the Apostles then have an *authority* though far different. Those gave rules that obliged the conscience only by the dictates and inspirations of the holy spirit of God, having no secular authority and so were only deliverers not makers of those laws which they themselves could not alter. Whereas the magistrate commands the obedience of the outward man by an authority settled on him by God and the people, wherein he is not to expect immediate inspirations but is to follow the dictates of his own understanding, and establish or alter all indifferent things as he shall judge them conducing to the good of the public.[93]

[*Secondly from the things they impose: 1. they call them a weight which is not unnecessarily to be laid on the shoulders of any.*‡] But the magistrate [p. 17] is the sole judge of that necessity. [*2. they forbid only those very necessary things, to show that necessary things only and not indifferent should be the matter of our imposition.*] I answer:

1. That things may be necessary, (i) in their own nature and so are all comprehended within the law of God; (ii) *ex suppositione*, as being the means to some requisite end, so meat is necessary to him that would live etc.,§ such were the things necessary here[94]—and

---

* Bagshaw, 1660 (*a*), p. 7; continuous quoting by Locke.

† Bagshaw, 1660 (*a*), p. 6, in fact.

‡ Bagshaw, 1660 (*a*), p. 7; Locke paraphrases three of his adversary's paragraphs in his treatment of this next argument.

§ An orthodox scholastic distinction deriving ultimately from Aristotle, *De partibus animalium*, I, I, 639 *b*, 23–5; but for the peculiar relevance of this distinction for Locke, cf. chapters I and II.

so things indifferent may become necessary before they are enjoined and oblige the prince before they are commanded the people, and such a necessity (which I say still the magistrate is judge of) is sufficient for their imposition.*

2. I answer against what he here contends for that those things enjoined to the Churches by the synod excepting only fornication were not in themselves necessary as appears, (i) because no law then in force commanded them† since[95] the positive moral law of God nowhere mentions them but only the same ceremonial law which was now abolished. Indeed eating of blood was forbidden Noah which precept our author thinks is *still obligatory to all his posterity*, p. 8,‡ though[96] contrary to the doctrine of St Paul *I Cor.* 8, concerning things offered to idols, and *Romans* 14. 14 where[97] he clears the doubt concerning them all, 'I know and am persuaded by the Lord Jesus that there is nothing unclean of itself but to him that esteems it', and v. 20, 'all things[98] indeed are pure', i.e., defile not the eater but are indifferent in their use. And[99] St Paul, *I Timo.* 4 calls the commanding to abstain from meats the doctrine of devils,[100] giving the reason, v. 4, 'for every creature of God is good and nothing to be refused if it be received with thanksgiving'. The same is also clear from *I Cor.* 10. 27. [*The Apostles' scope was to ease and free not tie up their brethren.*§] 'Twas indeed here as in all other places where it came into question the Apostles' intention to enlarge converts from a subjection to the ceremonial law; but whatever was the reason 'tis certain they did tie up their brethren by those injunctions in things that were in themselves most of them indifferent—if St Paul's judgment be to be taken before our author's.

After a large consideration of the circumstances of the decree¶

---

* In fact Bagshaw, 1660 (*a*), p. 7, recognizes this difficulty and argues that either there is an objective necessity—in which case the magistrate's judgment must come to a particular view—or that the means 'requisite' to one necessary end may be subversive of another—and, he argues, more important—one.

† Locke here deletes an explanation in terms of natural law, cf. n. 95. This deletion is worth noting as the principle Locke invoked was that which Towerson had already or was shortly to challenge—the principle repudiated in the fifth of the *Essays on the Law of Nature*: that the law of nature can be known from the general consent of men; cf. Von Leyden, 1954, pp. 160–79. The deletion was perhaps made as a result of Towerson's criticism, cf. chapter 1.

‡ Gen. ix. 4; Bagshaw, 1660 (*a*), p. 8.

§ Bagshaw, 1660 (*a*), p. 7.

¶ Bagshaw, 1660 (*a*), pp. 7–8; the 'decree' is that of Acts xv, concerning 'necessary' things.

(p. 9) and a discourse of the particulars contained in it[101] he thus closes: [*Hence I conclude for persons 1. who have no such authority,*] the magistrate may have[102] another authority and that sufficient though not such; as I have above proved. [*2. In things much more indifferent*]; those were not then under the obligation of any law and therefore as much in their own nature indifferent as any.* [*3. And where the necessity of conforming is nothing near so pressing*]; the lawmaker alone is the judge of that necessity and its urgency in those laws that he establishes and therefore from thence we can take no rise to question the equity of his injunctions. [*For such I say to take upon themselves an arbitrary and an imposing power is altogether unwarrantable and*

[p. 18] *therefore sinful.*†] It is not requisite he should have such an authority as the Apostles had.‡ Then all our laws must be necessarily the dictates of the spirit of God, nor could the magistrate appoint so much as a fast or determine any indifferent thing without a special revelation. It suffices if he have any authority at all nor is it requisite he should make known the reasons of his edicts, 'tis enough if he himself be satisfied of them. Indeed should anyone without authority impose on others he[103] might well be ranked with the greatest offenders and expect the sentence of the law as well as our author's censure to lay hold upon him, but the case is far otherwise with the magistrate, whose authority I have proved already. Or[104] should anyone make use of the lawful authority he hath needlessly[105] to burden his subjects, and without a necessity appearing to him sport himself with the liberties of his brethren, and confine them narrowly in the use of indifferent things, he would not perhaps be innocent and though he should not be liable to the censures of men, yet would not scape[106] the tribunal of God.§ However,[107] this would not discharge our obedience. And I think 'tis no paradox to affirm that subjects may be obliged to obey those laws which it may be sinful for the magistrate to enact.¶

---

* Bagshaw claims the opposite, 1660 (*a*), p. 7: 'That all these things they forbid were not indifferent, but long before prohibited by God, not only in the ceremonial but also in his positive law and therefore obligatory.'

† Bagshaw, 1660 (*a*), p. 9.

‡ Bagshaw, 1660 (*a*), p. 9, does not claim that it is; on the contrary he uses the theory of hierarchic and deduced authority to argue that the magistrate, precisely in respect of the indifferent things of religion, has less authority than the Apostles had.

§ Cf. Latin *Tract*, p. 7, and cf. MS Locke c. 28, fol. 25, *Essay Concerning Toleration*, *Letter Concerning Toleration*, p. 269, and above, chapter IV.

¶ Cf. Sanderson, 1660, v, vii, and VIII, xv; Latin *Tract*, p. 6; *Two Treatises*, II, sects. 131, 134, 137, 139, 222, 240, for Locke's later reversal of this doctrine.

All that the author says in his third instance from Paul's oppos-
ing the false brethren* is no more than hath been urged and
answered above in the same case of the Galatians, only there it is
brought as a precept, here as an example. From whence in the
close he comes to lay down a very strange position, *viz*: [*When any
shall take upon them to make a thing indifferent necessary, then the thing so
imposed presently loses not its liberty only, but likewise its*[108] *lawfulness.
And we may not without breach of the Apostle's precept submit to it.*†]
A conclusion that by no means can[109] be drawn from his instance,
Gal. 2, where those[110] the Apostle disputes against[111] were not any
that pretended a power to make laws, or imposed those as their
own injunctions, but urged them as necessary doctrines and the
laws of God which obliged their consciences. The Scripture, that
almost everywhere commands submission though contrary to the
whole bent of our inclinations, could never be thought to teach us
disobedience and that too contrary to our wills; this is an opinion
so monstrous that it cannot without a very great injury[112] be
fathered upon the Apostles. Who can believe that the magistrate's
authority should make anything unlawful by enjoining it; that if in
those things we are cheerfully doing ourselves his command
should come and encourage us we ought presently to stop, to turn
about and resist him and at once oppose his and our own wills too,
alone, as if a child going to church of his own accord being by the
way commanded by his father to go on ought straight to return
back again? If this doctrine be true, I know not how any law can be
established by the magistrate or obeyed by the subject, indifferent
things of civil as well as religious concernment being of the same
nature, and will alway be so, till our author can show where God
hath put a distinction between them,‡ this I'm sure that according [p. 19]
to his own rule the observation of a fast enjoined by the magistrate
must needs be a sin, it being an imposition relating to the worship
of God in indifferent things. An anniversary thanksgiving day will
be but an anniversary provocation, and those that assemble in

* Bagshaw, 1660 (*a*), p. 10; the texts are I Cor. ix. 19–23; Acts xvi. 3; Gal. ii. 4.
† Bagshaw's argument is again from the assertion of the moral priority of 'inward
impressions'; to accept the imposition of indifferencies is unlawful because 'we
thereby own that whose injunctions we obey had a power to impose'; thus,
Locke's reply is not altogether to the point.
‡ Cf. Bagshaw, 1661(*a*), p. 10, where he attempts such a distinction in a further
analysis of the nature of Christian liberty by developing the conception of 'things
doubtful' as an intermediate category of moral objects.

obedience to such a command instead of returning a praise to God for a blessing, would call down on their heads a curse.* This is truly[113] to ensnare the consciences of men and put them under a necessity of sinning, a doctrine which strikes at the very root and foundation of all laws and government and opens a gap so wide to disobedience and disorder as will quickly ruin the best founded societies. Let the people (whose ears are always open to complaints against their governors, who greedily swallow all pleas for liberty) but once hear that the magistrate hath no authority to enjoin things indifferent in matters of religion, they will all of an instant be converts, conscience and religion shall presently mingle itself with all their actions and be spread over their whole lives to protect them from the reach of the magistrate, and they will quickly[114] find the large extent of *inordine ad spiritualia*. Let but the ruler's power be excluded out of the sanctuary and it will prove an asylum for the greatest enormities, tithes will be as unlawful as sacrifice,† and civil respect to a man as impious as if it were divine adoration, the stubborn servant will beard his master with a charter of freedom under Paul's hand, *Be ye not the servants of men.*‡ Nor will our author's interpretation be able to prevent it. Magistracy itself will at last be concluded anti-Christian, (as the author himself confesses many do, p. 1).§ Let the multitude be once persuaded that obedience to impositions in indifferent things is *sin* and it will not be long ere they find it their *duty* to pull down the imposer. Do but once arm their consciences against the magistrate and their hands will not be long idle or innocent. But of inconveniencies I shall have more occasion to speak in his next argument.

(p. 10)   [*My last argument against impositions shall be taken from inconveniencies*

* Cf. 12. Car. II, c. XIV, 'An Act for a Perpetual Anniversary Thanksgiving on the nine and twentieth day of May'.

† An argument which suggests the limited scope of the audience Locke is addressing; the debate, like those of the Savoy Conference and the Convention Parliament, is between Anglican and Presbyterian positions: it was a characteristic Anglican device to alarm Presbyterians out of their opposition by pointing to the far more radical opposition based on the same principles to their left. Bagshaw, 1660(*a*), p. 15, does in fact face this long-standing weakness of Presbyterian ecclesiastical politics and escapes from it by advocating a general toleration.

‡ I Cor. vii. 23.

§ Matt. xx. 25: 'The princes of the Gentiles do exercise dominion over them and they that are great exercise authority upon them, but it shall not be so amongst you'; but Bagshaw concludes, 'I will…admit that a Christian may lawfully exercise the highest place of magistracy, only as the Apostle saith in another case, *in the Lord*, i.e. not extending his commission farther than the Word of God doth warrant him.'

that attend such a practice*.] If inconveniencies make things unlawful as well as sometimes unpleasant I know nothing could be innocent, all our *blessings* would have their seasons of being curses, we cannot doubt there can be anything so good or innocent which the frail nature or improved corruption of man may not make use of to harm himself or his neighbour since the Apostle tells us we may abuse the *grace of God* into wantonness.† Ever since man first threw himself into the pollution of sin, he sullies whatever he takes into his hand, and he that at first could make the best and perfectest nature degenerate cannot fail now to make other things so too.

[*In principles on which moral actions are grounded the inconveniencies do use to be weighed, and that doctrine for the most part seems most true, at least most plausible which is attended by fewest inconveniencies‡.*] Prin- [p. 20] ciples ought to be of unalterable verity and therefore are not to be established upon our uncertain and commonly partial judgment of their consequences, which are usually so many, so various and cross, that nothing then could stand firm, if every little inconvenience could shake it. The question being of lawful or unlawful[115] we are to be judged by some law and not by supposed inconveniencies which nobody can miss of, that will seek to discredit and dissuade any constitution, and study as he says to render the contrary doctrine plausible.§ If popular arguments were proofs I know no principles could stand secure, and the Gospel itself would not be free from question, in which the heathens found inconveniencies[116] and arguments enough to render it less plausible than their own absurdities and irrational superstitions. Who might not this way declaim government itself out of the world and quickly insinuate into the multitude that it is beneath the dignity of a man to enslave his understanding and subject his will to another's pleasure, to think himself so ignorant or imprudent as to stand in need of a

---

* Bagshaw, 1660 (*a*), p. 10; he adds, however, that he lays 'little stress upon such arguments', whereas Locke makes a great deal of his refutation of them.

† Gal. v. 13.   ‡ Bagshaw, 1660 (*a*), p. 10; continuous quoting by Locke.

§ This, however, is not the real difference between Locke and Bagshaw; it is rather a question of the character of the sanctions from which law is to be deduced (cf. chapters II and IV). Bagshaw, 1660 (*a*), p. 10, makes this same general point and urges, 'Truth is to be tried by its evidence and not by its consequences', but suggests that gross inconveniences are relevant evidence in assessing moral value. Locke in fact is *more* pragmatic than Bagshaw; in a sense his argument is drawn entirely from a consideration of consequences—see the sequel in this paragraph, and chapter III. Bagshaw in his *Second Part*, 1661(*a*), p. 14, is even more explicit: 'the question is not of convenience but of lawfulness, not *cui bono?* but *quo iure?*',

guardian, and not to be as God and nature made him, the free dis-
poser of his own actions?* To fight to support greatness and a
dominion over himself, and rob his own necessities to maintain
the pomp and pleasure of one that regards him not, to hold his
life as a tenant at will and to be ready to part with his head when
it shall be demanded, these and many more such are the disadvantages of government, yet far less than are to be found in its
absence as no peace, no security, no enjoyments, enmity with all
men and safe possession of nothing, and those stinging swarms of
miseries that attend anarchy and rebellion.† This I grant is a *ready*
but not a fair way to decry any doctrine, to point out all the
dangers that may follow from it and not at all to touch its advantages or obligation, and by showing only the black side of the
cloud persuade the beholder that even the Israelites are in darkness
and error whereas a better prospect would discover them guided
by a brighter illumination. 'Tis true everyone in those things that
fall under his choice ought well to balance the conveniencies and
inconveniencies on both sides, and to be poised on that side on
which the weightier consequences shall hang, and he sins at least
against discretion that shall do otherwise. And thus the magistrate
is to consider the consequences of those things which God hath
left free before he determine them by his public decrees, and the
subject to consider the consequences of those things which the
magistrate hath left free before he determine them by his private
resolution; and would all men thus limit their motions within their
[p. 21] own sphere they would not be so turbulent and troublesome.‡

[*The opposers of liberty have very little else to urge for themselves besides
inconveniencies.*§] But the defenders of the magistrate's power offer
something more when they tell you that a man cannot part with

---

* Locke shifts from one mode of argument to another in the course of the following paragraph—not altogether successfully. He starts by using the Hobbesian
mechanism, in which the concept of natural liberty is the indispensable premiss for
the validation of social authority. But the argument below ('in those things that fall
under his choice') makes nonsense of natural liberty; if men are at best only free
within prescribed spheres they cannot be free as individuals, only as individuals already
inside an authoritative moral order.

† Cf. Cranston, 1957, p. 62; Gough, 1950, p. 180; both cite this sentence as evidence of Locke's 'Hobbism'. The comparison is with *Leviathan*, I, xiii; *Leviathan*, II,
xix, 'Sovereign power not so hurtful as the want of it'; but see chapter III for some
discussion of this theme.

‡ For the idea of spheres of action within a function and law-bound hierarchy as an
axiom of the thought of Locke's immediate circle, see Allestree, *The Gentleman's Calling*
(1660), pp. 20 ff.; also, of course, Hooker, I, ix.   § Bagshaw, 1660 (*a*), p. 10.

his liberty and have it too, convey it by compact to the magistrate and retain it himself.*

[*The first inconvenience is the impossibility to fix a point where the imposer will stop. For do but once grant that the magistrate hath a power to impose, and then we lie at his mercy how far he will go.*†] An inconvenience as strong against civil as ecclesiastical jurisdiction:[117] do but once grant the magistrate a power to impose taxes and we then lie at his mercy whether he will leave us anything.‡ Grant him a power to confine anyone, and we cannot be long secure of any liberty: who knows how soon he will make our houses our prisons. Grant him a power to forbid assemblies and conventions, and who knows how long he will allow us the company of our friends, or permit us to enjoy the conversation of our relations. A practice not unknown to the Presbytery of Scotland, who took on them at pleasure to forbid the civil and innocent meeting of friends in any place but the church or market, under pretence to prevent evil and scandal. So far will religious and spiritual jurisdiction be extended even to the most indifferent of common actions when it falls into busy and unskilful hands. Grant once that the magistrate hath a power to command the subject to work, and limit his wages too, and who can secure us that he will not prove rather an Egyptian taskmaster than a Christian ruler, and enforce us to make brick without straw to erect monuments of his rigour and our slavery.[118]

(*vid: Burden of Issachar*)§

(*v. Stat: 5. Eliza. c. 4. 1. Jac. c. 6*)¶

---

* Cf. Hobbes, *Leviathan*, II, xxviii and xxi; here at least Locke makes no pretence that his use of the argument from compact is a hypothetical one.

† Bagshaw, 1660 (*a*), p. 10; cf. the consideration of this objection in Latin *Tract*, p. 17, where the argument is identical, 'observare libet, quod hae obiectiones... magistratus potestatem tam in adiaphoris civilibus quam ecclesiasticis oppugnare et convellere'. Either the magistrate must be trusted or there can be no government at all.

‡ Cf. Latin *Tract*, p. 17; Bagshaw returns to the problem of isolating religious indifferencies as a logically and morally distinct order of acts in 1661, pp. 10–11.

§ As Locke's only precise book reference in either *Tract*, and one that has not been hitherto observed, this marginal note deserves some attention. James Maxwell, Archbishop of Thuan, *The Burden of Issachar...or the Tyrannical Power and Practices of the Presbyterical Government in Scotland* (1646); Maxwell was Chaplain to the Royal Army in Oxford from 1643 and the book was published by the official printers. Locke seems to confuse two distinct points in Maxwell's book: p. 8, 'An act is enacted that if...two persons suspected of fornication or adultery, shall be seen to meet...except they meet in church or market, it shall be holden *pro confesso*...that they are guilty', and p. 9, 'the Edinburgh weekly market day on Monday prohibited by the Presbytery as violating the Sabbath'. Locke has transferred the explicit prohibition from one case to the other; and the former case is something less than 'the innocent meeting of friends', though his general argument about power is unaffected.

¶ These statutes are the 'Acte touching divers orders for Artificers' of 1564 and

These are inconveniences whose speculation following from the constitution of polities may often fright but their practice seldom hurt the people. Nor will the largeness of the governor's power appear dangerous or more than necessary if we consider that as occasion requires it is employed upon the multitude that are as impatient of restraint as the sea, and whose tempests and overflows cannot be too well provided against. Would it be thought dangerous or inconvenient that anyone should be allowed to make banks and fences against the waves for fear he should too much encroach upon and straighten the ocean? The magistrate's concernments will always teach him to use no more rigour than the temper of the people and the necessity of the age shall call for, knowing that too great checks as well as too loose a rein may make [p. 22] this untamed beast to cast his rider. Who would decline embarking himself because the pilot hath the sole guiding of the ship, out of fear lest he should be too busy and impertinently troublesome at the helm, and disturb the voyage with the ill management of his place, who[119] would rather be content to steer the vessel with a gentle than a stiff hand would the winds and waves permit him; he increases his forces and violence only with the increase of the storm and tumult; the tossings and several turns of the ship are from without and not begotten in the steerage or at the helm?* Whence is most danger to be rationally feared, from ignorant or knowing heads? From an orderly council or a confused multitude? To whom are we most like to become a prey, to those whom the Scripture calls gods, or those whom knowing men have always found and therefore called beasts?† Who knows but that since the multitude is always craving, never satisfied, that there can be

the 'Acte for the explanation' of it of 1603. See especially sections x and xi of the Elizabethan Act; and chapter 1.

  * If Locke's use of this analogy is a serious indication of his early political philosophy, his conception of civil society is not so much an authoritarian or Hobbesian one as that J. S. Mill was to describe as the regime of the 'besieged city' (referring to Comte); cf. chapter III.

  † This distinction was a commonplace of the age; cf. Ps. lxxxii. 6: 'I have said, ye are Gods', etc. Digges, 1644, and Maxwell, 1646, p. 20, 'By how much worse it is to be subjected to an untamed beast, the multitude, than to the tyranny of one.' And from another work certainly read by Locke before 1660:

Upon the law thy judgments always ground
  And not on man; for that's affectionless;
But Man in passions strangely doth abound,
  Th'one all like God: t'other like to Beasts.
                (Du Bartas, *Quadrains of Pibrac*, p. 265)

nothing set over them which they will not always be reaching at
and endeavouring to pull down, those constitutions in indifferent
things may be erected as the outward fences to secure the more
substantial parts of religion which experience tells us they will be
sure to be tampering with when these are gone which are therefore
fit to be set up, because they may be with least danger assaulted and
shaken and that there may be always something in a readiness to be
parted with to their importunity without injuring the indispensable
and more sacred parts of religion when their fury and impatience
shall make such an indulgence necessary. But I too forwardly
intrude myself into the council chamber, and like an impertinent
traveller, which am concerned only which way the[120] hand of the
dial points, lose time in searching after the spring and wheels that
give it motion. It being our duty not[121] curiously to examine the
counsels but cheerfully to obey the commands of the magistrate in
all things that God hath left us free.

But to my author's inconvenience I shall oppose another I think
greater, I'm sure more to be provided against because more pressing and oftener occurring. Grant the people once free and unlimited in the exercise of their religion and where will they stop,
where will they themselves bound it, and[122] will it not be religion
to destroy all that are not of their profession? And will they not
think they do God good service to take vengeance on those that
they have voted his enemies? Shall not this be the land of promise,
and those that join not with them be the Canaanites to be rooted
out?* Must not Christ reign and they prepare for his coming by
cutting off the wicked? Shall we not be all taught of God and the
ministry cast off as needless?† They that have got the right use[123]
of Scripture and the knack of applying it with advantage, who can [p. 23]
bring God's word in defence of those practices which his soul
abhors and do already tell us we are returning to Egypt,‡ would,
were they permitted, as easily find us Egyptians and think it their

* Num. xxxiii. 51–5.
† Again, the device is to frighten the Presbyterian into submission by raising the
spectre of the Anabaptist. Bagshaw had entered the 'ministry', with episcopal
ordination, the previous year; in the course of 1660–1 he acquired a living; he was
very vulnerable to the sort of argument Locke advances here, yet in his *Second Part*,
and again in the *Third Part*, he accepts the logic of a request for toleration for one sect
and extends his appeal generally.
‡ E.g. Milton, *A Ready and Easy Way to Establish a Free Commonwealth* (1659);
Milton concludes with a prayer for 'reviving liberty' in a time when he sees men
'now choosing them a captain back for Egypt'.

right to despoil us. Though I can believe that our author would not make this large use of his liberty,* yet if he thinks others would not so far improve his principles, let him look some years back he will find that a liberty for tender consciences was the first inlet to all those confusions and unheard of and destructive opinions that overspread this nation. The same hearts are still in men as liable to zealous mistakes and religious furies, there wants but leave for crafty men to inspirit and fire them with such doctrines. I cannot deny but that the sincere[124] and tender-hearted Christians should be gently dealt with and much might be indulged them, but who shall be able to distinguish them, and if a toleration be allowed as their right who shall hinder others who shall be ready enough to lay hold on the same plea?

Indeed [I have[125]] observed that almost all those tragical revolutions which have exercised Christendom these many years have turned upon this hinge, that there hath been no design so wicked which hath not worn the vizor of religion, nor rebellion which hath not been so kind to itself as to assume the specious name of reformation, proclaiming a design either to supply the defects or correct the errors of religion, that none ever went about to ruin the *state* but with pretence to build the *temple*, all those disturbers of public quiet being wise enough to lay hold on religion as a shield which if it could not defend their cause was best like to secure their credit, and gain as well pity to their ruin as partisans to their success, men finding no cause that can so rationally draw them to hazard this life, or compound for the dangers of a war as that which promises them a better, all other arguments, of liberty, country, relations, glory being to be enjoyed only in this life can give but small encouragements to a man to endanger that and to improve their present enjoyments a little, run themselves into the danger of an irreparable loss of all. Hence have the cunning and malice of men taken occasion to pervert the doctrine of peace and charity into a perpetual foundation of war and contention, all those flames that have made such havoc and desolation in Europe, and have not been quenched but with the blood of so many millions, have been at first kindled with coals from the

---

* In view of Bagshaw's activities in Oxford at this time, Locke might be thought to be indulging in a private irony here, cf. chapter II; but perhaps he is simply recognizing the claim in Bagshaw's *Preface* that the author would gladly submit to whatever the King chose to impose.

altar,* and too much blown with the breath of those that attend the altar, who, forgetting their calling which is to promote peace and [p. 24] meekness, have proved the trumpeters of strife and sounded a charge with a 'curse ye Meros'.† I know not therefore how much it might conduce to the peace and security of mankind if religion were banished the camp and forbid to take arms, at least to use no other sword[126] but that of the word and spirit, if ambition and revenge were disrobed of that so specious outside of reformation and the cause of God, were forced to appear in their own native ugliness and lie open to the eyes and contempt of all the world,‡ if the believer and unbeliever could be content as Paul advises to live together, and use no other weapons to conquer each other's opinions but pity and persuasion,§ if men would suffer one an- (I *Cor.* 7) other to go to heaven every one his one way, and not out of a fond conceit of themselves pretend to greater knowledge and care of another's[127] soul and eternal concernments than he himself, how much I say if such a temper and tenderness were wrought in the hearts of men our author's doctrine of toleration might promote a quiet in the world, and at last bring those glorious days that men have a great while sought after the wrong way, I shall leave every-one to judge.¶

But it is like to produce far different effects among a people that are ready to conclude God dishonoured upon every small devia-tion from that way of his worship which either education or interest hath made sacred to them and that therefore they ought to vindicate the cause of God with swords in their hands, and rather to fight for this honour than their own; who are apt to judge every other exercise of religion as an affront to theirs, and branding all others with the odious names of idolatry, superstition or will-

---

* Cf. Latin *Tract*, pp. 5–6. Grotius, an important source for Locke soon after 1660 if not before, was another author who saw a *trahison des clercs* of this order as a principal cause of unrest; cf. *De Veritate Religionis Christianae*, e.g. p. 154 (edition of 1669).

† Judges v. 23; the phrase was still being used for the purposes and in the sense deplored by Locke, twenty years later, cf. Edward Hickeringill, *Curse Ye Meros* (1680).

‡ This gloomy scepticism fills Locke's thought for almost a decade (1657–66); cf. the letters MS c. 24, fols. 172 and 231: 'As I do not credit all those glorious promises and pretences of the one side, so neither am I scared with those threats of danger and destruction which are so peremptorily asserted by a sort of men which would persuade us that the cause of God suffers whenever they are disappointed of their ambitious or covetous ends'; and chapter III.

§ I Cor. vii. 12–13.

¶ Cf. MS c. 27, fol. 12, the letter to 'S.H.', for a similar statement.

worship, and so looking on both the[128] persons and practices of others as condemned by God already, are forward to take commission from their own zeal to be their executioners, and so in the actions of the greatest cruelty applaud themselves as good Christians, and think with Paul they do God good service. And here, should not the magistrate's authority interpose itself and put a stop to the secret contrivances of deceivers and the passionate zeal of the deceived, he would certainly neglect his duty of being the great *conservator pacis*, and let the very foundations of government and the end of it lie neglected, and leave the peace of that society is committed to his care open to be torn and rent in pieces by everyone that could but pretend to conscience and draw a sword.*

After some enlargement and an innumeration of certain particulars and ceremonies of the Church of Rome, which whether indifferent or no concerns not our question,† he comes to make the

[p. 25] imposing of indifferent things the mark of Antichrist: [*If I understand anything of Antichrist his nature seems to me to consist in this, that*

(Rev. 13) *he acts in a way contrary to*[129] *Christ, instead of a spiritual he brings in a devised worship, and instead of freedom lays a constraint even upon our devotion, so that as John in his Revelation says of him, 'Men shall neither buy nor sell which have not his mark', i.e. who do not serve God in that outward way which he commands.‡*] St John who alone names and more than once describes Antichrist gives another character of him, and if we will take his authority we shall find his nature to consist in denying Jesus to be the Christ, *1 John* 2. 18, 22; *1 John* 4. 3; *2 John* 7. And here would we content ourselves with those discoveries the Scripture allows us, we should not grope for Antichrist in the dark prophesies of the revelations, nor found arguments upon our own interpretation wherein the mistakes of eminent men might teach us to be wary and not over-peremptory in our guesses.§

---

* Cf. Hobbes, *Leviathan*, 2, Of the Office of the Sovereign Representative.

† Locke is, to say the least, optimistic in this assertion. The 'inconveniency' Bagshaw urges in the passages passed over by Locke here follows from his last: he argues that the magistrate may under Locke's doctrine lawfully restore 'Papacy' since this 'consists not in particular imposed indifferencies but in the doctrine of imposition' as such, 1660(*a*), p. 10.

‡ Bagshaw, 1660 (*a*), pp. 10–11, draws a parallel here which Locke does not discuss—linking antichrist and the imposition of ceremonies by way of the Papacy: 'Whoever doth own the doctrine of imposition, though in the smallest circumstances, he brings in the essence, though not the name of Papacy.' The reference is to Rev. xiii. 17. § Cf. Daillé, *Traicté*; Sanderson, 1660, III.

[I know very well that the argument is specious and often urged why (p. 11)
should men be so scrupulous? Most pleading for ceremonies as Lot did for
Zoar, are not they little things? But I answer, 1. That a little thing un-
*warrantably done is a great sin.**] Unwarrantably against a positive
precept, not unwarrantably without a special commission. [*2. That*
a little thing, unjustly gained makes way for a greater.†] Though little
things make way for greater yet still they will be within the compass of indifferent, beyond that we plead for no allowance and
whether a power to impose these be *unjustly gained* must be judged
by the arguments already urged.

[*The second inconvenience is that it quite inverts the nature of Christian*
religion not only by taking away its freedom but likewise its spirituality.‡]
Our author here had forgot that rule, what God hath joined let no
man put asunder. That an outward set form of worship should
necessarily take away the spirituality of religion I cannot think,
since God himself that did then demand the worship of the heart
and spirit no less than now and made that the only way to please
him, did once erect an outward form of worship cumbered with
more ceremonies and circumstances than I believe ever any in the
world besides, which could yet no way shut out or clog the operations of his spirit where he pleased to enter and enliven any soul.

[*Our Saviour says that God will now be worshipped not in show and*
ceremony but in spirit and in truth.§] Show and ceremony are not in
the text, and might here have been spared without any injury to
the discourse of Christ which doth not usually need such supple-
ments. The words of our Saviour are, *John* 4. v. 24, 'The hour
cometh and now is when the true worshippers shall worship the
Father in spirit and in truth'; the discourse is to a woman of
Samaria,¶ the people whereof contended with the Jews about the [p. 26]
right place of worship, preferring their Mount Gerezime to Mount
Sion,130 between whom the controversy had bred such dislike and
aversion that it broke off all civil commerce as appears by the

* Bagshaw, 1660 (*a*), p. 11; Locke exaggerates the area of conceptual disagreement
between himself and Bagshaw here by not taking notice of Bagshaw's immediately
subsequent remark, 'In impositions we are not to consider how small and inconsiderable the thing imposed is, as how lawful it is.' The reference is to Gen. xix. 20.
† Bagshaw, 1660 (*a*), p. 11.
‡ Bagshaw, 1660 (*a*), pp. 11–12.
§ Bagshaw, 1660 (*a*), p. 12; continuous quoting by Locke; but (cf. Locke's next
sentence) Bagshaw does in fact indicate that the phrase 'in show and ceremony' is not
quoted.
¶ Cf. MS Locke, c. 18, fol. 196 v, for Locke's notes on this incident; and chapter 1.

woman's words, v. 9,* who being zealous for the religion of her country maintains it against that of the Jews; but Christ to put an end to the controversy and to prepare her for his doctrine, tells her first indeed that her religion was false, but that of the Jews too which was true, was then to cease and that therefore they should no longer contest which mountain stood nearest heaven nor in which place the worship of God was most acceptable, since God was now publishing a religion to the world not confined to any place, but wherever there were a heart inflamed with love to him and a spirit rightly disposed to his service there was a sacrifice acceptable to him.† All that can be drawn hence is that[131] the great business of Christian religion lies in the heart, that wherever there is a well set spirit there God may be worshipped wherever it be, but this excludes not an outward form, nor can it be from hence concluded inconsistent with it. God may be worshipped in spirit and in truth as well where the indifferent circumstances are limited as where they are free, a gracious heart may pray as fervently in the ancient form of the Church as the extemporary form of the minister, and an humble soul may receive instruction as well from the pulpit as the state; a surplice indeed will add but little heat to the body, but I know not why it should chill our devotions. There is no necessity why David should be thought less zealous when he danced with all his might in a linen ephod than when he was clad in his shepherd's coat.‡ He that judges that where he finds *ceremony* and *show* there *spirit and truth* are necessarily wanting may as rationally conclude that where he observes an uniform structure with a stately outside there is no fire or inhabitants within, or that handsome bodies have no souls.

[*Whereas the doctrine of impositions places it (viz. religion[132]) in such things in the observance of which superstition will be sure to outdo devotion.*§] This doctrine that the magistrate hath power to impose indifferent things places it in none, but leaves it to his arbitrary and uncertain determination, and should the magistrate prescribe such a form wherein *superstition*, (a word alway sounding ill and not seldom applied to very innocent actions)¶ would perhaps outdo *devotion*, yet this would be no better an argument against such injunction

---

* John iv. 9.   † John iv. 9-21; the reference is in fact to Jerusalem.
‡ I Chron. xv. 27.
§ Bagshaw, 1660 (*a*), p. 12; continuous quoting by Locke.
¶ Cf. Latin *Tract*, pp. 14-15.

than if he should endeavour to prove that the magistrate should not command truth and justice because they are things wherein [p. 27] Turks will be sure to outdo Christians. That the *superstitious* should be more zealous than the devout or a Turk honester than a Christian might indeed well shame the professors but could not at all discredit the doctrine of either.

[*But true religion like the spirits of wine or subtle essences whenever it comes to be opened and exposed to view runs the hazard of being presently dispirited and lost.**] Christ who best understood the nature of Christian religion hath fitted it with another simile, *Math.* 5. 25,† he fears not to trust it to the open view, nor thinks that the profession of the Gospel would have less heat or light upon an hill than in a corner, and makes it a kind of absurdity to endeavour to conceal that which was to be a light to those that sit in darkness and was to shine over all the world, this would be to confine the sun to a cave, and not to light or set up a candle for fear it should go out, which runs a greater hazard in a close confinement.

[*There is a vast difference between purity and pomp, between spirit and splendour.*‡] Not so vast a distance but that they may meet. The priest's robes many and specious did not make Aaron guilty, nor the whiteness of his garment diminish the innocence of his heart.§ *Spirit* and *splendour* are as far different as life and clothes, yet no man is persuaded to strip himself naked because his life consists in the inward motion of his heart and not the outward fashion of his habit, and those ornaments that make not a man more strong and vigorous in himself may render him more comely and acceptable to others.

[*Whereas the imposer only drives at and improves the latter (viz: splendour) but of the former (viz: spirit) is altogether secure and careless as is evident in those places where uniformity is most strictly practised.*¶] The imposer carries his religion as far as he can, and being not able to reach beyond the outside he must necessarily stop there, neither his commission nor power extending any farther, but that he is secure and careless of an inward purity, that he doth not wish and

---

* Bagshaw, 1660 (*a*), p. 12; continuous quoting by Locke.

† Matt. v. 15 must be intended here; v. 25 is meaningless.

‡ In Bagshaw, 1660 (*a*), p. 12, this sentence reads, 'In the service of God there is...', etc., and Bagshaw's point is not that purity and pomp may not meet, but that there is no necessary relation between the latter and the former.

§ Exod. xxviii.

¶ Bagshaw, 1660 (*a*), p. 12; continuous quoting by Locke.

pray for that too, is a very severe censure. The miscarriages of those where uniformity is most strictly practised are no more to be imputed to his law than the formality of the Jews to the ceremonial. As long as the greatest part of men shall be the worst,* and outward profession shall be more easy and cheaper than inward conversion, it will be no more wonder to find want of spirit with splendour, formality under uniformity, than ambition and faction, pride and hypocrisy under a toleration, and generally [p. 28] want of sincerity in all professions. And 'tis not to be doubted that many may find admittance in a church as well as conventicle here who will scarce get admittance into heaven hereafter.

[*Thirdly this doctrine making no provision at all for such as are scrupulous and tender supposes the same measure of faith in all.*†] This inconvenience was touched at above, page 4,‡ and generally this plea of scandal and offence is made use of by all sorts of men as a sufficient reason against whatever suits not with their humour, who cannot but be well pleased to find themselves always furnished with this argument against whatever cannot gain their approbation, and to think anything unlawful and ought to be removed because they dislike it. This is an inconvenience that Christ himself and his doctrine could not escape, this cornerstone which was a sure footing to some, was also a stumbling block whereat many stumbled and fell and were broken in Israel. Were offences arguments against anything, I know not who might not clap on a tender conscience and therewith sufficiently arm himself against all the injunctions of the magistrate, and no law could lay hold on him without encroaching on[133] this law of charity and his just freedom.§ How far we ought to part with our own liberty to gratify another's scruple[134] is a question full of niceness and difficulty. But this I dare say, that of what value soever the inward[135] and private peace of a Christian be, it ought not to be purchased at the settled and public peace of the commonwealth, especially where it will not remove

* Cf., for a comparable pessimism producing similar politics, Philip Nye, *The Lawfulnesse of the Oath of Supremacy*, pp. 17 ff.; Locke is emphatically more pessimistic than the average Anglican divine in his observations on human nature.

† Bagshaw, 1660 (*a*), p. 12; continuous quoting by Locke; but Bagshaw makes two points in this passage which Locke ignores the politically more important one; cf. chapter 1.

‡ The reference is to Bagshaw, 1660 (*a*), p. 4; see, too, the developed treatment of scandal in Latin *Tract*, p. 15; and Hammond, 1644, II, Of Scandal, for the theme 'Christ himself is a stumbling block'.

§ Cf. Latin *Tract*, p. 15; Hammond, 1644, I, Of Conscience.

the offence and only cast the scandal on the other side and disturb the peace of the contrary persuasion, since some men will be as much offended at the magistrate's forbearance as others at his injunctions and be as much scandalized to see a hat on in the public worship as others a surplice.* [*As the Apostle says of thing offered to idols so concerning ceremonies I may say that all have not knowledge. But to this day many there are utterly unsatisfied with the lawfulness of any, and most are convinced of the uselessness of them all.†*] Many too are unsatisfied of the lawfulness of a Christian magistrate, and yet who besides themselves think they are not obliged whilst they live within his dominions to submit to his laws, and may without any inconvenience be punished if they offend against them? And who will think a prince ought to betray his right and lay by his sceptre as often as anyone shall scruple at his power and plead conscience against his authority? [*The last inconvenience is that by impositions, especially when the penalty is severe, we seem to lay as much weight and stress upon these indifferent things as upon any the most material parts of our religion.‡*] If the [p. 29] magistrate employ his power only within those bounds that are set to his authority he doth not thereby slight or undervalue those things that are out of his reach. Were faith and repentance, the substantial parts of religion, entrusted to his jurisdiction and open to his knowledge we might possibly find his penalties severer in those things than in any other. But God, the judge of hearts, hath reserved both the knowledge and censure of these internal acts to himself, and removed those actions from the judgment of any tribunal but his own. We may well spare the magistrate the exercise of his sovereignty in those things wherein God doth not allow it, and we have as little reason to accuse him of usurpation because he makes use of the authority that is put into his hands as of negligence and lukewarmness because he goes not beyond his commission. Nor doth human impositions in indifferent things advance them above the more substantial and necessary which

---

* Again Locke confronts Bagshaw with the extreme sects—in this instance the Quakers; Henry Stubbe, *A Light Shining out of Darkness* (1659), had recognized the weakness of a limited appeal for toleration in this respect and had been led to demand a toleration for Quakers and Presbyterians alike—Bagshaw, in his *Third Part*, comes to the same view.

† Bagshaw, 1660 (*a*), p. 12; continuous quoting by Locke; the reference is to I Cor. viii. 7.

‡ Bagshaw, 1660 (*a*), p. 12; continuous quoting by Locke.

stand above them by the appointment of a superior law enjoined by divine authority, and therefore challenges the first and chiefest part of our homage and obedience, so that though he say [*that this rigid irrespective obtruding of small things makes no difference at all between ceremony and substance*],* 'tis certain it puts as much difference as is acknowledged between an human and a divine law, as between the commands of God and the injunctions of man. The magistrate whilst he reverently forbears to interpose his authority in these things lays a greater stress upon them by acknowledging them to be above his authority, and he that in all other things stands above and commands his people, in these descends to their level and confesses himself their fellow subject.

[*So that a man who were not a Christian at all would find as good, nay perhaps better usage from the imposer, than he*[136] *who labouring and endeavouring to live up to other parts of Christian faith, shall yet forbear to practise those ceremonies: which is not only harsh and cruel but very incongruous dealing, that a Jew or Mahomedan should be better regarded than a weak or scrupulous Christian.*†] Whatever other country do, England is clear of this imputation. Yet I shall further add that he who thinks he ought to allow a Turk as well as a Christian the free use of his religion, hath as little reason to force or abridge the one contrary to his Alcaron as the other contrary to his Gospel, and can as little forbid circumcision to the one as baptism to the other. But yet nevertheless he retains an absolute authority over all those indifferent actions which the respective law of each hath left undetermined, but the reason why perhaps he determines the indifferent things of his own profession whilst he leaves those which he disregards free is (by the example of the great lawmaker who though he strictly tied up his own people to ceremony in the true worship yet never prescribed a form to the idolators in their false) [p. 30] lest by enjoining positive ceremonies in their religion[137] he might seem to countenance and command its profession and by taking care for their worship acknowledge something good and right in it; it being irrational that the magistrate should impose (possibly he might forbid) any indifferent actions in that religion wherein he looks on the whole worship as false and idolatrous. The Christian prince that in any public[138] calamity should enjoin a fast and com-

---

* Bagshaw, 1660 (*a*), p. 12; continuous quoting by Locke.

† Bagshaw, 1660 (*a*), p. 12; continuous quoting by Locke: cf. MS Locke c. 28, fol. 22, *Essay Concerning Toleration*, where Locke makes this very point.

mand the Christians in their public place of worship to send up their prayers to God and implore his mercy might perhaps at the same time prohibit his subject Turks the ordinary works of their vocations, but would never send them in sackcloth and ashes to their mosques to intercede with Mahomed for a blessing (which he might be well supposed to do were he of their persuasion) and so encourage their superstition by seeming to expect a blessing from it; this would be to condemn his own prayers, to affront his own religion and to provoke God whom he endeavours to appease, and proclaim his distrust of him whilst he seeks help from another. Though those of different religions have hence small occasion to boast of the advantage of their condition, whatsoever is bated in ceremonies being usually doubled in taxes, and the charge their immunity puts them to in constant tributes will be found far heavier than the occasional penalties of nonconforming offenders.

Another reason why the magistrate possibly doth more severely tie up the liberty of those of his own profession, and exercise his power in indifferent things especially over them may be because they are most likely to disturb the public peace, the state religion being usually the[139] state trouble, which is not[140] seldom found to arm the subjects against the prince but when he is of the same profession, either because men generally when their fears are removed and have a free exercise of their religion allowed, are apt to grow wanton and know not how to set bounds to their restless spirits if persecution hang not over their heads; they will be ready to advance them too high, and if the fear of losing divert not their thoughts, they will employ them in getting; where nothing checks them, they will be sure to mount still and not stop so long as anything is above them, and those perhaps who under the Turks would be well content to be subjects[141] so they might be Christians will in England scarce digest that condition but be ready to think if the magistrate be their fellow Christian he is their brother too and will hence expect as our author pleads, p. 4,* to be used

* Bagshaw, 1660 (a), p. 4; a passage of which Locke might perhaps have taken greater notice, as his adversary here implicitly endorses the theory of government which he himself is so concerned to elaborate: '*As Christians not his subjects so much as his brethren: and therefore since they have left their natural and voluntarily parted with their civil, they ought not to be entrenched upon in their spiritual freedom.*' Bagshaw's case thus comes to rest upon the 'reasonableness' of toleration—an argument which Locke could meet forcefully on the ground of practicability; cf. his letter MS c. 27, fol. 12, and chapter 1.

THE FIRST TRACT ON GOVERNMENT

rather as brethren than subjects, equals than inferiors. Nor is the subtlety of malicious men wanting to make the magistrate's religion troublesome to him, wherein they will be sure to search out those arguments and spin those consequences (which a different profession could never afford them) which shall lay hold on the actions and, as they will represent them, mal-administrations of the prince. They will offer proofs from Scripture that he is not true to his own profession, that he either superstitiously innovates the worship, or is supinely careless of reformation or tyrannically abridges them of that liberty, which the law of their God, and that doctrine which he cannot deny freely and equally bestows on [p. 31] them, and pretend him as disobedient to the law of God as they will hence take leave to be to his, and at last will arrive at this, if he will not reform what they think amiss, they themselves may, or at last conclude that he cannot be a Christian and a magistrate at once. Thus are the public religions of countries apt by the badness of the professors to become troublesome to the magistrate and dangerous to the peace, if not carefully eyed and directed by a strong and steady hand, whilst underling and tolerated professions are quiet, and the professors content themselves to commend their doctrine by the strictness and sobriety of their lives and are careful not to rend their unity by needless disputes about circumstances and so lay themselves open to the reproach of their enemies; or if any difference creep in, mutual consent closes it, without appealing to force or endeavouring to carve out a reformation with the *sword*, an argument never made use of but when there are hands enough prepared to wield it.*

The remaining part of his discourse is taken up with answers to some objections which they are concerned to defend that first urged them, amongst others he mentions the learned and reverend Mr Hooker and Dr Sanderson,† two such eminent champions of truth that it would be an high presumption[142] in me to take upon me to be their second and adventure to make good their arguments which I am the more unfit to do as having never yet had the

---

* Cf. Latin *Tract*, p. 1.

† 'amongst others'; but Bagshaw, 1660 (*a*), pp. 13–14, mentions no others by name. This is Bagshaw's 'third objection' in a list of four. Locke considers only two of these objections—the two easiest from his own point of view. Bagshaw's first and principal objection is in fact the emotional focus of Locke's whole argument: the argument from 'disorder and confusion'. Locke is surely cheating in passing over Bagshaw's substantial treatment of this view; cf. chapter 1.

opportunity to peruse the writings of the former beyond his preface, and the lectures of the latter at their first appearance in public* I run over with that haste and inadvertency that I could be able to give but a very slender account of their reasonings. Yet[143] I shall take the boldness to say that their argument mentioned by our author is not so slight as he makes of it. Their[144] argument as it is quoted by him stands thus: [*That[145] since things necessary to the* (p. 14) *worship of God be already determined by God, and over them the magistrate hath no power; if likewise he should have no power in indifferent things, then it would follow that in things appertaining to religion, the Christian magistrate would have no power at all. Which they think to be absurd,*†] which well they might that the magistrate should have no power at all, for if you once deny his power in any sort of indifferent things you take it away in them all for they are all of the same nature, and there is no law of God which confines his power to this or that kind of them.‡ But let us see the author's answer:

[*1. That it is no absurdity at all that princes should have no more power in ordering the things of God than God himself hath allowed them. And if God nowhere hath given them such an imposing power they must be content to go without it.*] If they have no imposing power till God by a positive express commission somewhere hath given it them, they will be found to have as little in civil as religious indifferent things and no right of tying up our liberty in either. But that they have a power in both and how they came by it I have shown above. [*But* [p. 32] *in this case where will the Christian magistrate find his warrant?*] In whatever text of Scripture the magistrate's charter for jurisdiction in civil indifferent things is to be found, in the very same or next verse is his warrant for impositions in religious. [*The Scriptures being utterly silent that he is now to take such authority upon him which because the things concern not man but the worship of God had it been thought necessary and fit would certainly not have been omitted.*§] The Scripture speaks very little of polities[146] anywhere (except only the government of the Jews constituted by God himself over which he had a particular care) and God doth nowhere[147] by distinct and particular

---

* Though this was not so long before the writing of Locke's *Tract*. The lectures *De Obligatione Conscientiae*, though delivered in 1647, were not published until December 1659, less than a year before Locke wrote; cf. chapters I and III.

† Bagshaw, 1660 (*a*), p. 14; Bagshaw is in fact quite scrupulous in his account of the views of Hooker and Sanderson; cf. *Hooker, Preface* VIII, 4; bk. III, viii, 6, and Sanderson, 1660, VI, xxvi.　　　　　‡ Cf. Latin *Tract*, p. 14.

§ Bagshaw, 1660 (*a*), p. 14; continuous quoting by Locke.

prescriptions set down rules of governments and bounds to the magistrate's authority, since one form of government was not like to fit all people,* and mankind was by the light of nature and their own conveniencies sufficiently instructed in the necessity of laws and government and a magistrate with power over them,† who is no more to expect a commission from Scripture which shall[148] be the foundation and bounds of his authority in every particular[149] and beyond which he shall have none at all, than a master is to examine by Scripture what power he hath over his servant,‡[150] the light of reason and nature of government itself making evident[151] that in all societies it is unavoidably necessary that the supreme power (wherever seated in one or more) must be still supreme, i.e. have a full and unlimited power over all indifferent things and actions within the bounds of that society.§ Whatever our author saith there[152] 'tis certain there be many particular things necessary and fit now, that are yet omitted in Scripture and are left to be determined by more general rules. Had the questions of paedo-baptism, church government, ordination, excommunication etc. been as hotly disputed in the days of the Apostles as in ours, 'tis very probable we should have had as clear resolutions of those doubts and as positive rules as about eating thing strangled and blood. But the Scripture is very silent in particular questions, the discourses of Christ and his Apostles seldom going beyond the[153] general doctrines of the Messiah or the duties of the moral law, but where either the condition of the persons or their enquiry made it necessary to descend to particulars and possibly had there not some miscarriages sprung up in the Church of Corinth we had never received that command of decency and order, and 'twas their enquiry that occasioned Paul's resolution of those their private doubts, *1 Cor.* c. 7, c. 8. It was not therefore requisite that we should look for the magistrate's commission to be renewed in Scripture who was before even by the law of nature and the very condition[154] of government sufficiently invested with a power over all indifferent actions. Nor can we rationally conclude he hath none

[p. 33] because we cannot find it in the Bible.

* Cf. Latin *Tract*, p. 8, where the same point is made again.

† This is Hooker's theory of the origins of government; Hooker, I, x, I; it is also Locke's a generation later, cf. chapter IV.

‡ There follows a deleted passage in which Locke makes direct use of a 'consent' theory of government, cf. n. 150 and chapter I.

§ Cf. Latin *Tract*, p. 3.

His second answer* is no more but an affirmation that things indifferent cannot be determined which is the question between us and no proofs of it. (p. 15)

[*Lastly it is much more suited to the nature of the Gospel that Christian princes should reform religion rather by the example of their life than the severity of their laws.*†] 1. I answer that it is not easy to be guessed what our author means here by *reformation of religion*. The outward moral acts of virtue and obedience to the second table he makes no part of *religion*, at least in the sense we dispute of, which is the worship of God. Or if he will grant them to be religion and within the compass of our question he will not, I believe, deny the magistrate a power of making laws concerning them, unless instead of pleading for tender consciences he become a patron of hardened and deboshed offenders. And as for the observance of outward ceremonies in the worship (they being in his opinion *either unlawful or useless*), he will readily exclude them from reformation, and how the magistrate's example of life can any way reform except in one of these two is beyond my apprehension. Since *true religion*, i.e. the internal acts of faith and dependence on God, love of him and sorrow for sin, etc.‡ are (as our author says) *like the spirits of wine or subtle essences* I'm sure in this that they cannot be seen and therefore cannot be an example to others. 2. I answer that it is a very good way, for the prince to teach the people the service of God by his own example and 'tis very likely the paths of virtue and religion will be trodden by many when they lead to credit and preferment and the prince will be sure to have a large train of followers which way soever he goes. But all men live not within the influence of the court, nor if they did are all so ingenuous to be thus easily won over to goodness. This is one but not the only means of drawing men to their duty, nor doth it forbid[155] the magistrate the rigour of laws, and the severer applications of his authority where the stubbornness and peevishness of the people will not be otherwise [p. 34] reclaimed.

* Bagshaw, 1660 (*a*), p. 15; the passage meant is: '*It is so far from being an argument for impositions to urge that the thing imposed is indifferent, that there cannot be a stronger argument against them, since it is as requisite to Christian practice that things necessary be held necessary*'; by avoiding this last point Locke escapes having to admit that he has in fact eliminated the whole category of indifferencies; cf. chapter 11.

† Bagshaw, 1660 (*a*), p. 15, and cf. Thomas Collier, 1644, who also concludes with this argument, making this 'the only role the magistrate has in matters of religion'.

‡ Cf. Latin *Tract*, p. 3.

Sir*[156]

In obedience to your commands I here send you my thoughts of that treatise which we not long since discoursed of, which if they convince you of nothing else, yet I am confident will of this,[157] that I can refuse you nothing that is within the reach of my power. I know not what entertainment they will deserve from you, yet I am sure that you have this reason to use them favourably, that they owe their original to you. Let not the errors may appear to you in their perusal, meet with too severe a censure, since I was neither led to them by the beaten track of writers, nor the temptation of interest, but they are, if any, the wanderings of one in pursuit of truth, whose footsteps are not always so clear as to leave us a certain direction or render our mistakes unpardonable, but very often so obscure and intricate that the quickest sighted cannot secure themselves from deviations. This candour I may with justice expect from you since I should never have gone out of my way had not you engaged me in the journey. Whatsoever you shall find in these papers was entertained by me only under the appearance of truth, and I was careful to sequester my thoughts both from books and the times, that they might only attend those arguments that were warranted by reason, without taking any upon trust from the vogue or fashion. My greatest fear is for those places of Scripture that fall in my way, whereof I am very cautious to be an over-confident interpreter, as on the other side I think it too servile wholly to pin my faith upon the not seldom wrested expositions of commentators,[158] whom[159] therefore, in the haste I make to satisfy you[160] I have not been much encouraged to consult on this occasion being only content with that light which the Scripture affords itself, which is commonly the clearest discoverer of its own meaning. I have chose† to draw a great part of my discourse from the supposition of the magistrate's power, derived from, or conveyed to him by, the consent of the people, as a way best suited to those patrons of liberty, and most likely to obviate their objections, the foundation of their plea being usually an opinion of their natural freedom, which they are apt to think too much intrenched upon by impositions in indifferent things. Not that I intend to meddle with that question whether the magis-

---

* This letter is discussed above, chapter 1.

† Cf. *The Preface to the Reader*, where the text of the letter from this point on is reproduced virtually unchanged; and chapter 1.

trate's crown drops down on his head immediately from heaven or be placed there by the hands of his subjects, it being sufficient to my purpose that the supreme magistrate of every nation what way soever created, must necessarily have an absolute and arbitrary power over all the indifferent actions of his people. And if his authority must needs be of so large an extent in the lowest and narrowest way of its original (that can be supposed) when derived [p. 35] from the scanty allowance of the people, who are never forward to part with more of their liberty than needs must, I think it will clearly follow, that if he receive his commission immediately from God the people will have little reason thereupon to think it more confined than if he received it from them until they can produce the charter of their own liberty, or the limitation of the legislator's authority, from the same God that gave it.* Otherwise no doubt, those indifferent things that God doth not forbid or command[161] his vicegerent may, having no other rule to direct his commands than every single person hath for[162] his actions, *viz:* the law of God. And it will be granted that the people have but a poor pretence to liberty in indifferent things in a condition wherein they have no liberty at all, but by the appointment of the great sovereign of heaven and earth are born subjects to the will and pleasure of another. But I shall stop here having taken already too tedious a way to tell you that I am

Sir,

Your most obedient servant
JOHN LOCKE[163]

Pensford 11 Dec.
1660

NOTES

The Preface to the Reader

1 The following eighteen words are inserted in the MS; the version printed by King omits the parenthesis. Above, the MS has *premise*, but elsewhere Locke uses this spelling.

2 *this Majestic* in the MS.

3 The next two sentences as far as *and I believe...* are inserted in the MS.

4 MS Locke e. 7, fol. 36, reads *doth not forbid*.

* Observe that in the *Essay Concerning Toleration* it is the defenders of government *jure divino* whom Locke requires to produce their 'charter'.

First 'Tract'

1 Indifferencys (?).

2 This paragraph to *unalterable condition of society and government* is added on the facing page of the MS. An original opening to the paragraph, *That it is the sole foundation of government and unalterable condition of society* is deleted. In the substituted sentence the words *either a full, entire or limited liberty and so . . .* are deleted after *owner of*; also *which the free* after *to any other.*

3 *native right to his primitive liberty* is the original reading.

4 *if anywhere to be found*, added by Locke.

5 *Excepting* deleted.

6 *My author* substituted for *nobody* and *not* added.

7 *'tis pleaded* added.

8 *line* deleted before *person* above, and *his* substituted for *their.*

9 *thing* in the MS.

10 *he cannot abridge* deleted between *therefore* and *much less.*

11 *of* (?) deleted here and 1° above the line.

12 *ther* deleted.

13 *used* deleted and a second *be* added.

14 *the second and chief* deleted in the MS and the paragraph from *Upon supposition* to *A second reason* added as a substitute opening on the facing page. In the substituted paragraph the following changes are decipherable: after *derived from the people: which I believe nobody that pleads for liberty will . . . deny . . . and reason against*; and after *patrons of freedom: . . . they usually . . .* —both passages deleted.

15 *is* deleted and *will be* added.

16 *more immediate* deleted and *nearer* added.

17 This sentence is marked for deletion by Locke; the word *on* could possibly be *with* in Locke's usual abbreviated form.

18 *undetermined* deleted and *exterior, indifferent* added.

19 *had he enjoined the pictures of Christ or any of the Apostles to have been hung up in their churches* deleted after *place.*

20 *have* added.

21 *these* deleted and *in those that are determined* added on the facing page.

22 *who endeavo*[ured] deleted in MS.

23 *did not* deleted in MS.

24 *in indif-* deleted in MS.

25 *as* added by ed.

26 *incroaching* added in MS.

27 *when they* deleted in MS and the passage from *when they joined* to *Deut. 12, 32* added on the facing page.

28 *determine* deleted in MS and *limit* added.

29 *law* added in MS.
30 *in this place* added.
31 *hypocritical* added.
32 *But* deleted in MS and the passage from *And the reason he gives* to *And if we will observe* is added on the facing page.
33 *be* deleted in MS.
34 *because they* added in MS.
35 *life and* deleted in MS.
36 *it* deleted, *we* added and *where* deleted after *places*.
37 *as men* added in MS.
38 *as traditions* added in MS.
39 *lest* deleted in MS and *such* deleted after *countenance*, below.
40 *ease* deleted in MS.
41 *they had* repeated and deleted in MS.
42 *too* added in MS.
43 *example and* deleted in MS and *and their example too* added after *Apostles*.
44 *formerly* added in MS.
45 *St* added in MS.
46 *the* deleted in MS.
47 *to whom* deleted in MS.
48 *better* added in MS.
49 *Scripture* in MS.
50 *they* deleted in MS; *others* added.
51 *action* deleted in MS, *outward action* substituted.
52 *Indeed* deleted before *imposing*.
53 *But* deleted in MS and *What* added.
54 *begin* deleted in MS.
55 *gov-* deleted before *magistrate*.
56 *some and* deleted before *a great part*.
57 *und-* deleted in MS.
58 *and in gen-* deleted in MS.
59 The rest of this sentence, *the argument* to *rules of worship*, and *Though* are deleted in the MS.
60 *be* deleted in text, *is* added.
61 *that* deleted in MS.
62 *St* added in MS.
63 *but* added in MS.
64 *St* added both times in MS, and the question that follows, *Or in denying his master?*, is inserted on the facing page.
65 *cannot* deleted before *know*.
66 *appointed* deleted in MS.
67 *scarce hence follow* deleted in MS and *be no very good consequence* added.

68 Locke has a stop here, as he does below after *from it* and *duty*. The sense clearly requires commas or semi-colons.

69 The passage that follows from *such traditions* to *any more than tribute* is added on the facing page of the MS. Locke's notation suggests that he wrote this passage after writing the paragraph that follows it, rewrote that paragraph, and then inserted these sentences; see n. 71.

70 *as* added in MS.

71 This whole paragraph to *and not of God's owning* is added on the facing pages of fols. 14–15. It replaces the following passage, which is deleted: [*And Christ leaves two unanswerable arguments which are of equal validity in things of the same nature.*] *But here the things are not of the same nature. There they were determined in the negative, and their imposition was peremptorily forbidden here they are free and indifferent.* [*As first, that this was not a plant of his father's planting*] *whether this plantation as the original hath it, were meant of the Sect or the Doctrine it matters not much.* [*From whence I gather this rule, that when once human inventions become impositions*] *contrary to the declared will of God* [*and lay a necessity upon that which God hath left free*] *and more than once forbidden, his conclusion must stand so or else it will be besides the premises and then he may infer* [*that then we may lawfully reject them as plants of man's setting and not of God's owning*].

72 An ambiguous sign in the MS.

73 Parenthesis added by ed.; cf. n. 71.

74 *thing* in MS.

75 *how a surplice* deleted in MS, and again, after *any*, *surplice* is deleted and *habit* added.

76 *-ly* is repeated here in the MS—possibly a copying mistake; the original phrase was perhaps meant to read *willingly given and acceptable*; *acceptable* is changed to *acceptably*.

77 Part of this word is obscure in the MS.

78 This paragraph, *But our author* to *a freewill offering* is added on the facing page of the MS.

79 *rights* deleted and *rites* added in the MS.

80 *on sunder* in the MS.

81 The remainder of this paragraph, *But the yoke* to *necessary*, is added on the facing page of the MS.

82 *the* is repeated.

83 *bele-* deleted in the MS here.

84 *on* deleted in MS.

85 *converted* deleted in MS and *believers* added.

86 *tacitl-* deleted in MS.

87 *have* deleted before *can*.

88 *yet* deleted before *already*.

89 There is a rather obscure deleted marginal note in the MS here.

I read it as follows: *vd: this being of the Question Act. 15.* A reference in Acts xv. is discussed on the next page.

90 This last sentence is added in the MS.

91 *the* and *of* added in MS.

92 *remarkable* deleted after *very* in the MS.

93 *society* deleted and *public* added.

94 The last six words are added in the MS.

95 The following passage is deleted in the MS here: *for we have no reason to think them any part of the law of Nature, since the practice and doctrine of all the world (bating only the Jews) the usual and best interpreter of that law was wanting bating only the Jews in obedience to their Ceremonial laws and—.* The parenthesis is not deleted but plainly belongs at the point indicated.

96 *Paul and the greatest part of Christians since his time will be found to be scarce of his judgment. Secondly from* is deleted in the MS here; *contrary to* is added.

97 *where* added by ed.

98 *thing* in MS.

99 This sentence *And St Paul* to *1. Cor. 10. 27* is added on the facing page of the MS.

100 *and affirms, v. 4* is deleted here in the MS.

101 *them* deleted in MS.

102 *hath* deleted after *magistrate.*

103 The rest of this sentence from *he might well* to *proved already* is added on the facing page.

104 *should* is added in the MS.

105 *without a necessity appearing to him* is deleted in the MS before *needlessly.*

106 *sape* in the MS.

107 *But the case is far otherwise with the magistrate* deleted in the MS before *However.*

108 *it* in MS.

109 *can* is added in the MS.

110 *those* is added in the MS.

111 *discourse is against* is deleted in the MS after *Apostles.*

112 *fondness to our own opinion* is deleted in the MS after *great; our own conceits* is added and itself deleted; *injury* is added.

113 *indeed* deleted and *truly* added.

114 *quily* in MS.

115 *or unlawful* repeated in the MS and deleted.

116 *enough* deleted in MS here.

117 I have been unable to decipher four or five deleted words here.

118 *These* is deleted here in the MS, which has no para. break.

119 Locke has a new sentence here in the MS.
120 *of* deleted in MS.
121 *too* deleted in MS.
122 *and* added in MS.
123 *knack of* deleted in MS after *got*.
124 *and tender* deleted and restored in MS.
125 *haveing* in the MS; the sense requires this form, however.
126 *sord* in MS.
127 *an other soul* in MS.
128 This word is obscure in the MS.
129 The word after *contrary to* is obliterated in the MS; Bagshaw 1660 (*a*), p. 10, has *Christ*.
130 *Jerusalem* deleted before *Mount Sion* in the MS.
131 *'tis* deleted in the MS after *that*.
132 *viz. religion* added in the MS.
133 *interfering with* deleted and *encroaching on* added.
134 *freedom* deleted in MS before *scruple*.
135 *peace* deleted after *inward*.
136 An undecipherable deletion here in the MS (but the quotation from Bagshaw is continuous).
137 *the true worship* is deleted before *their*.
138 *public* added in MS.
139 *usual ye* in MS.
140 *not* added in MS.
141 *Turks* deleted in MS after *be* and *that* after *so*; *they* added.
142 *presuption* in MS.
143 *that* deleted in MS.
144 (*Viz*) *Their* deleted in MS; *stands* deleted after *it* and *is* added.
145 Brackets added by ed.
146 *government* deleted in MS and *polities*, or *politics*, added.
147 *by them* deleted in MS.
148 *confirm and limit* deleted here in the MS.
149 *and bounds* and *in every particular* are added in the MS.
150 The following passage is deleted here: *it being the consent of parties and not an immediate grant from God that confers it on both, hence it is that one princes* (sic) *hath a different powers* (sic)—*some larger others narrower according to their different constitutions of their countries which could not be were there laid down in Scripture one stand-Charter for them all. Only this I say.* The words *of their countries* and *stand-* are additions.
151 These eleven words, *the light of reason* to *evident*, are added on the facing page of the MS.
152 *'tis certain there* added in MS.
153 *the* is added.

154 *foundation* deleted and *condition* added in MS.

155 *make* deleted before *forbid* and *the magistrate* added after it.

156 Everything that follows is deleted in the MS. Some passages are deleted within the deletion—see the notes below.

157 *at least* deleted here.

158 Some twenty words are added here on the facing page; they appear to be written over an earlier addendum and are only in part legible. I read these words as, *fearing to be too tedious a way...there is no security where...the present...and.*

159 *whom* added in MS.

160 *serve you* deleted in MS.

161 *commanded* in MS.

162 *for* is added in the MS.

163 The address and signature are heavily deleted; the signature and some letters of the address are just legible, however. Gough, 1950, p. 177, reads the latter as *Oxford*, but Locke's usual Oxford address was *Christ Church* or *Ch. Ch.*: for my reasons for preferring to read *Pensford*, see chapter 1.

THE SECOND TRACT ON
GOVERNMENT

———

LATIN TEXT AND
TRANSLATION

SECOND TRACT ON GOVERNMENT: LATIN*

An Magistratus Civilis possit res adiaphoras in divini cultus ritus asciscere, easque† populo imponere? Affirmatur.   MS Locke c. 28, fol. 3

Veritas haec in controversiam hodie deducta, tot iam disputationibus vexata tantis partium iactata odiis, utinam aliquando in quaestione versari desineret et eam in omnium animis quam meretur sedem adepta, securitatem singulis, pacem universis stabilita tandem largiretur, nec defensores diutius posceret sed agnosceret cultores. Et acri nimis animorum, et armorum contentione fessos,‡ libertate et tranquilitate nostra velit nos esse contentos. verum cum mecum in animo reputo quas clades dederit una haec lis; quas inter armatos pariter ac togatos civerit procellas quarum hactenus pene audiuntur murmura, et vixdum omnis componitur tempestatis trepidatio; quum cogito quod raro in publicum prodit nisi tam armorum quam argumentorum stipata satellitio bellicosa nimis quaestio in qua res plerumque verba sequitur nec otiosos et languidos patitur auditores, sed incendit, animat armat et inter se furiosos et infensos committit, videor mihi non in gymnasium et ad umbratilem velitationem sed in arenam et aciem discendere,§ nec tam proponere thesin quam classicum canere. Quotusquisque enim pene est qui in hac re sibi temperare potest, qui sedato animo huiusmodi disputationibus se patitur interesse, nec credat suam rem serio agi summis viribus ne dicam vi et armis propugnandam, quum opinione, vel spe, vel conscientia actis in diversum studiis, hinc nimia licentia religionem pacem et ecclesiam periclitari anxie queruntur, illinc libertatem Evangelii, optimum illud Christianorum privilegium, tyrannide oppressam, conscientiae ius violatum¶ vehementius vociferantur, hinc magistratus contemptus legum violatio, omnia tam sacra quam profana susque deque habita et quicquid libet sibi licere autumant dum

---

* See Editorial Preface, pp. 112–13, for a description of the editorial procedure used in presenting this work and the translation.

† *Eosque* in the MS.

‡ *contentione fractos velit tandem nos libert-*, the original reading, is deleted here.

§ Locke uses vulgar and classical spellings quite arbitrarily and in general I have not tried to standardize his usage.

¶ MS A begins here.

libertatem et conscientiam prae se ferunt, duas illas voces in con-
ciliandis animis mire efficaces,* et† sane horum zelus praefervidus
non raro in populare‡ incendium prorumpit omnia invasurum, qui
temeritatem imperitae et concitatae multitudinis conscientiae
authoritate armare sciunt.§ Huic veritati fidem facit cladibus insig-
[p. 1]¶ nis Germania,‖ et O utinam haec nostra aetas haec regio alias
felicissima peregrinis contenta exemplis, huius rei propriis et
domesticis vulneribus** tam lugubre non daret documentum, nec
in se experire vellet quantas calamitates post se traheret sub specie
libertatis Christianae et religionis grassata libido, quarum sane
recordatio esset admodum molesta nisi consolaretur praesens
fortuna et nova rerum facies et bene compositus ordo, nec aliter
has miserias respicimus quam qui tuti in littore stantes non sine
voluptate contemplantur quos nuper evaserunt undarum tumultus
et inanes minas,†† et cum iam deus O M‡‡ nobis tranquilitatem
restituit non sine miraculorum longa serie sperandam cuius ut
laetior esset adventus effecit proximi temporis discordia.§§
Optandum est,¶¶ neminem tam obstinata fore pervicacia ut novis
in posterum rebus studeat, nec magistratus circa res adiaphoras
detrectabit imperium, sed cum iam deferbuit‖‖ turbidus ille et en-
theus animorum aestus discet aliquando mens sedatior obsequium
civile etiam in rebus adiaphoris divini cultus non inter ultima
religionis Christianae officia numerandum, necque aliud esse usquam nisi in cura parendi auxilium,*** nec aliam spero in posterum
haec controversia pugnam excitabit nisi huiusmodi ludicram quam

---

* This seems the most satisfactory reading of these two words which are altered in
the MS.

† *quorum* deleted here in A.

‡ *populare* added in A.　　　　　　　　§ *norunt armare* in A.

¶ I.e. MS Locke c. 28, fol. 3, but page 1 of the *Tract*. I have given page references
rather than folio references here as previously.

‖ *nec pauciores Gallia hac in re numerat tumultus* is added here in A, and *externis* is
deleted after *utinam*.

** *malis* in A.

†† There are several classical images evoked by this phrase; cf., especially,
Lucretius, *De Rerum Natura*, Bk II, init.

‡‡ *Optimus Maximus.*

§§ The last part of the sentence from *cuius* is added in A.

¶¶ *nemo sperandum est in posterum* in A (deleted) and no stop.

‖‖ *de* for *circa* in this sentence in A, and a stop after *imperium*; *detrectabit* should perhaps be *detrectet*, and the following verb is written as (most probably) *desorbuit* in both
A and B; Cicero uses *absorbeo* in a possible sense for this passage but *defervesco* seems
more likely to be the intention here; *insanus* is deleted in A in favour of *turbidus*.

*** *necque ullam est usquam nisi in cura parendi auxilium* is added in A.

ut melius instituamus acies quodammodo explicanda est, et
termini excutiendi, ut sciamus quid intelligitur hic per magistratum quid per cultum divinum et quid per res adiaphoras.*

1° Per magistratum† hic intelligimus illum qui curam gerit communi-
tatis qui summum in reliquos omnes obtinet imperium, et cui
denique condendarum abrogandarumque legum delegata est
potestas, hoc enim summum est illud imperii ius in quo uno consistit vis illa magistratus qua caeteros regit et moderatur et pro
libitu res civiles, et quoquo modo‡ ad bonum publicum popu-
lumque in pace et concordia continendum ordinat et disponit, nec
opus est singula enumerare imperii insignia, et iura dicta regalia,
qualia sunt ultima provocatio, ius vitae et necis, belli et pacis
monetae procudendae authoritas, vectigalia, tributa, et id genus
multa§ quum certum sit omnia haec potestatem legislativam sequi,
et ab illa aliter in hac aliter in illa republica pro more gentis posse
determinari, nec huius praeterea loci est rerum publicarum formas
recensere, gubernantium numerum definire, id demum nobis
sufficit et pro rata habemus ut ille dicatur magistratus sive coetus [p. 2]
quis velit sive monarcha¶ sit qui iure suo potest leges in subditos
ferre et sancire.

2° Cultus divinus varias habet significationes:

1° Aliqui sunt quibus idem sonat cum religione, et utramque vocem
in lata admodum significatione sumunt‖ pro omni illo obsequio
quod legibus divinis debemus, et quicquid aliquo modo obligat
conscientiam, quicquid iussi a deo praestamus id omne religionem**
et partem divini cultus (minus tamen proprie) dicunt esse, adeo ut
omnes pene actiones humanae in cultum divinum transirent,
deumque edendo bibendo dormiendo, quum in his aliqua potest
esse rectitudo,†† coleremus. Ita sane in hoc verborum sensu nemo,
puto, negabit magistratum res adiaphoras posse in cultum dei

---

* The organization of this sentence is much changed between A and B; the object
of the main clause is plural in A.

† This section is headed *Magistratus* in the margin of A.

‡ *aliquomodo* is deleted in A.

§ *et huiusmodi non pauca* in A; and *regnantium* for *gubernantium* at the end of the
sentence.

¶ *sive coetus sit sive monarcha* in A; *quis velit* is enigmatic here unless some such
parenthesis as that offered in the translation was intended.

‖ *utrumque premunt* for this clause in A.

** *totum id religionem* in A.

†† *quoquo peccare possimus* deleted in A, then *deum coleremus* and *sed* and *adeo ut*
deleted and replaced by *ita sane*.

asciscere* et subditis imponere, quamvis hoc concesso non adeo
fortasse manifestum erit cur idem ius in reliquo† rerum divinarum
apparatu et publicis coetibus necessario negaretur, quum utrimque eadem sit ratio ἀδιαφορίας‡ quum nullubi his rebus magistratus potestatem exclusit, summus legislator deus, sed hac de re
plura in sequentibus.

2° Magis proprie sumitur cultus divinus pro internarum virtutum
actionibus quarum omnium obiectum est deus ut amor dei reveren-
tia timor fides Etc.§ Hic est internus ille animi cultus quem poscit
deus, in quo vis et anima religionis consistit, quo ablato caetera
omnia ad cultum divinum spectantia provocant deum potius quam
conciliant nec magis gratum numini sacrificium praestant quam
depraedatarum bestiarum lacera cadavera, et hinc est quod deus
tam frequenter tamque unice cor et spiritum sibi vendicat¶ corda
et intima pectoris penetralia templa vocat suo cultui dicata, et
animum poscit sibi obsequentem et quasi unicum quem respicit
cultorem, hic autem cultus tacitus omnino et secretus, ab oculis et
observatione hominum remotissimus, nec legibus humanis sub-
iicitur nec subiici quidem potest, unus est cordium scrutator deus,
qui intimos animi rimatur recessus qui solus internas mentis cogi-
tationes aut cognoscere‖ potest aut de eis sententiam ferre.

3° Externae religionis actiones cultus divinus etiam dicuntur,** cum
deus hominem e corpore uti ex anima constare voluit, quorum
altero sibi soli servire iubet, altero hominibus†† inter ipsos societatem et coniunctionem conciliavit, non enim sine interventu et
auxilio corporis homines animi sui sensa proferre‡‡ et mutua bene-
volentia frui possunt, deus autem utriusque postulat obsequium,
et exigit ab utroque quod solvi§§ potest tributum, cumque honorem
sibi in terris et nomen quaerit, non tacito illo et quasi furtivo
solummodo cultu contentus est, cultores suos nomen palam pro-
fiteri voluit quorum exemplis edocti reliqui mortales ad cultum et
[p. 3] reverentiam divini numinis incitarentur; ideoque externos illos

* *transferre* in A, and the same deleted in B.
† *reliquis et publicis rebus* in A.
‡ *necessario magistratui* deleted in A and B and no ἀδιαφορίας in A.
§ *timor, fides, spes* in A, and *spes* deleted in B.
¶ *vindicat* ?; but Locke's spelling is clear in both MSS.
‖ *agnoscere* in A.
** The para. begins *Dico tertius quod cum deus*... etc. in A.
†† *ex corpore uti et anima*, above and ...*servire postulat, altero homines*... in A.
‡‡ The phrase following is *et in vicem patefacere possunt* in A.
§§ *quod solui posset ab utroque* in A.

postulat actus quibus internus ille mentis cultus exprimitur imo et augetur* quales sunt praecationes publicae, gratiarum actiones, psalmodiae, sacramentorum participatio,† verbi divini auditio, quibus omnibus aut animi amorem fidem et obsequium in praesentiarum testatum facimus vel in futurum iuvamus,‡ et hic externus dicitur cultus qui a deo in lege sua passim mandatur quem ex praescripto praestare debemus nec in hunc ius aliquod obtinet magistratus quum a nullo nisi ipso legislatore deo mutari possit.

4° Cum nullae sint actiones quarum non multae sunt circumstantiae quae continuo eas comitantur§ cuius modi sunt Tempus, Locus, Habitus, Gestus, etc., cultus etiam divinus hoc carere non potest famulitio, hae igitur actionum appendices propter connexionem quam cum rebus divinis habent et quia solemnibus et publicis cultus religiosi actionibus semper et ubique aliquo modo inserviunt, itaque haec etiam cultus divinus vulgo audiunt et ritus dicuntur, hos autem ritus deus sapientissimus et ubique benignus magistratus prudentiae permisit¶ et in eius‖ qui imperium obtinuit et ecclesiae gubernandae ius habet** manus tradidit pro arbitrio, prout temporum et morum ratio, et ecclesiae utilitas†† postularet in mutandos abolendos renovandos vel quo quo modo iniungendos. Qui dummodo praecepta eius de vero et spirituali cultu sarta tecta habentur, dum religionis substantialia salva sint, caetera ecclesiis ipsis hoc est earum rectoribus permisit prout visum fuerit instituenda, una hac lege atque omine scilicet ut honestati ordini et decori stud[e]atur, quia diversis in locis, diversimode se habent, nec certa in lege divina norma et regula praescribi poterat, quae doceret, quid ubique gentium deceret, quidve minus. Deus igitur clementissimus quo minus impedita variis gentibus esset ad Christianam religionem transitio, et ut facilior in evangelio, ad religionem novam, et ad Christum pateret aditus, doctrinam Christianam solum animis et fide amplectendam‡‡ et cultum illum verum in coetibus et externis actionibus praestandum proposuit

---

* *imo et augetur* added in A.
† *sacramenta et conciones* in A.
‡ *et testatum facimus et in futurum iuvamus, et hic*... was the original form in A.
§ *circumstantiae omnino necessariae*... in A.
¶ *igitur*...*deus sapientissimus magistratui permisit* in A.
‖ *eorum* in A.
** *et ecclesiae gubernandae ius habet* added in A, and *tradidit* is at the end of the sentence.
†† *ecclesiae exigentia* in A.
‡‡ *amplectendam exegit* in A, and the following clause seems to be added in B.

non autem tam difficile obsequium a tyronibus expectavit ut illico omnes gentis suae mores ritusque deponerent, adeo plerumque gratos, adeo longo usu charos et educatione ac opinione venerandos ut fortunas, libertatem vitam et omnia plerisque citius quam harum aestimationem usumque extorquebis. Quam inviti, quam aegre, conversi ad Christianismum Judaei onerosam illam et gravem demiserunt ceremoniarum pompam gentili consuetudine iam familiarem, nec iugum cervicibus suis grave, a Christo emancipati excuti voluerunt. Fando nuper audivimus urbem inter Sinenses* in oriente positam, obsidione longa ad deditionem†

[p. 4] tandem coactam hostiles copias apertis portis admisisse,‡ incolasque omnes se triumphantis victoris voluntati permisisse, cumque se, uxores, familias, libertatem, opes, omnia denique tam sacra quam profana hosti in manus tradidissent, ubi capilli cincinnum quem in capite, more gentis alebant detondere§ iuberentur, resumptis armis usque dum omnes caesi¶ ad internecionem animose demicarunt, et qui hostibus capita sua venalia tradi paterentur, illis in crinem patrio ritu gestum‖ vel minimum licere ferre non poterant, adeo ut vilissima et nullius momenti res** etiam ipsa corporis excrementa opinione omnium et gentili consuetudine quasi consecrata vitae ipsi†† et solidis naturae bonis facile praeferantur. Et sane qui motus nostros civiles secum reputare velit, fatebitur aliquando fortasse non gravioribus de causis etiam apud nos, tanta atrocitate, tanta animorum contentione ab aliquibus pugnatum fuisse, sed rursus in viam. Hi sane ritus hae actionum circumstantiae tam contrario sunt‡‡ et vario in usu, apud omnes gentes, ut frustra expectares, frustra in Evangelio quaereres, unam eandemque venustatis normam.§§ non facile persuaderes orientis incolae vel sectae mahumedanae devoto,¶¶ ut fidem amplecteretur Christiani aperto capite deum suum (et ut ille putaret) contumeliose colentis, non levius videretur piaculum, insolens apud illos consuetudo quam apud nos tecto capite precari, nemo sane transitionem meditaretur in religionem ritibus ridiculam, quales

---

* No *inter Sinenses* in A. † *ditionem* in A.
‡ *accepisse* in A. § *detrudere* in A.
¶ *ad omnium*... the original version deleted in A.
‖ *suam* for *in patrio ritu gestum* in A.
** *adeo ut vel minima res*... in A. †† *ipsae* in A.
‡‡ *hae...circumstantiae...contrariae*... in A, and *frustra a deo*.
§§ *decoris normam* in A.
¶¶ *vel...devoto* not in A and *religionem* for *fidem*.

omnes sunt omnium gentium invicem mores; deus igitur humanae
imbecilitati consulens cultum suum pro more uti ferret hominum
sententia externis ritibus ornandum in medio* reliquit, nec magis
ex his cultores suos quam rex subditos fidemque et obsequium
eorum ex corporis habitu aut vestium ornatu aestimat, nec fideles
magis aut Christiani aut cives habendi sunt qui negligentius aut
vilius ornantur. Id vero omnibus constare videtur magistratum†
iudicem esse quid sit ordo, quid sit quod deceat, eumque solum
pulchritudinem et venustatem posse definire.‡ nec sane (quicquid
in contrarium nonnulli aggerunt) hanc ego minimam Christianae
libertatis partem arbitror quod liceat magistratui eodem tempore et
paci publicae et religionis incremento et magestati consulere
iisdemque legibus utrique providere.§ Haec de cultu divino dicta
sint. Proximo explicemus¶ quid hic intelligendum est cum dicitur
potest subditis imponere inter Iuris consultos axioma est‖ id possumus quod iure possumus, his autem quaestionis nostrae terminis
duo significari** puto, 1° Magistratus ius et legitimam potes-
tatem†† 2° Subditorum obligationem i.e. quid magistratus potest
sine culpa sua, et quid potest cum obligatione subditorum quae
ut clarius elucescant una et altera praemittenda est destinctio.

1° In magistratus sanctionibus duplex potestas observari potest
quam liceat mihi appellare potestatem materiae et potestatem
praeceptionis, obiecti, et actus: 1° potestas materiae quando res
ipsa quae iubetur‡‡ licita est et adiaphora nec praecepto divino§§ [p. 5]
contraria, 2° potestas praeceptionis est quando ipsa praeceptio
licita est nam et in rebus liberis iubendis peccare potest magi-
stratus¶¶ nec ei licet omnia libera et adiaphora restringere et legum
finibus concludere‖‖ et populo imponere, cum vero magistratus

---

* No *in medio* in A. Above, *pro more* seems more likely in A, *promere* cancelled in B.
† *magistratum* replaces *authoritatem publicam* in B.
‡ The two sentences from *aestimat* not in A.
§ The para. ends here in A, with a marginal note, *hic inferenda quae sequuntur ad notam (i) pag: 213*. A then continues as B, fol. 6, line 27, *q.v.* The bracket opened in B after *sane* is not closed before *hanc*.
¶ *ultimo explicare oportet* in A.
‖ *posset* for *potest* in A, and *regula* for *axioma*.   ** *intendi* in A.
†† *legitima potestas 2 Subditorum obligatio* in A, and the following clause to *quae ut clarius* is added in A.
‡‡ *considerari* deleted for *observari* and *praecipitur* for *iubetur* in B.
§§ *dei praeceptis* in A.
¶¶ *et iniusta iniusta [sic] potest esse lex* is deleted in A, which also has *lex* for *magistratus* in B.
‖‖ This phrase not in A.

ideo populo praeponitur et praesidet ut bono publico et saluti communi prospiciat, ideo clavum tenet ut in portum non in scopulum navem dirigat, huius potestatis regula a fine, vel intentione Legislatoris desumenda est, adeo ut id magistratus potest imponere quod saluti* rei publicae conducere arbitratur id vero non potest imponere (hoc est) sine peccato, quod huic fini inservire et subordinari non putat.

2° De obligatione subditorum sciendum est† potestatem magistratus aliam esse directivam aliam coercivam, cui in subditis respondet duplex obligatio, 1° obligatio ad agendum, 2° obligatio si ita dicam ad patiendum sive ut vulgo dicitur obedientia activa et passiva.‡ His praemissis dico:

1° Obligatur subditus ad obedientiam passivam in quacumque magistratus sanctione sive iusta sive iniusta, nec quavis de causa licet privato vi et armis magistratus mandatis resistere, si vero materia sit illicita magistratus iubendo peccat.

2° Dico, si lex licita sit tam materia quam praeceptione, magistratus iure sancire potest et subditus ad omnimodam obedientiam praestandam tam activam quam passivam obligatur.

3° Dico, si lex sit licita materia praeceptione vero et intentione illicita, scilicet non in bonum publicum directa sed privatum, nempe cum magistratus aut crudelitati aut avaritiae aut vanitatae§ suae morem gerens legem fert ideo solum ut ditescat ut insultet ut sibi placeat, huiusmodi inquam lex magistratum quidem reum facit et tribunali divino obnoxium, nihilominus subditum ad obedientiam etiam activam obligat, quia in materia licita non legislatoris intentio quae cognosci non potest sed voluntas, quae obligationem inducit, regula est obedientiae.

Restat ultimo¶ ut de rebus adiaphoris verba faciamus et quae sint, cum de his non minima lis sit, statuamus. Dicuntur autem res adiaphorae respectu bonitatis et malitiae moralis;‖ ita ut omnes res quae nec bonae nec malae sint moraliter dici adiaphoras.**

---

* *saluti populi* in A.
† *dicendum est* in A, and then *cui respondet in subdito* below.
‡ *uti dicitur* in A. § No *nempe* in A, and *vanitati* here.
¶ In A this follows the discussion of divine worship which ends on fol. 7 (p. 5, above) of B. In A the paragraphs which intervene in B are on p. 213 of the MS. At the end of them Locke has a reference back to p. 227 and another to 'pag. 6', of MS B, presumably.
‖ *malitiae naturalis* in A deleted.
** *plane adiaphoras* in A and Locke has a long miscopying in B deleted.

quum vero morales actiones supponunt legem boni et mali
normam, ad quam vitam actionesque nostras exigere et probare
debemus, certum enim est, si nulla daretur lex omnes res actionesque
esse plane adiaphoras et indifferentes ut pro arbitrio cuiusque vel
fieri vel omitti potuissent: ut igitur res adiaphorae plenius innotes-
cant legum aliqua habenda ratio, cuius generalissima[m] natura[m]*
ita describit doctissimus Hooker l. 1. c. 2, quicquid assignat
unicuique rei genus qui[c]quid vim et potentiam moderatur,
quicquid praescribit et modum et mensuram operandi, id legem
dicimus,† apud authores occurrunt legis definitiones voce non [p. 6]
re discrepantes, uti et multiplices divisiones et destinctiones,‡
verbi gratia in naturalem et positivam divinam et humanam
civilem et ecclesiasticam etc., quibus omissis mihi in praesentiarum
novam viam insistenti liceat legem dividere: in Divinam sive
Moralem, Politicam sive humanam, Fraternam sive charitatis, et
Monasticam sive privatam quae destinctio etiamsi fortassis minus
usitata fuerit,§ et minus quam par est accurata ad praesentem
tamen causam magis fortassis accomoda¶ et in explicandis rebus
adiaphoris non plane inutilis,‖ haec legum destinctio ab authoribus
praecipue desumitur divinam enim eam vocamus** quae a deo,
humana quae ab homine potestatem habente†† lata est, et hi legum
authores potestate legibus ipsis et subditis quibus imperant
superiores sunt. lex fraterna vel charitatis authorem etiam agnoscit
deum, sed occasio obligationis a Christiano quovis aequali vel
forte inferiore‡‡ oriri potest ac solet, ultimae legis quam privatam
dicimus author est privatus quispiam, qui nec superior est se ipso
legi isti obnoxio nec in latam de se legem authoritatem habet ut
rescindat. Verum horum terminorum ratio ex sequentibus clarius
elucescet.§§

* *generalissimam natura* in A.

† *sive ut venerandus Epis: Lincolnensis definit est regula agendi subdito a superiore potes-*
tatem habente imposita, aliae passim follows here in both A and B but is deleted in B.

‡ Locke uses this word in this form three times on this page alone; his spelling is
clear. *Wase* gives *distinctio*.

§ A has *ego alia contentus* deleted after *quibus omissis,* and some minor changes in
word order at the end of this passage.

¶ Locke has one *m* in both MSS. *Wase* gives *accommodus*.

‖ The para. ends here in A; the last sentences are added opposite.

** *a legum authoribus* deleted in A, which has no *praecipue*.

†† *authoritatem habente* in A; see ch. 1, above.

‡‡ *aequali vel inferiori* in A.

§§ *quid sibi volunt hi termini ex sequentibus pateret* in A, and *constabit* deleted for
elucescet in B.

1° Lex divina illa est, quae a deo hominibus tradita, illis regula et norma vivendi est, quae prout vel lumine rationis naturali et insito mortalibus innotescit, vel supernaturali revelatione declarata promulgatur* rursus dividitur in naturalem et positivam quae utraque cum eadem prorsus sit re et materia, solum promulgationis modo et praeceptorum perspicuitate differant in vicem, ego utramque eadem appellatione moralem dico, haec enim magna illa recti iustique norma est et fundamentum aeternum omnis bonitatis et malitiae moralis, quae etiam in rebus adiaphoris interventu inferioris legis reperiri possit.† quicquid igitur vel vetando vel iubendo attigerit haec lex semper et ubique necessario bonum aut malum est reliquae res omnes quae inter huius legis limites non coercentur, liberi sunt usus et natura sua adiaphorae.

2° Lex humana‡ illa est quae sancitur ab aliquo imperium et ius in alios obtinente, imo mandatum aliquod superioris in suum inferiorem in quem legitimam habet potestatem, velut parentum in liberos, domini in servum, sub nomine legis humanae venire potest et obedientiam requirit, quamquam decreta publica communitatum a magistratu sancita quum praecipua sunt, et privata iura vel tollant vel confirmant vel mutant pro libitu, hic praecipue sub nomine legis humanae intelligi volumus,§ propria materia sunt res adiaphorae quae superioris, scilicet divinae legis finibus non concluduntur¶ nec adeo restrictae et determinatae sunt, licet enim magistratus furtum prohibere castitatem iubere possit actum tamen agere nec tam novam legem ferre‖ quam veterem promul-

[p. 7] gare et inculcare videtur, huiusmodi enim res vel illo tacente necessariae sunt et subditorum conscientias obligant, verum cum magistratui a deo societatis cura demandatur, nec infinita legum multitudine omnia mala reipublicae eventura praecaveri poterant** nec eadem instituta populo semper esse utilia deus res multas indifferentes legibus suis solutas magistratui vicario suo†† permisit quasi utilem gubernandi populi materiem, quae prout usus postularet vel iuberentur vel vetarentur et earum prudente moderatione saluti reipublicae prospiceretur.

* *supernaturali revelatione se vel dei ipsius vel filii vel prophetarum voce declarata* in A.
† *appellatione divin-* deleted above in A and a comma here.
‡ *lex humana sive civilis* in A and deleted in B.
§ *praecipue intelligi volumus harum legum* in A.
¶ *scilicet divinae legis cancellis nondum definitae aut restrictae* in A.
‖ *sancire* in A.   ** *possint* in A.
†† No *vicario suo* in A.

194

3° Lex fraterna* vel charitatis dicta ea est qua libertas nostra inter angustiores adhuc cancellos coercetur, nec liberum rerum tam divina quam civili lege permissarum usum habemus, scilicet quum frater infirmus in nos nullam potestatem habens, libertatem tamen nostram in rebus adiaphoris et a deo et a magistratu concessam suo quodam iure restringere potest, et efficere ut id nobis quoad hic et nunc (uti loquuntur) non liceat quod alteri et alias plane liceret,† haec scandali lex vulgo audit, cui paremus‡ cum Christiani cuiusvis libertatis suae non bene conscii saluti et innocentiae consulentes, ea coram uti libertate in licitis nolumus, qua forte ille libertatis Christianae non bene gnarus nostro exemplo in fraudem inductus id perpetrat quod sibi minus licere persuasum habet et ita criminis se aligat, v[erbi] g[ratia] ἰδολυθυλα edere Christianis licitum erat nec prohibuit ulla vel divina vel humana lex, res proinde erat adiaphora et plane licita, cum autem multi erant huius libertatis ignari et ut loquitur Ap[ostolus] Paulus ad Cor[intios] c. 8. v. 7 et sequentibus§ ubi etiam monet ut a liberis abstineamus ne forte fratri offendiculo simus — cuius praecepti summa huc demum redit, scilicet, rebus adiaphoris et omnino¶ licitis abstinendum esse si metus sit ne ea libertate offendatur frater, hoc est, non ne irascatur, vel aegre ferat vel indignatur quod alter peccat vel peccare videtur, sed ne nostro exemplo id ipse faciat, quod illi non licet, quia ipse sibi non licere arbitratur.‖

4° Praeter iam dictas leges altera restat Monastica sive privata dicta, quam homo sibi imponit et res adhuc adiaphoras et prioribus legibus solutas superinducta nova obligatione necessarias reddit** et haec duplex est vel conscientiae vel pacti,†† altera a judicio altera

---

* *tertia lex* in A.

† This example from *scilicet quum frater infirmus*... above is set as an addition on the facing page of MS A; the verb is *cohibere*.

‡ *cui obedientiam praestamus* in A.

§ *cum igitur multi erant*... etc. in A and *Divus Paulus*, and the text is then quoted, *non in omnibus est ea cognitio nonnulli enim cum conscientia Idoli usque ad hoc tempus ut Idolis immolatum edunt et conscientia eorum infirma cum sit inquiratur qua propter monet ut abstineamus quamvis esca nos deo non commendat* i.e. *plane adiaphora est, sed videte inquit, v. 9, ne quo modo facultas illa vestra imperigendi causa sit infirmis et enim si quis viderit te*, etc.; the text of A then continues *cuius praecepti*, etc., as in B below; the — in B after *offendiculo simus* is presumably for this passage of quotation.

¶ *plane licitis* in A.

‖ *et hoc dici potest lex scandali* ends this para. in A.

** *facit* in A.

†† The order is reversed in A; thus *duplex est vel pacti vel conscientiae, altera a voluntate, altera a judicio*...; and see next note.

a voluntate profecta,* conscientiae legem vocamus ultimum illud intellectus practici de quacunque propositionis moralis de rebus agendis veritate iudicium, nec enim sufficit ut res sua natura adiaphora sit nisi id nobis persuasum fuerit, Deus pectoribus lumen naturale indidit et legislatorem quasi domesticum nobis semper adesse voluit cuius edicta transgredi ne latum quidem unguem liceret, adeo ut libertas nostra in rebus adiaphoris parum satibilis† sit et cum opinione cuiusque coniuncta, ut certum sit eam vere [p. 8] nobis libertatem deesse, quam (quam) nos non habere putamus, huc facit illud praeceptum Apostoli ad Rom[anos] c. 14, v. 5, unusquisque in animo suo plane certus esto, et ver. 14, novi et persuasum habeo per dominum Jesum nihil esse impurum per se (de esculentis loquitur)‡ sed ei qui reputat aliquid esse impurum id ei impurum esse, et v. 23, qui vero dubitat si ederit condemnatus est quoniam non edit ex fide quicquid vero ex fide non est peccatum est, fides haec nihil aliud est quam libertatis suae certa opinio uti ex contextu patet.§ Altera lex privata a voluntate dependens pactum est quod cum deo vel cum vicino inimus, prius peculiari nomine votum dicitur quale fuit istud Jacobi Geneseos c. 28. Jacobus vovit votum dicendo, quum fuerit deus mecum et servaverit me in via ista qua ego profecturus sum dederitque mihi panem ad comedendum et vestimentum ad induendum, tum haec strues lapidum quam disposui in statuam erit domus dei et quicquid dederis mihi eius decimas sum omnino daturus tibi. voti obligationem videre est Deuteron: c. 23. vv. 21, 22, si voveris votum

---

* The text of A is here marked *Postponatur* and then continues, *votum est cum homo modo deus inceptum hoc vel illud secundet, vel alia quacunque de causa spondet hoc vel illud se facturum quod cum alias ille integrum liberumque omnino esset voti iam damnatus sit necessarium sic Jacobus Gen. c. 28...* and then as in B, fol. 9 (p. 7), l. 9, as far as *daturus tibi* and then, *Deutr.* XXIII *v. 21, 22...* and as in B again to *erit in te peccatum*; and A then continues, *quod prodiit elabiis tuis observato ut facias quem admodum voveris Jehova deo tuo voluntariam oblationem quod dixeris ore tuo.* [i.e. *v.* 23] *ex quibus efficitur quem vis posse res adiaphoras quas praedictarum legum nulla iusserit sibi ipsi imponere et libertatem suam sibimet adimere. sic Nazareus omnibus diebus voti sui et nulla re quae sit ex vite vinifera vel ipsis nucleis acinorum et ante comedere debuit, et alias plures res plane adiaphoras ac reliquo populo licitas usurpare fas erat. uti patet Numerorum, c. 6* [i.e. *vv.* 3–4] *huc ennumerari potest pactorum et promissorum obligatio quorum etiam uti votum libertatem in adiaphoris tollet, eo solum inter se differunt quod in votis deo aliquid promittimus promissionibus cum homine pacificeremur, utriusque libertas nostra nostri iuris est quam vel amittere vel servare pro libitu possimus. Altera lex privata illa est quam conscientiae legem vocamus...* and then as in B, fol. 10 (p. 8), l. 32.

† *evanida est et parum stabilis* in A; *evanida est* deleted in B, and *stabilis* is obviously intended here.　　　　‡ *eduliis* for *esculentis* in A.

§ *e contextu patet* in A; and the rest of this para. is missing in A.

Jehovae deo tuo ne differto solvere illud, nam omnia reposceret
illud deus tuus abs te et esset in te peccatum quod si abstinueris
a vovendo non erit in te peccatum, et dicitur ibi voluntaria oblatio.
promissiones itidem homines inter ipsos obliga[n]t, utrimque
libertas nostra nostri iuris est, quam vel exuere* vel servare pro
libitu possimus. His ita positis

1° Dico, Omnes has leges respectu obligationis esse plane divinas,
hoc est, nullam aliam legem directe et per se obligare hominum
conscientias praeter divinam cum aliae non virtute propria et
innata ennergia† obligant homines sed virtute alicuius divini
praecepti in quo fundantur obligare nec alia de causa magistratibus
parere tenemur nisi quia iussit dominus dicens omnis anima
potestatibus supereminentibus subiecta esto, et necesse est subiici
non solum propter iram sed etiam propter conscientiam.

2° Dico, Leges humanas aliasque modo enumeratas excepta una
divina rerum adiaphorarum non mutare naturam, adeo ut harum
legum authoritate fiant ex indifferentibus omnino et ex se
necessaria sed quoad nos tantum, quoad hic et nunc et respectu
obligationis quam pro tempore induxerit novum et humanum
praeceptum, a quo obedire, facere vel abstinere tenemur, abolita
vero illa lege vel quovis modo cessante nos libertati immutata
re restituimur.

3° Dico, Talem inter leges has esse subordinationem ut inferior
superioris authoritatem aut obligationem tollere aut rescindere
nullo modo possit, haec enim esset inverso rerum ordine dominum
servo subiicere, nec in mundo imperium et regimen stabilire sed
anarchiam, nec alium agnoscere Legislatorem quam quemvis e
plebe infimum et ignarum.‡ A tribunali divino ad humanum
provocare non licet nec edicta magistratus irrita§ reddere potest [p. 9]
subditi votum aut conscientiae privatus error, hoc enim concesso,
nusquam stat disciplina, pereunt iura omnia, evanescit ex ter-
rarum orbe omnis authoritas et turbato pulchro rerum ordine et
soluta regiminis compage¶ sibi Legislator sibi quisque deus esset.

4° Et ultimo dico, quod res adiaphorae omnes superioris legis sunt
obiectum et materia inferioris et authoritatem uniuscuiusque,

---

* *exuere* replaces *restringere* in B.

† *vi sua et innata energia* in A; *Wase* gives *energia*; in the next phrase A has *divini alicuius.*

‡ *a plebe vilissimum et ignarum* in A, and deleted in B; perhaps *a plebe* in B.

§ *rescindere potest* without *irrita* and *nusquam stat disciplina* (below) in A.

¶ *evanescit et rerum natura omnis authoritas et eversa rerum compage...,* etc. in A.

imperium et ius habere in omne illud quod lege superiore non omnino praescribitur quaeque in aequilibrio quasi relicta* nec huc nec illuc in bonum aut malum inclinant, a proxima et subordinata potestate in utramvis familiam adoptari et adscisci possunt, ubi enim terminat se divina lex ibi incipit magistratus authoritas, et totum illud indeterminatum et adiaphorum illius iuris factum potestati civili subiicitur, ubi cessant reipublicae edicta locum invenit scandali lex, his demum omnibus tacentibus conscientiae et voti audiuntur edicta[†] nec quicquam est legibus superioribus solutum[‡] quod privatus quisque suae libertatis dominus sibimet ipsi vel opinione vel voto vel pacto facere non possit necessarium[§] et sane mirandum est qua de causa illi ipsi qui in reliquis omnibus hanc potestatis ordinem et latitudinem libenter admittunt[¶] soli magistratui et civili[||] authoritati negatum volunt, si modo publicam privatae potestatem praeferendam censent, et imperium aliquod et politicam societatem inter homines esse aut posse aut debere. Hi praeter[**] dei omnipotentis summum illud imperium reliquas etiam modo enumeratas leges minime dubitant,[††] scandali, conscientiae, voti, pacti, in rebus adiaphoris determinandis limitandisque quantumvis absolutam magnamque facile agnoscunt authoritatem, magistratus vero nihili homuncionis et praecaria,[‡‡] non (uti loquitur sacra pagina) a deo ordinata potestate imperantis ius nullum in rebus adiaphoris saltem ad cultum dei pertinentibus, esse contendunt[§§] contrariam autem sententiam uti ex legum praedictarum analogia et subordinatione ut ex Apostoli[¶¶] praeceptis ubi omnem animam potestatibus supereminentibus subiectam esse iubet hoc in loco confirmari niteremur, uti etiam ex Ep[istola] Sancti Petri c. 2, v. 13, proinde subiecti estote cuivis humanae ordinationi propter dominum sive regi supereminenti aliquid asstruere liceret.[||||] Ex quibus pateret, in rebus adiaphoris

---

* *quasi relinquuntur* in A. † *leges* in A.
‡ *legibus istis* in A.
§ *quam iuris vim et latitudinem qui in omnibus aliis* deleted in A.
¶ *et sane miror. . .latitudinem facile concedunt* in A.
|| No *civili authoritati* in A, and *authoritatem* below for *potestatem*.
** *omnes praeter* in A; *omnes* deleted in B.
†† *enumeratas leges fatentur et agnoscunt* in A.
‡‡ *praecaria potestate* in A, and *constituta* for *ordinata*.
§§ *saltem ad cultum dei pertinentibus* is added in A.
¶¶ *contrariam autem sententiam nostramque thesin hoc in loco confirmare niteremur, ex Apostoli praeceptis. . .,* etc., in A.
|||| *aliquid asstruere liceret* not in A, and *ex quibus patet* follows.

aliquam magistratum habere potestatem, quia ubi requiritur obedientia et subiectio* ibi necesse est esse imperium, necque subiici quis potest nisi aliqua sit superior persona authoritate publica praedita. Quae uti aliqui volunt† non solum res ex lege divina prius bona vel mala subditis imponere potest sed res etiam adiaphoras quod inde manifestum est 1° quia Apostolus illic Magistratui obsequium praestare iubet non deo. Et si tantum dei mandata repetere deberet et populo praeco potius quam legislator iussa divina praelegere et inculcare, non videtur supereminentior [p. 10] magistratus potestas quam privati cuiusvis, quum lex divina eandem obtinet vim et obligandi rationem sive e principis sive e subditi ore prolata, nec tam imperat alteruter quam docet. 2° quia subi[i]ci iubet propter conscientiam, quod frustra adiiceretur nisi in rebus adiaphoris aliquam haberet magistratus potestatem nemo enim Christianorum dubitare poterat rebus necessariis etiam vel tacente magistratu conscientiam obligare quia ideo tantum sunt necessaria quod‡ conscientiam obligant, intelligi igitur hic aliquid debet quod ex praecepto supereminentioris potestatis obligat quod nihil aliud potest esse quam res adiaphora.§ 3° quia res adiaphoras in exemplum vocat Apostolus, tributum inquit cui debetur tributum, cum certum sit quod nisi imperante magistratu nullum debetur tributum, et pecuniae ius et proprietas omnino libera est, et cuique vel opes suas servare, vel cuiquam possidendas donare et quasi tran[s]ferre, et an nostrae sint vel alienae prorsus indifferens est.¶ Sed quorsum haec! Dicat aliquis, quis negat magistratus in rebus adiaphoris civilibus potestatem? Dicam quod res est, qui alteram alteram [sic] harum negat potestatum utramque negat, imo nonnulli totidem verbis negant, quod alii interrogati fatentur, disputantes quidem negant adeo verum est, aut haec cum illa habenda est aut illa cum haec omittenda. Illud igitur imprimis firmandum est quo probato, iure optimo inde sequetur, res etiam adiaphoras ad cultum dei spectantes principi potestati subiici debere,‖ quum

---

* No *et subiectio* in A.   † *uti aliqui volunt* is deleted in B.   ‡ *quia* in A.

§ *conscientiam ad obedientiam quod antea quidem non obligabat quod nihil aliud . . .* in A.

¶ *prorsus indifferens, sed hac ex parte non magnopere laborandum est quum in res civiles adiaphoras magistratum potestatem habere fortassis impetravero quo concesso (licet adversariis vehementer negant eandem magistratus potestam esse in rebus sacris admittendam) inde tamen secuturum iure optime videtur res adiaphoras tam ecclesiasticas quam civiles principi potestati subiici debere* is the reading in A; there is no sign of the 8-line passage that now follows in B.

‖ B now once more follows the text of A: immediately below A has *utriusque eadem ratio,* and *imo et materia . . . in templo* is inserted.

enim omnium eadem prorsus sit ἀδιαφορία et utrimque eadem
ratio imo et materia cum diverso solum respectu, nec inter se magis
differunt quam toga in foro differet ab eadem in templo, constat
magistratus authoritatem tam hanc quam illam rerum indif-
ferentium amplecti familiam, nisi deus aliquo suo mandato angus-
tiore limite magistratus potestatem circumscripsit, nec inter
pomoeria civilis ditionis templum suum locari permittat, ut*
autem clarius innotescat veritas, paulo altius res repetenda est
civilis imperii† fontes adeundi et ipsa authoritatis fundamenta
eruenda, fundamenta autem duo apud authores qui hac de re dis-
putant plerumque invenio, quorum neutrum est cui nostra haec
thesis inniti, et alterutro concesso stabiliri non potest‡ alii enim
supponunt homines in servitute alii ad libertatem natos. hi pari-
tatem§ inter mortales naturae lege affirmant, illi paternum ius in
liberos et inde ortum imperium asserunt,¶ ut ut sit hoc certum est,
si princeps ad imperium natus sit si dei instituto et naturae ac
nascendi beneficio sceptrum et solium possidere[t], constare,
eundem et terrae et incolarum unicum sine pacto et conditione
[p. 11] esse dominum et‖ ei licere quicquid a deo (cui soli subi[i]citur a
quo solo et legem vivendi et regnandi accepit) non prohibetur,
nec quisquam negare potest omnes actiones indifferentes cuiuscun-
que demum sint generis, sub eius potestate, cuius arbitrio subditorum omnium libertas fortunae et vita ipsa** permittitur, quod
si homines communi nascendi sorte aequales iure pari libertate
utuntur, nulla sane coniunctio hominibus inter ipsos contingere
potest, nulla vitae societas, nulla lex, nec reipublicae forma qua
mortales inter se quasi in unum corpus coalescant nisi quisque
prius libertatem illam (quam supponunt)†† nativam exuat et in
alterum quempiam sive principem sive senatum‡‡ transferat prout
de reipublicae forma convenire contingit in quo summam potestatem residere necesse est, res publica enim sine legibus humanis
nulla unquam aut fuit aut esse potuit, leges ab alia nisi a summa

---

* *verum ut clarius* in A.
† *paulo aliter res...civilis magistratus* in A, and *eruenda sunt.*
‡ *quorum neutrum est in quod nostra haec thesis inniti et stabiliri non possit* in A.
§ *naturae lege* is added here in A.   ¶ No *et inde ortum imperium* in A.
‖ *potestatem et solium possidet* in A, followed by *negari non posse*, deleted, and *et terrae et incolarum unicum esse dominum et cum sine pacto vel conditione...*
** *fortunae* added in B, and the list is changed several times in A, thus *vita et libertas*, deleted; *libertas*; *fortunae*, deleted.
†† No *quam supponunt* in A.
‡‡ *et coetum* in A.

potestate sancire non possunt, quis enim in superiores, aut aeque liberos quicquam iure statuere valeat?* Suprema vero illa est potestas quae aliam superiorem in terris non habet cui actionum suarum rationem reddere tenetur, talis autem potestas nunquam constitui potest nisi unusquisque totam illam suam libertatem naturalem quanta quanta sit legislatori deferat ei concedit† qui quasi vicaria omnium authoritate et delegato singulorum consensu leges in illos ratas fert‡ ex quibus efficitur ut quicquid licet cuiquam facere id et magistratui liceat imperare, quum singulorum authoritatem et ius naturale communi pacto ipse in se continet, resque tam sacras quam profanas adiaphoras omnes illius imperio et potestati legislativae omnino subiici.§ His tertius fortasse civilis potestatis constituendae modus addi potest in quo authoritatem omnem a deo, personae autem eam potestatem gerentis¶ nominationem et designationem a populo esse supponatur, quum alias ex paterno iure ius ad imperium ex populari ius vitae et necis haud facile constabit, verum de his nihil statuo, nec utrum hoc vel illud verum sit in praesenti disputatione‖ quicquam moror. Hoc dico. Voluit deus inter homines societatem ordinem et regimen esse, quam rempublicam nominamus,** in omni republica debet esse aliqua suprema potestas sine qua res publica esse non potest, illa suprema potestas ubique in omni imperio prorsus eadem est, legislativa scilicet, legislativae potestatis obiectum et materiam esse omnes res adiaphoras supra probavimus et iam iterum dicimus†† quod aut in has est summi magistratus potestas aut plane nulla est quum vero satis constat magistratum in res civiles adiaphoras potestatem habere, et plurimi hoc concedunt,‡‡ sequeretur secundum ipsos illos, quod si nulla esset religio omnes res adia- [p. 12] phorae authoritati magistratus subiicerentur ideoque cum nostra

---

* *potest* in A.

† Several attempts to find the appropriate verb for this clause appear in A, *refert, delegit, deferat,* not *concedit.*

‡ *facit* in A; in the next clause *ut quicquid* is repeated in B.

§ The text of A here continues *Hanc Magistratus potestatem sive huic sive illuc fundamenta innitentem convellere inter adversarii pluribus argumentis*; this is deleted and the para. which follows in B is set on the facing page.

¶ *authoritatem istam gerentis* in A.

‖ *in praesenti disputatione* not in A.

** *quam rempublicam nominamus* not in A.

†† *iam iterum dico aut in has est suprema magistratus potestas* in A.

‡‡ *quum vero nemo pene sit qui agnoscit magistratum in res civiles adiaphoras potestatem habere sequeretur secundum...* for this sentence in A.

religio Christiana sit si* nulla lex e religione Christiana adduci potest† qua aliqua pars rerum adiaphorarum magistratus potestati subtrahitur, qua has vel illas res adiaphoras huc vel illuc spectantes determinare prohibetur magistratus,‡ potestatem in omnibus rebus adiaphoris prorsus eandem esse ac si nulla omnino esse[t] religio, quum solum huiusmodi legis Christianae praetextu§ magistratus authoritas in nonnullis rebus adiaphoris negatur, verum an aliqua huiusmodi potestati civili adversaria lex inter Evangelii statuta reperiri possit ex sequentibus dissentientium argumentis patebit.¶

1° Inter quos primi sunt qui rectam viam ingressi legem Evangelii hanc magistratus authoritatem adimere affirmant et civilem rectorem a rebus divinis arcere et ne se suamque potestatem cultui religioso immiscere audeat prohibere novum testamentum asserunt.‖ Se iam hac servitute emancipatos gestiunt** et nil nisi libertatem crepant Christianam in hanc rem firmandam intenti, Sanctae Scripturae locos congerunt, apostolorum testimonia citant†† exemplorum agmen explicant et his copiis confisi facilem et indubitatam sperant victoriam. Verum cum singula recensere, nedum excutere, et ad examen revocare longum esset sic breviter respondeo, magnam sane libertatem a redemptore nostro humano generi datam‡‡ et in Evangelio saepius promulgatam, verum hanc libertatem eorum causam parum admodum iuvare constabit testimonia illa paulo attentius intuenti.§§ Libertas enim illa cuius toties in Evangelio fit mentio omnino duplex est. Altera qua Christus subditos suos e potestate et servitute diaboli in libertatem manu asserit, altera qua legis ceremonialis triste illud iugum Judaeorum cervicibus excussit quod nec ipsi nec patres eorum portare valuerunt uti loquitur Ap[ostolus] Petrus,¶¶ et antiquata illa lege qua diu coacti et oppressi ingemuerant in communem populi sui sortem et gratam regni sui libertatem vindicavit, quum vero novum testamentum de magistratus authoritate‖‖ coercenda aut

---

* *sequitur si nulla lex* in A; and *si nulla lex* repeated in B.
† *proferri potest* in A.
‡ *prohibetur magistratus, sequitur inquam eandem prorsus esse in omnibus rebus adiaphoris ac si* in A.
§ *praetextu et obtentu* in A.
¶ *adversaria* deleted in A, and then *lex in pagina sacra* deleted and *oppugnantium* in A for *dissentientium.* The main text of A resumes here.
‖ *immiscere prohibitum* in A.   ** *emancipatos exclamant* in A.
†† *testimonia asserunt* in A.   ‡‡ *largitam* in A.
§§ *hanc concessionem . . . paulo attentius consideranti* (deleted), *pensitenti* (deleted) in A.
¶¶ *excussit et sua antiquata lege illa . . .* in A.   ‖‖ *libertate* in A.

limitanda nullibi mentionem facit, cum nullum aut in Evangelio
aut epistolis praeceptum magistratui civili destinatum appareat
verum de republica et civili imperio plerumque silet imo Christus
ipse occasionem saepe ea de re disserendi nactus, quasi dedita
opera rebus civilibus se immiscere recusat, nec aliud regnum nisi
divinum spirituale suum esse agnoscens iura civilia reipublicae
immutata praetermisit hoc idem* doctor gentium I Cor[inthios]
c. 7 affirmat ubi docet religione et libertate Christiana conditiones
hominum non omnino immutari sed servos etiamsi Christi facti
sin[t] subditi, servos adhuc civiles esse et idem quod ante dominis
suis debere obsequium nec alia sane ratio principis et subditorum [p. 13¹
quum mandati alicuius quo imminuta sit magistratus in rebus
quibusvis adiaphoris potestas in sacra pagina appareat nec vola
nec vestigium.

2° Alii negant licere magistratui res adiaphoras in cultu divino im-
ponere† quia scriptura perfecta est et vitae et morum regula.
Respondeo, perfectionem scripturae hoc argumento tollere magistratus authoritatem aeque in rebus civilibus quam ecclesiasticis,‡
si enim ita scriptura morum perfecta regula sit, ut piaculum sit,§
alias de moribus corrigendis dirigendisque leges ferre civilia edicta
hanc ob rationem omnia aeque illicita futura ac ecclesiastica nec
fas erit magistratui de quavis re legem sancire, quum nulla lex ferri
potest quae non aliqua sit vitae et morum regula;¶ quo potius iure
vestium habitum iudicibus et iuris consultis lege praescribere
possit, quam praesbyteris et sacrarum rerum ministris, quidvel‖
audeat Rhetori potius quam Evangelii praeconi** locum, modum et
tempus concionis habendae statuere, cum par sit ratio utrimque, et
perfecta illa vitae regula non aliam (non aliam) ad mores Rhetoris
Christiani vel concionatoris formandos†† requirit aut admittit. dico
autem‡‡ regula haec perfecta dici potest dupliciter; 1§§ quatenus
generales morum normas tradit a quibus reliquae omnes particulares emanant et deduci possunt, et sic scriptura dici potest regula

---

* *quod idem A. Paulus eandem sententiam . . . in A.*
† No *in cultu divino* in A.
‡ *respondeo perfectionem scripturae tollere magistratus authoritatem in rebus ecclesiasticis*
quam civilibus in A.
§ *et plane illicitum* added in A.   ¶ *morum norma* in A.
‖ *vel quid audeat* in A.   ** *praedicatoris* in A.
†† *formando* in B, *-os* in A.   ‡‡ *respondemus* in A.
§§ The number is given in A, omitted in B; *emanant et,* and *regula* in the following
clause are not in A.

perfecta, nec aliquod vel magistratus vel parentis vel domini iustum reperiri potest mandatum quod non continetur et fundatur in scriptura, uti illud praeceptum omnia fiant decenter et ordine particulares leges de ritibus cultus divini ab ecclesiae rectoribus* postea sanciendas in se continet,† 2 Regula morum perfecta dici potest quae singula et particularia‡ vitae nostrae officia complectitur et quid cuique in unaquaque re§ agendum quid omittendum sit praescribit, qualis nulla unquam perfecta fuit regula vitae nec esse potuit, vel si malint scriptura est perfecta regula interni et necessarii cultus¶ divini rituum autem et circumstantiarum numerum et modum nec tradidit usquam nec descripsit, sed ecclesiis ipsis ut cuiusque loci consuetudini consuleretur permisit et pro necessitate temporum hominum opinione‖ et rerum ipsarum dignitate omnia statuerentur.

3° Obiicitur in cultu divino inventa humani ingenii admiscere, superstitionem esse sacras res, quas ad mentem et praescriptum divini numinis fieri debent humanos ritus non admittere, nec impune licere temerariis hominibus** sacram illam provinciam et dei legislatoris unici regnum invadere, hinc si in cultu divino, solemne aliquod quod eorum palato minus arridet praescribatur†† acrius statim in legislatorem invehunt, et severa censura rem ipsam et authorem condemnant, verum quoniam superstitio vox sit, quae [p. 14] plerumque male audit quo quasi spectro aliquo imperitos vulgi animos terrere solent qui exter[n]um dei cultum aut vituperare aut innovare laborant, et hanc apellationem‡‡ tanquam larvam honestis rebus et satis venustis induunt.§§ Apud Latinos proprie significat superstitum cultus et respondet¶¶ δαιμονία quae apud Graecos varias habet significationes, 1° enim idem sonat quod daemonum id est spirituum cultus, 2° heroum, 3° dei unius veri timor (uti loquuntur servilis) quo nimirum perculsi deum tanquam severum implacabilem crudelem animo effingimus, 4° cuiusque sectae et religionis

---

* *gubernatoribus* in A and *stabiliendos*.

† *continet, nec qui postea modeste et reverenter flexis genibus ad preces publicas se componeret etiamsi magistratus id non iuberet contra scripturam perfectam illam vitae regulam peccant etiamsi ingenua latio nullibi inter praecepta eius reperitur* follows in A; only the deleted *nec* remains in B.

‡ *particularia* not in A. §§ *quid singulis hominis* in A.

¶ *veri cultus divini* in A. ‖ *temporum et... in A.*

** *nec licere sine summa audacia et temeritate* deleted in A, and *quasi dei* below.

†† *usurpetur* in A. ‡‡ *volunt, hanc quo appellationem... in A.*

§§ *et satis venustis induere. liceat ergo paucis huius vocis sensum excutere* ends the para. in A. ¶¶ *respondet vocabulo* in A.

cultus divinus, ab aliis superstitio vocatur quia cuiusque sectae
initiati* alios omnes praeter suum divini numinis cultum condem-
nantes superstitionem appellare solent.† Sic Festus Christianam
religionem superstitionem vocat, Actorum c. 25, v. 19 sed quaes-
tiones quasdam de sua superstitione habebant adversus eum et de
quodam Jesu defuncto quem aiebat Paulus vivere. dicimus ergo,
licere iis idem quod licuit Festo instituta ecclesiastica et ritus
religiosos lege praescriptos superstitionem nominent cultus vero
inde nihilo magis illicitus.‡ Efficitur, nec ideo magis reiiciendus
quam a beato Paulo audita superstitionis appellatione Christiana
exuenda erat fides, quod vere dicunt deum unicum esse Legislatorem eodem modo intelligendum est quo scriptura dicitur
unica et perfecta vitae regula, scilicet deum solum imperium habere
in hominum conscientias, solus sua authoritate leges sancire, omnia
iusta mandata tam publica quam privata ab illius voluntate pro-
ficisci et in ea fundari, quamvis haec verba unus est Legislator qui
potest servare et perdere ex Epistola Jacobi desumpta ad praesentem causam non omnino spectant uti patet ex contextu.

4° Obiectio est Scandalum, scilicet non licere magistratui ritus
imponere quia scandala sunt.

1°] Respondeo, 1° Illud non est scandalum quod alium irritat, quod
alter§ fieri indignatur qualis plerumque est animi adversariorum
habitus, irascendo non immitando¶ in quo natura scandali consistit plerumque peccant.

2° Dico, Omne illud quod scandalum dicitur in quod aliquis im-
pingere ita ut corruat potest non illico malum esse Christus enim
ipse saepius s[c]andalum dicitur et plurimi in eo dicuntur offendi.

3° Dico, Quod qui offenditur semper peccat qui offendit non ita.

4° Dico, Si magistratui nihil statuere liceret nisi quod nullos offendere
potest nullam legem iure potuit sancire, quia nihil ita‖ omnibus
arridet, nihil tam iustum et aequum omnibus videtur in quo aliquis
non inveniat quod condemnet quod illo iudice illicitum videatur.

5° Dico, Quod forte aliquis ritibus a magistratu constitutis vere
offendatur non igitur** sequi legem esse iniquam et eo ipso non
obligare, quia inferioris cuiusque mala mens vel privata opinio vel

* *initiati* added in B; *quaeque sectae alios...* in A.
† *vocare solet* in A.   ‡ *illicitus nihil magis* in A.
§ *quodque alter* in A; *quod* deleted in B.   ¶ *aut agendo* deleted in B.
‖ *quod nullos offendere[t] possit nullam legem unquam iure potuit quia nihil tam...* in A.
** *non ideo* in A.

[p. 15] scrupulum,* publico magistratus iuri nequaquam officit,† nec inferioris aliqua conditio superioris potestatem tollere possibile est, tum enim legum obligatio non a magistratus voluntate sed nostro penderet assensu‡ et e subditis quispiam pro libitu iura omnia a principe rata ipse irrita facere valeret, fieri non potest ut magistratus omnes subditorum animos sciat, cum consuetudinum depravatio, opinionum vanitas, voluptatum illecebrae, affectuum impotentia, partium studium tam varie animorum imbecilitatem torqueat et flectat, aut si sciret quidem, cuiusque tamen aut opinioni aut scrupulis consulere aut potuit aut debuit sufficit ad legis rectitudinem et obligationem si quid in materia libera et adiaphora statuat quod ipsi qui curam reipublicae gerit populi saluti et paci publicae aliquo modo conducere videatur.§

5° Alii¶ ut magistratui se subtrahant et legum ab ipso latarum obligationem illudant‖ in semet ipsos refugiunt, et ubi tuto lateant in conscientiae suae penetralibus quaerunt asylum, conscientiae sacram obtendunt libertatem,** ritibus legibusque ecclesiasticis minime violandam, libertatem illam conscientiae omnino sacram esse et divinae voluntati†† solum obnoxiam, quam si magistratus suae ditionis esse asserit contumeliam majestati‡‡ numinis vim et iniuriam fratri non sine gravi delicto facere. adeoque omnes leges qui hanc libertatem quoquo modo premunt et circumscribunt§§ ipso facto iniustas esse et irritas. verum ut intelligatur quae leges libertati conscientiae adversantur, cum manifestum sit¶¶ omnes iustas magistratus leges tam civiles quam ecclesiasticas obligare subditorum conscientias praemittenda est aliqua et obligationis et libertatis destinctio.

Dico igitur, Quod legum humanarum obligatio duplex esse potest 1° Materialis 2° Formalis. 1° Obligatio materialis est cum res ipsa quae est materia legis humanae per se obligat conscientiam, quae scilicet ex vi legis divinae ante latam legem humanam esset omnino

---

* No vel scrupulum in A. † No nequaquam in A.
‡ consensu in A.

§ B has almost no punctuation for this paragraph; A has a stop after possibile est, and a comma after flectat; breaks after quidem and aut debuit are required by the sense. A has videtur.

¶ The para. begins Obiicitur non licere ceremoniam impositionem illicitum esse (deleted) in A.

‖ A has eludant. ** praedicant libertatem in A.
†† B has divini, A gives divinae and ...quod si magistratus.
‡‡ numinis divini in A. §§ premunt et coercunt in A.
¶¶ No verum in A and cum certum sit here.

necessaria, 2° obligatio formalis est cum res alias adiaphora, legitima magistratus potestate populo praecipitur et conscientias obligat, harum altera materia sua obligat [altera] virtute tantum praeceptionis magistratus.* Deinde libertas haec qua de loquimur duplex etiam est 1° libertas iudicii 2° libertas voluntatis 1° libertas iudicii est quando non requiritur necessario assensus iudicii, ut hoc vel illud sit sua natura necessarium et in eo consistit libertas omnis conscientiae, 2° libertas voluntatis est cum non requiritur assensus voluntatis ad hanc vel illam actionem et haec tolli potest salva interim† conscientiae libertate.

His praemissis dico

1° Si magistratus praecipiat quod a deo ante praeceptum erat,‡ verbi gratia, ut subditus a furto vel adulterio abstineat, huius legis et materialem et formalem esse obligationem, qua tollitur et iudicii et voluntatis libertas adeoque ipsius conscientiae.§ non est tamen lex [p. 16] ea iniusta, quoniam nova nulla vincula conscientiae inicit nec alios aut angustiores conscientiae libertati limites magistratus ponit quam deus ipse.

2° Dico, Si magistratus authoritate sua¶ prout potestate legislativa praeditus est rem liberam et adiaphoram edicto subiectis imperat haec lex cum obligatio illius formalis tantum sit non materialis id est res necessaria facta, non natura sua sed vi praeceptionis magistratus civilis conscientiam quidem obligat verum illius non tollit libertatem, quum requirat assensum voluntatis tantum ad obediendum non iudicii ut habeatur in se necessaria, dico itaque‖ omnes magistratus leges tam civiles quam ecclesiasticas, tam quae cultum divinum quam quae communem vitam respiciunt** esse iustas et ratas quae obligant homines ad agendum non ad iudicandum, et utrique simul prospicientes obedientiae necessitatem cum conscientiae libertate coniungunt.

3° Dico, Si magistratus rem adiaphoram obligatione materiali subditis imponere velit hoc est ita praecipiat tamquam res sua [natura] necessaria ante legem†† a se latam cum re vera non esset sed

---

* *harum alteram natura sua obligat altera virtute... in A.*
† *manente salva conscientiae in A.*   ‡ *quod a deo ante mandatum erat in A.*
§ *et conscientiae libertatem coercetur in A; no magistratus at the end of the following sentence in A.*
¶ *si magistratus authoritate sua sibi demandata...et plane adiaphoram in A, deleted.*
‖ *dico igitur hoc modo in A.*
** *tam civiles quam ecclesiasticas tam morum quam religionis in A.*
†† *tamquam res sua natura esset necessaria in A.*

prorsus adiaphora, huiusmodi lege libertatem conscientiae illaqueat et imperando peccat, verum leges ecclesiasticae hoc modo non feruntur, quibus res in ritus ceremoniales translatae, non ideo iubentur quia necessariae sunt sed ideo dicuntur necessariae quia iubentur.*

Ultimo† agmen claudunt qui de authoritate magistratus male ominantur‡ et dicunt quod ea de causa nec legitima est nec ferenda§ tanta potestas quia malorum esse potest feracissima, quia periculorum plena,¶ ubi tandem se sistet magistratus incertum est, quid non tandem nobis imponet‖ vel onerosum vel absurdum impotens fortasse legislator si tali et tantum non infinita potentia praeditus clamitant. cur rationem cur religionem nobis largitus est deus, quorsum homines nati sumus, quorsum Christiani facti, si nec ratio nec religio nostra ad mores formandos cultum deo praestandum sufficiat, et huiusmodi plurimae querelae et varia in ipsorum animis male providis efficta levium ingeniorum terriculamenta,** verum hic observare libet, quod hae obiectiones uti praecedentes†† magistratus potestatem tam in adiaphoris civilibus quam ecclesiasticis oppugnare et convellere, unde etiam intelligamus quanta sit coniunctio et affinitas inter res omnes adiaphoras tam ad ritus quam ad mores spectantes adeo ut si magistratus authoritas ex altera saltem parte auferatur ex altera etiam corruat. Sed‡‡ breviter respondeo, nihil in rerum natura tam undique perfectum et innocuum ex quo malum aliquod sequi aut saltem timeri nec possit§§ nec soleat, et multa iusta et legitima saepe a quibusdam inutilia et onerosa sentiuntur, verum ea incommoda quae mihi ex alterius iure eveniunt aut evenire possunt, illius iuri minime obstant.

[p. 17]

Sic tandem¶¶ hostiles copias levi adumbratione depictas exhibui‖‖ et argumentorum capita currente calamo perstrinxi, media,

---

* *quia iubentur* X (Christo?) *modestia-* in A.
† *6° et ultimo* in A, and *qui de tanta....*
‡ *potestate magistratus* in A.
§ *quod igitur non legitima est non ferenda* in A.
¶ *malorum feracissima et periculorum plena* in A.
‖ *imperabit* in A.
** A number of small differences in this last passage in A.
†† *praecedentes omnes* in A.
‡‡ *verum breviter respondeo* in A.
§§ *ex quo malum aliquod sequi nec potest nec soleat* in A; *innocens* changed to *innocuum* in B.
¶¶ *Ita currente calamo*, deleted, begins this para. in A.
‖‖ *numeravi* in A.

instantias, et authoritates omnes recensere longum esset, nec singula persequi temporis patitur ratio aut argumentorum momenta postulant, quicunque contra nos militat inter praedictos ordines locum inveniet.* [p. 18]†

* *aut temporis patitur angustia aut argumentorum momenta postulant, quicunque puto, contra nos militat inter praedictos ordines locum inveniet, quorum arma diutior non enim difugiam in A.*

† I.e. MS Locke c. 28, fol. 20.

SECOND TRACT ON GOVERNMENT: TRANSLATION

Whether the civil magistrate may incorporate indifferent things into the ceremonies of divine worship and impose them on the people: Confirmed.

If only this truth which is now drawn into dispute and which has already been the subject of so many hot debates, and has been bandied about in such bitter party quarrels, would finally stop being challenged! If only, having achieved the place that it deserves in every mind, it would, being settled, at last grant security to each and peace to all! If only it might demand advocates no longer, but rather recognize worshippers!* Exhausted as we are by so bitter a clash of opinions and of arms, we ought to rest content with our liberty and quiet. But when I remind myself what disasters this one issue has caused, what tempests, military no less than civil, it has provoked—tempests of which distant rumblings are heard even now, and of which the whole ferment has hardly yet subsided; when I consider that this exceedingly provocative question, in connection with which deeds almost always follow words, is hardly raised in public but it is attended by a train of as many violent acts as there are points of view, and that it does not permit of calm or passive listeners, but inspires, excites and arms them and sets them, bitter and incensed, against one another; when I consider all this, it looks to me as though I am not approaching a gymnasium and a private fencing-match so much as a public arena and a field of battle, and not so much proposing a thesis as raising a war-cry.

For there is hardly anyone who can contain himself on this subject, or bear to take part soberly in controversies of this sort without imagining that his own interests are seriously at stake and must be defended with the greatest energy, not to say by force of arms, when, their enthusiasms driven this way and that by opinion, hope or conscience, some here anxiously complain that peace, religion and the church are imperilled by excessive licence, and there others

---

* Locke's rhetorical training is apparent in several passages of 'fine' Latin writing such as this—so is the tendency of scholastic rhetoric (a tendency of which he himself complained) to surrender meaning to style; I have tried to stay as close as possible to what Locke actually says.

vehemently cry out that the liberty of the Gospel, that greatest privilege of Christians, is despotically suppressed and the right of conscience violated. And hence follows the belittling of the magistrate, the violation of laws; all things sacred as well as profane are held as nothing and so long as they march under the banners of liberty and conscience, those two watchwords of wonderful effect in winning support, they assert that each may do what he will. And certainly the overheated zeal of those who know how to arm the rash folly of the ignorant and passionate multitude with the authority of conscience often kindles a blaze among the populace capable of consuming everything.*

Germany, which is notorious for civil disasters, provides evidence of this.† And I only wish that this age and country of ours, [p. 1] so happy in other respects, had been content with foreign examples and had not provided such wretched evidence of this truth in its own domestic misfortunes or wished to learn by experiment on its own body how many calamities a predatory lust under the guise of Christian liberty and religion brings in its wake —calamities of which the very memory would in truth be thoroughly distressing did not our present good fortune, the new posture of affairs and the well-composed order of society reassure us. Nor do we now look back at those miseries but as men who, standing safely on the shore, gaze, not unsatisfied, at the tossing and vain threats of the waves from which they have just escaped. And now that Almighty God has restored peace to us—which was not to be hoped for without a long chain of miracles, the discord of the immediate past making its arrival still more welcome—it is to be hoped that nobody will be so obstinate and stiff-necked as to attempt further civil changes or to disparage the magistrate's

* Parry, 1660, has a very similar passage: 'and if once active burning spleen be set on fire by an ignorant zeal we may quickly expect all to be in flames'; and cf. *The Preface to the Reader*, 'the several bands of Saints would not want their Venners to lead them', etc., and p. 66 above, for Locke's 'conspiracy' theory.

† In his letter to Henry Stubbe, Locke stresses the relevance of the recent experience of other countries to the discussion of contemporary English religious politics; he suggests Holland, France and Poland as cases in question. The reference to France in A is omitted here, perhaps because French disorders at this time were more generally interpreted as purely civil troubles. Balzac, *The Prince*, advanced this interpretation, as Locke noted (MS e. 6). Among other authors Locke read before 1661, Richardson, *State of Europe*, and Ascham, *Of the Confusions of Governments*, are possible sources for his view of German history. But the instance is almost a commonplace of seventeenth-century political commentary.

power in respect of indifferent things.* Rather, it is to be hoped that now that that chaos has abated along with the heady ferment of passions, a more sober view will eventually recognize that civil obedience, even in the indifferent things of divine worship, is not to be counted among the least duties of the Christian religion, and that there is no other help but in eagerness to obey. And I hope that in future this controversy will excite no further conflict, unless it be a mock battle of the present sort. And in order that we may the better undertake such a combat we must set forth the debate and define its terms in such a way that we shall understand what is meant here by *magistrate*, what by *religious worship*, and what by *things indifferent*.†

(1) By *magistrate* we here understand one who has responsibility for the care of the community, who holds a supreme power over all others and to whom, finally, is delegated the power of constituting and abrogating laws; for this is that essential right of command in which alone resides that power of the magistrate by which he rules and restrains other men and, at will and by any means, orders and disposes civil affairs to preserve the public good and keep the people in peace and concord.‡ Nor is there any need to enumerate the particular tokens of sovereignty and the rights defined as regal,§ such as the final appeal, the right of life and

---

* I have reconstructed this sentence somewhat. The stop after *discordia* seems doubtful in view of the different version in A.

† 'Proceeding as the schools do, *ad determinandum*', in Selden's phrase, Locke's technique here should be contrasted with his professed contempt for scholarly distinctions in the letter to Henry Stubbe. He proceeds with just the 'regulated motion which a pedantical fencer would prescribe' that he ironically urged on Stubbe— further proof perhaps of the academic occasion of this *Tract*, and of Locke's intellectual conservatism at this stage of his career.

‡ Edward Gee, *The Divine Right and Original of the Civil Magistrate* (1658), part III, ch. VII, and Philip Nye, *The Lawfulness of the Oath of Supremacy*, pp. 2 ff., both derive a definition of magistracy from a distinction between *potestas* and *potentia*; *potestas* implies lawful as against natural dominion, that is, dominion recognized by an act of the subject's will; the conventional extreme of authority, 'tyranny', is thus ruled out of Locke's discussion.

§ Of the works in Locke's reading lists before 1660, Bodin, *Methodus*, III, Of Sovereignty, lists five 'functions' of a sovereign: making subordinate magistrates, proclaiming and annulling laws, declaring war and peace, the final appeal, the power of life and death; chief among the 'attributes' of sovereignty are levying taxes and striking coins; and the 'Hobbist', Antony Ascham, 1649, observes, p. 131, 'No state hath a capacity to go higher than, First to make or take away a Law, Secondly to make warre or Peace, Thirdly to judge of life and death, Fourthly to fix all appeals in itself'; or cf. Bodin's identical list of 'the marks and Ensigns of supream power' in *Republic*, I, x. This, incidentally, is quoted by Ascham in another work, *Of the Original*

death, of making war and peace, the authority to coin money, to raise revenue and taxes, and many things of that sort, since it is certain that all these are adjuncts of the power of making law* and may be prescribed on the authority of that power in different ways in different commonwealths according to the custom of the people. Nor, above all, is it necessary in this context to review the forms of government or prescribe the number of the governors.† It is sufficient for our purpose, in effect, and we may take it as settled that that [institution] may be called 'magistrate' which can, [p. 2] of its own right, impose laws on subjects and sanction them, whether it be an assembly—as some desire—or a monarch.‡

(2) 'Divine worship' has several meanings.

(i) There are some§ for whom the phrase has the same meaning as 'religion' and they take both expressions in a very general sense as referring to the whole of that obedience which we owe to divine laws. Whatever in any way binds the conscience, anything we perform as commanded by God, all this they declare—not at all correctly, however—to be 'religion' and a part of 'divine worship', taking the definition so far that almost all human actions turn into divine worship, and we worship God in eating, drinking and sleeping, since there can be some degree of righteousness in these actions.¶ And I conclude that in this sense of the phrase, surely, no one will deny that the magistrate can determine indifferent things in the worship of God and impose them on his subjects. Although when this is granted, it will not perhaps be altogether clear why the same right is necessarily denied in the remaining ceremonial

and End of Civil Power, also of 1649. Hobbes's various definitions of sovereignty are more elaborate, but in *Leviathan*, II, ch. XVIII, he includes among the 'essential rights of sovereignty' all those listed here by Locke.

* Cf. Hooker, I, x. For both Sanderson and Hobbes a 'deductive' arrangement of power starts on the other hand from the *ius gladii*, and the right of making law is itself an adjunct of that. See Sanderson's *Preface* to the 1661 edition of Ussher's *Power Communicated by God to the Prince*, sect. xv, 'the *Ius gladii* (which is really the Sovereign Power)...', etc.

† Note here again Locke's preference for the more 'constitutional' word.

‡ Hobbes's definition, *Leviathan*, II, xxvi, is also in terms of action *iure suo*, as is that in his *De Corpore*, v, xix, and cf. Dudley Digges, 1644, pp. 2 ff., and of course Filmer, *The Anarchy of a Mixed Monarchy* (1648).

§ Locke's discussion of divine worship is closely modelled, to say no more, on that of Sanderson, 1660, VI; this first paragraph alone is not echoed in Sanderson's treatment. It is characteristically a Quaker and extreme Baptist position, cf. Richard Sibbes, 1639.

¶ In view of the subjunctive used in A I have read *possit* for Locke's *potest* here—a non-causal use of *cum* hardly makes sense in the context.

trappings and the public gatherings of religion, since the same argument of indifferency applies in each case, as God, the supreme legislator, has nowhere excluded the power of the magistrate from these matters. But more of this below.

(ii) 'Divine worship' is more correctly understood* as being the actions of the inner virtues of all of which God is the object, as the love of God, reverence, fear, faith, etc.; this is that inner worship of the heart which God demands, in which the essence and soul of religion consists, and in the absence of which all the other observations of religious worship provoke God rather than propitiate him, offering a sacrifice no more pleasing to the divine will than the mutilated carcasses of slaughtered beasts would be. And this is why God so frequently and so particularly claims the heart and spirit for himself, and calls the mind and the inner depths of the soul shrines dedicated to his worship, and requires a spirit obedient to himself as if it were the only worshipper that he prizes.† But this worship, wholly silent and secret as it is, completely hidden from the eyes and observation of men, is neither subject to human laws, nor indeed capable of such subjection. God who lays bare the most secret corners of the mind, and who can alone either know the private deliberations of the mind or pass judgment upon them, is the only examiner of men's hearts.‡

(iii) The outward acts of religion are also called 'divine worship'.§ Since God ordained that man should be composed of

* Sanderson, 1660, VI, sect. xxix, opens his discussion of the nature of worship in almost identical phrases, *Imprimis, Cultus Dei proprie dictus et praecipuus est internus ille animi cultus, qui consistit in exercitio virtutum internarum, Fidei, Spei, Dilectionis, Invocationis, Fiduciae*, etc. But this much was common theological ground for Protestants; cf. William Ames, 1633, and Gabriel Powel, 1606, who also both start from this position but develop 'positions Theologicall and Scholasticall' in opposite directions. Or William Bradshawe, *A Treatise of Divine Worship* (1605), re-edited in *Several Treatises of Worship and Ceremonies*, in 1660, who again sets out from the distinction of internal and external worship, 'internal...is merely spiritual and performed only within the temple of man's heart...it is all inward motions Faith, Hope, Love, Fear, Joy, etc.'

† The most familiar texts are: I Cor. iii. 16; I Cor. vi. 20; II Cor. vi. 16; Eph. ii. 21–2; Heb. iii. 6; Rom. viii. 9, and Ps. xxxiv. 18—which Locke uses in the English *Tract*, p. 15. William Perkins, *The Whole Treatise of Cases of Conscience* (1651), is conspicuous among the authorities Locke is likely to have read for taking 'worship' in this sense; he too uses the standard list of 'inward motions' followed by Locke, 'Fear, Obedience, Patience, Thankfulnesse...Faith Love Hope and invocation', Bk. II, ch. v.

‡ Ps. xliv. 21 is the most quoted source for this standard Protestant tenet.

§ Locke is still on non-controversial ground so far as the differences between Anglican and Presbyterian are concerned; cf. Sanderson, 1660, VI, sect. xxix, 2;

body as well as soul, he orders that he alone should be served by one of these, while by means of the other he has secured society and mutual association for mankind; for men cannot express the sentiments of their mind or benefit from mutual good will without the mediation and service of the body. But God requires the obedience of both, and he exacts from each the tribute it is able to pay; and since he seeks due service and recognition for himself on earth he is not satisfied with that silent and almost furtive form of worship alone, but he has required his worshippers—taught by whose example the rest of mankind are to be roused to the worship and reverence of his divine majesty—to acknowledge his name openly. And therefore he demands those outward performances [p. 3] by which that inner worship of the spirit is expressed, and indeed enlarged, such as public prayers, acts of thanksgiving, the singing of psalms, participation in the holy sacraments and the hearing of the divine word, by all of which we either bear witness here and now to the love, faith and obedience of the soul, or else strengthen it for the future; and this is the worship called external which is everywhere ordained by God in his law, and which by holy writ we are bound to fulfil, nor does the magistrate possess any right over this worship since it can be altered by none but the divine Lawgiver himself.*

(iv) Since there are no actions without a host of circumstances which always attend them, such as Time, Place, Appearance, Posture, etc., even divine worship cannot be free from this attendance; and thus these attributes of actions, by virtue of the necessary association they have with divine affairs, and because

William Bradshawe, *A Treatise of Divine Worship*, and *English Puritanisme*, where the 'second tenet' of the Puritan is said to be that 'all means instituted and set apart to express and set forth the inward worship of God are parts of Divine Worship'. One of the fullest expositions of the nature of worship is that of Dr John Burges in his *Answer rejoyned to the . . . Reply to Dr Morton's General Defence of the Innocencie of Three Ceremonies* (1631). Writing 'by the King's demand', Burges, ch. II, sects. i–xvi, sets out the official 'definition and distinctions of worship' in terms which are in substance those of Locke twenty-nine years later.

* Cf. Sanderson, 1660, VI, sect. xxix, *secundo, actus illi externi, quibus internus ille animi cultus, partim exprimatur, partim adjuvatur et fovetur: cuiusmodi sunt Praecationes publicae, Gratiarum actiones, Psalmodiae, Auditio verbi, participatio Sacramentorum*, etc. But, while there may be little doubt as to Locke's source here, he is still not on controversial ground, cf. Bradshawe, 1660(a), 'worship . . . is external also [which] expresses inward by outward signs and rites . . . it is a corporeal adumbration of some hidden thing in the mind', and Perkins lists the 'particulars' of external worship in the same terms as Locke and Sanderson—with the exception of psalmody and the addition of fasting. The body and soul analogy is employed to similar effect by Bishop Andrewes, *Discourse of Ceremonies* (1653).

they everywhere and always in some way serve the end of the solemn and public forms of religious worship, are therefore themselves popularly taken for worship itself and styled devotion. But God in his great wisdom and beneficence has relinquished these rites to the discretion of the magistrate and entrusted them to the care of him who holds power and has the right of governing the church, to be amended, abolished, renewed, or in whatever way soever enjoined as he should judge best in the light of the times and the customs of the people, and as the needs of the church should demand.* And so long as his injunctions concerning the true and spiritual worship are kept inviolate, so long as the substance of religion is secure, he has allowed everything else to the churches themselves, that is, to their governors, to be established as it should seem necessary under this single law and token, namely that dignity, decency and order be sought after;† for in different places different customs prevail, and a constant rule and standard could not possibly have been laid down in the divine law which would make clear what was proper for the several nations and what was not. Therefore, to make the path to the Christian religion as free of obstacles as possible for all the various nations, and in order that the approach to Christ and the new religion might lie more easily open in the Gospel, God in his great mercy appointed that Christian doctrine should be embraced by the soul and faith alone and that that true worship should be fulfilled in public gatherings and outward actions. But he by no means looked for so onerous an obedience from proselytes as that all men should forthwith abandon the customs and practices of their race, which

* Sanderson, 1660, VI, sect. xxix, 3, *tertio, cum sit impossibile actionem aliquam externam...sine circumstantiis, Quibusdam...locorum, temporum, gestuum, etc. praestari; inde fit ut ipsae illae circumstantiae...interdum Cultus appellationem accipiant,* and below, where Sanderson also concludes *pro locorum, temporum et occasionem rationem mutabiles, ad eos qui sub Christo regendarum Ecclesiarum jus et potestatem habent pertinere* (speaking of the determination of *ipsi cultui accidentales*). It is with the introduction of this fourth aspect of worship that the Anglicans part company with the Puritans, cf. the third tenet of Bradshawe's *English Puritanisme*. But note too that Locke does not pursue the traditional point of controversy—the theological standing of circumstances—here (cf. Powel, 1606, p. 70). Without committing himself as to whether these are or are not 'divine worship' he proceeds directly to his political conclusion. Owen's *Discourse of Liturgies* (ch. VII) may have shown Locke the dangers of overprecise definitions in this context.

† I Cor. xiv. 40; this text, 'the general command to Order', is the point of departure for the first extended treatment of indifferency as such, Gabriel Powel, 1606, *Epistle Dedicatory*; Sanderson quotes it for the same purpose as does Locke.

are so generally agreeable, so dear to them through long use, and so honoured through education and esteem that you shall wrest fortune, life, liberty and all from most of them sooner than their respect and use of these things. How reluctantly, how bitterly, the Jews, when converted to Christianity, laid down that grievous and burdensome train of ceremonies already familiar to their race by custom; nor when freed by Christ did they want the heavy yoke to be shaken off their necks. We have recently heard reports of a city, situated in the East, among the Chinese, which after a prolonged siege was driven at last to surrender. The gates were [p. 4] thrown open to the enemy forces and all the inhabitants gave themselves up to the will of the triumphant victor. They had abandoned to their enemy's hands their own persons, their wives, families, liberty, wealth, and in short all things sacred and profane, but when they were ordered to cut off the plait of hair which, by national custom, they wore on their heads, they took up their arms again and fought fiercely until, to a man, all were killed. These men, although they were ready to allow their whole civil existence to be reduced to slavery by their enemies, were so unable to allow them even the least interference with their hair, worn according to an ancestral custom, that the slightest of things and one of no significance, a mere excretion of the body, but all but sacrosanct by general esteem and the custom of their race, was easily preferred to life itself and the solid benefits of nature.*

* The closest account to that given by Locke in the contemporary travel literature is in Martinus Martini, *Bellum Tartaricum*, which was published in England in 1655 as an appendix to the *Relations* of Alvarez Semmedo. The English version has this story in Martinus' account (p. 283) of the Tartar assault on the city of Hangchow: 'When they commanded all by proclamation to cut off their Hair, then both Soldier and Citizen took up armes and fought more desperately for their Hair of their Heads than they did for King or Kingdom.' This is the first recorded indication of Locke's deep and continuing interest in China (cf. the very extensive notes from all periods of his life on Chinese manners, beliefs and institutions in the *Adversaria 1661*). The English edition of Olearius, *Voyages and Travels of the Ambassadors*, was published in London in 1662. Locke was interested in this work, took notes from it, and sent a copy to Strachey on 7 January 1664; it notes the Chinese addiction to their hairstyle but has no similar story. Neither do any of the other travel books published in England in the 1650s. The story reappears in Thevenot's book of 1667 where it is transferred to the war in Formosa. 1655 would perhaps count as 'recent' in comparison with the usual classical and biblical references of theological controversy; cf. Locke's appeal for contemporary examples in his letter to 'S. H.' below, Appendix I. However the version of the story in Locke's final library is that in the Amsterdam edition of Martinus' *Regni Sinesis a Tartaris tyranice devastiti*—the edition of 1661; if this was his source in the Latin *Tract* he could quite reasonably have called the information 'recent'.

And, certainly, whoever cares to contemplate our own civil commotions will confess that perhaps even among us war has at times been waged by some with equal barbarity and similar bitterness over issues of no greater weight.

But to return to the point: clearly, these ceremonies, these concomitant circumstances of actions, are so diverse and so unlike in practice among all peoples that you would look in vain, and comb the Gospel to no purpose, for a single common standard of propriety.* You would not easily persuade an inhabitant of the East or a devotee of the Mohammedan profession to embrace the faith of a Christian worshipping his God (as he would consider) offensively with a bare head. It would seem no lighter an offence to them, the custom being unknown among them, than praying with the head covered would to us.† And certainly, no one would consider going over to a religion as ridiculous in its ceremonies as all the customs of every nation are to every other. Therefore God, indulging the weakness of mankind, left his worship undetermined, to be adorned with ceremonies as the judgment of men might determine in the light of custom;‡ and he no more judges his worshippers by these things than a king judges his subjects and their loyalty and obedience by their physical condition or the style of their clothes. But neither as Christians nor as subjects are those to be considered more faithful who are carelessly or meanly arrayed.

It seems, then, to be agreed by all that the magistrate is the judge of what constitutes order and of what is to be considered decent, and that he and he alone is able to determine what is appropriate and seemly. Nor, indeed (whatever some may assert to the contrary), do I think it the least part of Christian liberty that the magistrate is permitted to consult at the same time the interests of both public peace and the growth and dignity of religion, and to provide by the same laws for them both. So much may suffice regarding 'divine worship'.

* The impotence of the Gospel in this respect was of course just the point and the source of anxiety and uncertainty to which Locke constantly returned, cf. above, p. 95.

† Cf. English *Tract*, p. 15; it is in his remarkable development of and emphasis on human partiality and the bias instilled by custom, education, and interest that Locke's treatment of his subject, so conventional hitherto, begins to show originality; this, too, was of course a continuing theme of his thought, cf. above p. 96; in this respect Locke is closer to Hooker than to Sanderson or Hobbes, cf. e.g. Hooker, 1, x, 4.

‡ Cf. Sanderson, 1660, VI, sect. xxix. Locke's argument here reverts, as closely as before, to the model set by Sanderson.

We shall next explain what is to be understood here when it is said that the magistrate 'can impose on his subjects'. It is an axiom with the lawyers that we 'can' do that which we do by law, but I think two things are indicated by the terms of our question: (1) the right of the magistrate and his lawful power, and (2) the obligation of subjects—that is to say, what the magistrate can do without fault on his own part, and what he can do given the obligation of his subjects. In order that these may be more clearly defined we must start with a number of distinctions.*

(1) A double power can be observed in the sanctions of the magistrate which I may call the material power and the preceptive power,† a power over the object and a power in the act. (i) Power is material when the thing itself which is commanded is lawful and [p. 5] indifferent and contrary to no divine precept. (ii) Power is preceptive when the command is itself lawful; for, on the one hand, it is possible that the magistrate may sin in commanding unrestricted things,‡ and, on the other hand, it is not lawful for him to bind all free and indifferent things and enclose them within the boundaries of the laws and impose them on the people, since in truth a magistrate is set above a people and governs them for this reason, that he may provide for the common good and the general welfare; he holds the helm so that he may guide the ship into harbour and not on to the rocks.§ The measure of this power is to be taken from the end or intention of the legislator;¶ that is to say, the magistrate

---

* Locke's argument now adopts a different form from that of Sanderson; but again the model for his distinction is that of the *De Obligatione Conscientiae*, Praelect. VI, sect. ii; cf. Gee, *The Divine Right and Originall of the Civil Magistrate*, where power is divided into natural and moral and the moral then subdivided into 'a coactive as well as a directive power'.

† Sanderson presents a distinction in the same terms as Gee, *directiva* and *coerciva*; later on Locke reverts to this model; still later, p. 16, he relies even more closely on Sanderson's structure: *Formal* and *Material* emerge as the major categories of analysis, *coactive* and *directive* as subdivisions; cf. Sanderson, 1660, VI and VIII; VI is concerned with the matter of law, in respect of which power is directive or coercive, VIII with the forms of law. The emphasis on the *matter* of law nevertheless constitutes an advance on Locke's part.

‡ The substitution of *magistrate* here for *law* in A is not unimportant. Locke is determined to maintain the normative objectivity of law throughout his argument; hence the tautologous developments below.

§ For the recurrence of this image in Locke's thought cf. MS Locke c. 24, fol. 14, and above, p. 64.

¶ Hobbes, *Leviathan*, II, xxx, 'The office of the sovereign consisteth in the end for which he was entrusted with the sovereign power', and cf. Sanderson, 1660, IX, *De legum humanorum obligatione ex parte causae finalis*.

can impose whatever he judges to serve the well-being of the community but, on the other hand, he cannot—without sin, that is—impose that which he does not consider to serve or be subordinate to this end.

(2) As to the obligation of subjects,* it must be understood that the power of the magistrate is on the one hand regulatory and on the other coercive, to which corresponds a double obligation, (i) the obligation to act, (ii) the obligation, if I may put it thus, to suffer; or, as it is commonly put, an active and a passive obedience.

On which premises I hold: (1) That the subject is bound to a passive obedience under any decree of the magistrate whatever, whether just or unjust, nor, on any ground whatsoever may a private citizen oppose the magistrate's decrees by force of arms, though indeed if the matter is unlawful the magistrate sins in commanding.† (2) That if a law is 'lawful'‡ in respect of its matter as well as its precept, the magistrate can legitimately sanction it and the subject is bound to execute obedience in all its forms, active as well as passive. (3) That if a law is 'lawful' as to its matter but in the precept and intention is unlawful, that is, if it is designed not for public but for private benefit, as for instance when the magistrate, indulging his own cruelty or greed or vanity, introduces a law only to enrich himself, to abuse his subjects or to flatter himself, then, though such a law certainly renders the magistrate guilty and liable to punishment before the divine tribunal, yet, nevertheless, it binds the subject even to an active obedience, for where the matter is lawful the standard of obedience is not the

---

* This obverse aspect of magisterial power is essential to Locke's argument. Bagshaw, in his *Second Part of the Great Question*, had argued at length that, though it might be lawful for the magistrate to impose, it did not follow that subjects ought to obey; obligation was a separate moral phenomenon; cf. above, p. 19. For the form of Locke's argument, cf. Sanderson, 1660, IV, sect. vi, and VI, sect. ii, *duplex etiam quod utrique potestati respondeat, subditi debitum. Debitum Obedientiae, respectu potentiae directivae et debitum Subiectionis, respectu potentiae coercitivae.* Sanderson has a further, but in this context trivial, distinction between *debitum* and *obligatio*.

† Sanderson, 1660, IV, sect. vi, *Leges omnes ab habente legislativam potestatem latas obligare...ad subiectionem; ita ut subdito non liceat supremae potestati vi et armis resistere, sive is iusta praeceperit sive iniusta.*

‡ *Si lex licita sit...*, Locke's examination of law involves him in many such quasi-tautologous expressions; and these are necessitated by his insistence on the distinction between natural and moral power, and by the political rather than the moral-theological bias of his own mind. Sanderson avoids this awkwardness by using a different formula, *ubi id sine peccato fieri potest*; Locke's text is so close to Sanderson here that I think we may consider this variation significant.

intention of the legislator, which cannot be known, but his expressed will, which establishes obligation.*

Lastly, it remains to say something of *indifferent things* and what they are, since this is a hotly disputed subject. Now things are said to be indifferent in respect of moral good and evil, so that all things which are morally neither good nor evil are called indifferent.† Since, however, moral actions imply a law as a standard of good and evil, against which we ought to measure and test our life and actions (for it is certain that if no law were provided all things and actions would be entirely indifferent and neutral, so that they could be done or left undone at the will of each individual), therefore, in order that indifferent things may be more clearly understood, some account must be given of laws, the general nature of which the learned Hooker describes, Book I, ch. 2, thus: 'That which doth assign the force and power, that which doth appoint the form and measure of working, the same we term a Law.'‡   [p. 6]

Definitions of law occur in the writings of the authorities disagreeing in the way they are expressed but not in their substance—in the sense that there are manifold divisions and distinctions, for example, into natural and positive, human and divine, civil and ecclesiastical and so forth. Leaving these on one side I may perhaps be allowed in the present controversy to venture a new way of subdividing law—into divine, or moral; political, or human; fraternal, or the law of charity; and monastic, or private. And although this distinction may be less familiar than others, and is less exact than is proper, it will perhaps be more suited to our present purpose for

---

* Sanderson, 1660, VIII, sect. xv, *voluntas Legislatoris, quae est adaequata mensura eius obligationis quam Lex inducit*, and v, vii–viii, *sed aut turpis lucri cupiditate, aut exercendae tyrannidis mera libidine, aut pravo alio quocunque animi affectu adductus; iniusta quidem esset Lex ex parte imperantis subditus tamen ad parendum nihilominus obligaretur.* Sanderson's eighth lecture is concerned entirely with the means by which will can be expressed properly: so, too, Hobbes, *Leviathan*, II, xxvi, 'civil law is...those rules...commanded...by...sufficient sign of the will'.

† This is the standard definition and in itself not subject to dispute; cf. above, p. 42. There were few who rejected or even questioned it between 1640 and 1667. Sanderson, who uses it himself, 1660, VI, sect. xxii, knew of only two writers to deny it: cf. Jeanes, 1660, 'An indifferent action then is that which is neither morally good nor evil...'

‡ Hooker, I, ii, 1; but in fact Locke does not argue from this functional conception of law virtually unique to Hooker but from that explicitly rejected by him, I, iii, 1, 'the learned...apply the name of Law unto that only rule of working which superior authority imposeth; whereas we...'. Yet Locke also deletes in the MS the considerably more voluntaristic definition of law he had quoted from Sanderson, 1660, v, sect. iii.

all that, and far from useless in the explanation of indifferent things.* This mode of distinguishing between laws is derived mainly from their authors; for we call that law 'divine' which is instituted by God, and that 'human' which is instituted by a man invested with power; and these authors of laws are, by their power, superior to the laws themselves and to the subjects they govern. The fraternal law, or law of charity, also owns God as its author, but the occasion of its obligation can and usually does spring from some equal or even inferior fellow Christian. The author of the last law, which we call 'private', is any single individual, who is neither superior, he himself being obliged by this law, nor does he have the authority, in respect of a law relating to himself, to abrogate it once it has been introduced. But the grounds of these distinctions will appear more clearly in what follows:

(1) The divine law is that which, having been delivered to men by God, is a rule and pattern of living for them. And according as it either becomes known by the light of reason which is natural and implanted in men, or is made manifest in divine revelation, it is in turn divided into natural and positive law.† And each of these I describe under the same head as 'moral' since each is exactly the same in its content and matter and they differ only in the manner of their promulgation and the clarity of their precepts. For this is that great rule of right and justice and the eternal foundation of all moral good and evil and which can be discovered even in things indifferent by the mediation of an inferior law. Whatever, then, this

---

* It is not, however, clear that Locke's own distinctions differ more in their substance than in their terms from those of his predecessors. To consider only his major suggested sources, Hobbes, *Leviathan*, II, xxvi, prefaces his discussion much as Locke does, 'The difference and division of Laws has been made in divers manners...it is a thing that dependeth not on nature, but on the scope of the writer', and he goes on to identify laws as 'natural and positive', 'human and divine', 'fundamental and not fundamental'; and Sanderson, with whom as usual the comparison is closest, 1660, IV, sect. v, 1, and v, sect. ii, specifies the heads of his discussion as divine law, human law, 'fee-will' law—by which he means oaths and compacts—and the law of scandal; in effect exactly Locke's divisions, and here, too, the distinction is based on an analysis of the sources of authority. Hooker, I, iii, 1, and I, xvi, 7, classifies laws quite differently but includes the 'divine and human' and 'civil and ecclesiastical' categories; Hammond, 1644, I, Of Conscience, treats laws as Christian, Moral, Civil, Natural, of Scandall and of Liberty.

† This point is standard; it is made by Hobbes, though he chooses to make the natural/positive distinction basic and the human/divine one a subdivision. Sanderson, 1660, IV, uses this conception at length.

law reaches, either by prohibition or command, is always and everywhere necessarily good or evil, and all other things which are not confined within the bounds of this law are indifferent by nature and their use is free.*

(2) Human law is that which is enacted by anyone maintaining law and command over others. Or, rather, I should say that any command of a superior to his inferior over whom he holds legitimate power, for instance of parents to children, of master to servant, can come under the head of human law and requires obedience, although the public ordinances of societies enacted by the magistrate, as they are particularly important and either abolish or confirm or alter private rights at will, are what we specially want to be understood here under the title of human law.† Its proper matter is indifferent things which are not comprised within the limits of a higher, that is, of the divine, law, and are to that extent not already bound up and determined.‡ For although the magistrate can forbid theft and demand chastity this is to act superfluously and seems to be not so much to make new law as to declare and enforce the old.§ For things of this sort are necessary [p. 7] and oblige the conscience of subjects even if he is silent. But since the responsibility for society is entrusted to the magistrate by God and since on the one hand all the evils likely to befall a commonwealth could not be guarded against by an unlimited number of laws, while on the other to have exactly the same constitution would not always be an advantage to a people, God left many indifferent things untrammelled by his laws and handed them to his deputy the magistrate as fit material for civil government, which, as occasion should demand, could be commanded or prohibited, and by the wise regulation of which the welfare of the commonwealth could be provided for.¶

* Cf. Sanderson, 1660, IV, sect. viii, *Deus solum merum et directum habet imperium*... etc., and VI, xxii; also Hooker, I, x, 1; Jeremy Taylor, *Ductor Dubitantium*, Bk. III, ch. i, sect. 13; Ralegh, *History of the World*, Part I, bk. 2, ch. iii.

† Cf. Sanderson, 1660, VII, *passim*, an extended argument associating the ideas of 'legitimate power' and 'superiority': this conception is essentially unlike the contrived superiority of Hobbes's legislator (*Leviathan*, II, xxvi): Locke and Sanderson are proposing a natural moral phenomenon *a priori*.

‡ This modest proposition is the core of the controversy; cf. above, p. 19, and Sanderson, 1660, VI, sect. xxvi.

§ Sanderson, on the contrary (1660, V, sect. x), holds that such law-making is indeed law-making in that it establishes a new obligation.

¶ Cf. Sanderson, 1660, V, sect. xxvi, VI, sect. xxii.

(3) That law is styled fraternal or the law of charity by which our liberty is confined within an even narrower compass and we lose the use of things left free both by divine and civil law. This happens when a weak brother, holding no power over us, can in his own right tie up our liberty in indifferent things although allowed us both by God and the magistrate, and consequently cause that to be unlawful for us 'here and now'—as they say*— which might be entirely lawful elsewhere and for another. This is commonly known as the law of scandal,† which we obey when, taking account of the welfare and innocence of any Christian not fully informed of his liberty, we are unwilling to make public use of our liberty in things lawful lest he, perchance unacquainted with his Christian liberty, and led into error by our example, performs that which he is far from convinced is lawful for him to do and thus becomes guilty of a crime. For example, eating meat offered to idols was lawful for Christians, nor did any divine or human law forbid it, and the action was accordingly indifferent and entirely lawful. But since many were unaware of this liberty and in the words of the Apostle Paul, I. Cor. c. 8, v. 7, *in all men there is not that knowledge*, etc., he even warns us in that passage to abstain from free things lest we provide a stumbling-block for our brother‡—the sum of which precept comes simply to this: that things indifferent and altogether lawful should be refrained from if there is any fear that a brother may be offended by that liberty. That is, not lest he is angered or takes it ill or is enraged because another sins or appears to sin, but lest on our example he should do that which is not lawful for him because he himself does not consider it lawful for him.§

(4) Besides the above-named laws there remains the other called monastic or private, which a man imposes on himself and by a

* Cf. Sanderson, 1660, v, sect. ii, and Jeanes, *Concerning the Indifferency of Human Actions*, pp. 20 ff.

† Hammond, 1644, I, Of Conscience, 'the law of scandall for matters of scandall'; Locke's terms at least have the advantage of avoiding definitions as vacuous as this; Sanderson, 1660, v, sect. xi, classifies obligations *ex accidenti* as the *lex Scandali*; Jeanes, 1659, also calls this the law of Charity.

‡ Locke leaves a space in B for the insertion of the Pauline text: it is necessary to understand at least verses 7 and 13 here to complete the sense of his sentence.

§ Cf. Hammond, 1644, II, Of Scandall, 'to be angry, grieved, troubled at any action of another is not [to be offended] in the Scripture sense' (sect. xxxiii); Hammond's conclusion is also followed by Locke; and we know (MS Locke f. 14, p. 42) that Locke possessed this work early in his life, possibly before 1660.

new, superinduced obligation renders necessary things hitherto indifferent and not bound by previous laws. And this law is two-fold, either of conscience or of contract, the one originating from the judgment, the other from the will. The law of conscience we call that fundamental judgment of the practical intellect concerning any possible truth of a moral proposition about things to be done in life. For it is not enough that a thing may be indifferent in its own nature unless we are convinced that it is so.* God implanted the light of nature in our hearts and willed that there should be an inner legislator (in effect) constantly present in us whose edicts it should not be lawful for us to transgress even a nail's breadth. Thus our liberty in indifferent things is so insecure and so bound up with the opinion of everyone else that it may be taken as certain that we do indeed lack that liberty which we *think we lack*.† That injunction of the Apostle to the Romans, c. 14, v. 5, [p. 8] is to the point here: *Let each man be fully assured in his own mind*, and verse 14, *I know and am persuaded in the Lord Jesus, that nothing is unclean of itself* (he is speaking of things to be eaten); *save that to him who accounteth anything to be unclean, to him it is unclean*, and verse 23, *But he that doubteth is damned if he eat, because he eateth not of faith; and whatsoever is not of faith, is sin*—this faith being nothing but a fixed opinion of one's own liberty, as appears from the context.

The other private law is derived from the will and takes the form of compact, which we enter into with God or with our fellow man. The former is called by a special name, a vow, an example of which was that of Jacob, Genesis, c. 28, *And Jacob vowed a vow, saying, If God will be with me, and will keep me in this way that I go, and will give me bread to eat, and raiment to put on, Then this stone, which I have set up for a pillar, shall be God's house; and of all that thou shalt give me I will surely give the tenth unto thee.* And the obligation of a vow is shown in *Deuteronomy*, c. 23, vv. 21, 22, *When thou shalt vow a vow unto the Lord thy God, thou shalt not be slack to pay it; for the Lord thy God will surely require it of thee; and it would be sin in thee. But if thou shalt forbear to vow, it shall be no sin in thee.* And this is here described as a

---

* Cf. Sanderson, 1657, vii, *Ad Populum*, sect. xl, 'The liberty of a Christian to an indifferent thing consisteth in this: that his judgment is throughly persuaded of the indifferency of it...it is the determination of the judgment...', etc.; and cf. Hammond, 1644, II, Of Scandall, sect. xxii.

† My italics: cf. Hammond's definition of the 'weak brother', 1644, II, Of Scandall, sect. xxii; and cf. above, p. 44.

freewill offering.* Promises between men bind in the same way and in both cases our liberty is in our own hands so that we may abandon or preserve it as we will.†

These points being made, I argue:

(1) That all these laws are, in respect of their obligation, plainly divine, that is, that no other law immediately and of itself binds the consciences of men except for the divine, since the others do not bind men by virtue of their own innate force but by virtue of some divine precept on which they are grounded; nor are we bound to obey magistrates for any other reason than that the Lord has commanded it, saying, Let every soul be in subjection to the higher powers, and that it is necessary to be subject, not only because of the wrath but also for conscience sake.'‡

(2) That human laws and the others detailed just now, with the single exception of the divine, do not change the nature of indifferent things so far that, on the authority of these laws, from being altogether indifferent they become, of themselves, necessary, but only so far as we are concerned, 'here and now', and with regard to the obligation which a new and human injunction may have temporarily induced and by which we are bound to obey, to act or to abstain. However, when that law is abolished or is in any way inoperative, we are restored to our former liberty, the thing itself remaining unchanged.§

(3) That the subordination of these laws one to another is such that an inferior law cannot in any way remove or repudiate the obligation and authority of a superior. For this would be to overturn the order of things and subject master to servant, to establish not order and government in the world but anarchy, and to own no other legislator than the meanest and most ignorant member of [p. 9] the mob. To appeal from the divine tribunal to man is not lawful, nor can a subject's vow or a private error of conscience nullify the

* Sanderson, 1660, IV, sect. vi, *ex libera cuiusque electione*... and *De Juramenti*, I, xi and cf. Jeanes, 1659, who discusses the same texts as demonstrating limitations on the free use of indifferencies.

† Sanderson, 1660, VII, sect. iii.

‡ Sanderson, 1660, IV, sects. ii–vii, and v, sect. xxii, where the same point is made on the basis of the same texts (Rom. xii. 1 and 5); and v, sect. xxxviii, *leges humanas non obligare directe et per se aut vi propria (sed) ex consequenti et virtute praecepti divini.*

§ Sanderson, 1657, *Preface*, 'Such necessity of obedience notwithstanding the things remain in the same indifferency as before...'; but the point is a common one, cf. Morton, 1619; Powel, 1606; Burges, 1631; and above, p. 45; also Sanderson, 1660, VI, xxiv.

edicts of the magistrate, for, if this is once granted, discipline will be everywhere at an end, all law will collapse, all authority will vanish from the earth and, the seemly order of affairs being convulsed and the frame of government dissolved, each would be his own Lawmaker and his own God.*

And lastly I hold:

(4) That all the things that are indifferent so far as a higher law is concerned are the object and matter of a lower, and the authority of the individual prevails in all matters that are not wholly prescribed by superior law, and whatever is left, as it were, in the balance, inclining neither to this side nor to that, towards neither good nor evil, can be adopted and appropriated to either class by an adjoining and subordinate power. For where the divine law sets bounds to its action, there the authority of the magistrate begins, and whatever is classed as indeterminate and indifferent under that law is subordinate to the civil power. Where the edicts of the commonwealth are wanting, the law of scandal will find a place; and only when all these are silent are the commands of conscience and the vow observed.† Nor does anything remain free from the higher laws which each individual as master of his own liberty cannot, by opinion, vow or contract, make necessary for himself.

And it is indeed to be wondered for what reason the very men who freely allow this arrangement and extent of power in all other respects wish it to be denied exclusively to the magistrate and the civil authority if, as one must suppose, they believe that public power ought to be ranked above that of the individual and that there either can or should be some government and political society among men. In addition to that supreme power of almighty God they have no doubts either about the other laws listed here. They readily own as extensive and absolute an authority as you please of scandal, conscience, oath and compact in the determination and limiting of indifferent things. But they firmly maintain that there is no right over indifferent things on the part of the magistrate—whom they call a contemptible little creature governing with a power obtained by entreaty and not (as holy Scripture holds) ordained by God with a power of command—at least not over

---

* As usual the point can be traced to Sanderson, 1660, IV, sect. vii; but the intensity of feeling is Locke's own; cf. above, p. 65.

† Sanderson, 1660, V, sect. vii, *cedant ergo oportet quantum ad obligandi vim leges humanae divinis, privatae pactiones et promissiones constitutionibus publicis, hisce demum omnibus Scandali lex.*

those concerning the worship of God.* But we would argue that
the opposite conclusion is confirmed in this matter, by, for instance, the analogy and subordination of the laws mentioned
above, as, too, by the precepts of the Apostle where he commands
all creatures to be obedient to the higher powers,† and again by the
Epistle of Saint Peter, [1.] c. 2, v. 13, *Be subject to every ordinance of
man for the Lord's sake: whether it be to the king as supreme.* And one
might be permitted to add some other evidence to this. From
which instances it would appear that the magistrate does have
some power in indifferent things, for where obedience is required,
and subjection, there there must necessarily be power, nor can
anyone be subjected unless there is some superior personage endowed with public authority—a personage who can not only
impose things already good or evil under the divine law on his
subjects, as some would have it, but things indifferent as well.‡

And this is apparent from the fact: (i) That the Apostle in that
place commands the performance of obedience to the magistrate,
not to God. And if his only duty were to repeat the command-
[p. 10] ments of God, and as a herald rather than a legislator only to
declare the divine commands and impress them on the people, the
power of the magistrate seems to be no greater than that of any
private citizen. For divine law possesses the same force and the
same grounds for obligation whether it is made known through
the mouth of the prince or through that of a subject; and neither of
them commands but rather teaches. (ii) That he commands subordination for conscience sake, which would be a pointless addition unless magistrates have some power in indifferent matters.
For no Christian could doubt that in necessary things even when
the magistrate is silent the conscience obliges—because things are
'necessary' just because they do bind the conscience. And therefore what ought to be understood here is something that obliges
by virtue of the command of a superior power, and this can be
nothing but a thing indifferent. (iii) Because the Apostle takes
indifferent things as an example. Tribute, he says, to whom tribute

---

* Cf. Bagshaw, who fits this description neatly, 1660 (*a*), Preface, and Jeanes,
1659—which was printed again in Oxford in 1660 by the University printer; Jeanes
acknowledges all the laws specified by Locke, under other names, but defines their
spheres of action in such a way as to preclude the 'pressing of ceremonies' (pp. 42 f.);
or John Milton, *A Treatise of Civil Power*, 1659.   † Rom. xiii. 1.

‡ It would seem that Locke intends *res* and *bona val mala* to agree with each other
in this sentence; I have taken them in this sense.

is due,* although it is certain that no tribute is due unless the magistrate commands it, both ownership and the rights of property being in general entirely free, it being open to everyone individually either to harvest his wealth or to give away his riches to anyone else and, as it were, to transfer them; and whether they are ours or another's is a matter of complete indifference.

But what is the point of all this? Who, you will ask, denies the power of the magistrate in civil indifferent things? I will tell you: the fact is that he who denies either of these powers denies them both. And there are indeed some who flatly and openly do this, denying what others admit when pressed, although they [too] deny it when disputing; so true is it that either both [powers] must be kept or both must be abandoned.†

We must therefore start by establishing that general principle from which, once it is proved, it will follow with perfect justice that indifferent things, even those regarding divine worship, must be subjected to governmental power. Now as the indifferency of all things is exactly the same and on both sides we find the same arguments and indeed the same matter, the only difference being in the way they are viewed, there being no greater distinction than there is between a gown worn in the market-place and the self-same gown worn in church, it is clear that the magistrate's authority embraces the one type of indifferent things as much as the other unless God by some decree of his own has circumscribed the magistrate's power within narrower limits, not allowing his sanctuary to be set within the bounds of the civil jurisdiction.

But for the truth to be more clearly evident the subject must be examined a little more profoundly. The sources of civil power must be investigated and the very foundations of authority uncovered.‡

---

* Rom. xiii. 7.

† The body of this sentence is not at all clear; the link which presumably exists between the first clause and the last has not emerged; I have presumed a stop after *negant*. The first position mentioned by Locke is that of the Fifth Monarchists, cf. William Aspinwall, *The legislative power is Christ's alone* (1656), where the implications of Locke's point are seen and seized in a denial of the magistrate's legislative competence, 'Magistrates have a law-ordering power, law-making...is Christ's alone' (p. 19).

‡ This is Locke's first unorthodox step; few previous participants in the debate on indifferency had pushed their inquiry back as far as this; rather, one or other of the positions examined by Locke is usually taken for granted: cf. Sanderson, 1660, VII, sect. xix; Taylor, *Ductor Dubitantium*, Bk. III, ch. I, and above, p. 42.

Now I find that there are, among the authors who discuss this question, commonly two such foundations.* It is not impossible for our present thesis to be grounded on either of these foundations or to be established whichever of the two is accepted. For some suppose men to be born in servitude, others, to liberty. The latter assert an equality between men founded on the law of nature, while the former maintain a paternal right over children and claim that government originates thence.† However that may be, this much is certain, that, if the magistrate is born to command, and if he possesses the throne and sceptre by divine institution and by the distinction of his character and nature, then it is beyond dispute that he is the sole ruler of the land and its inhabitants without

[p. 11] contract or condition and that he may do whatever is not forbidden by God, to whom alone he is subjected and from whom alone he received his title to live and to rule. Nor can anyone deny that all indifferent actions, of whatsoever sort they may be, lie under the power of him to whose discretion are delivered the liberty, fortunes and the life itself of every subject. But, if men enjoy a right to an equal liberty, being equal by virtue of their common birth, then it is clear that no union could occur among men, that no common way of life would be possible, no law, nor any constitution by which men could, as it were, unite themselves into a single body unless each one first divests himself of that native liberty— as they suppose it to be—and transfers it to some other, whether a prince or a senate (depending on the constitution on which they happen to agree) in whom a supreme power must necessarily reside.‡ For a commonwealth without human laws never has

* This 'finding' is itself a commonplace; cf. Hobbes, *De Corpore Politico*, pp. 81–2, *De Cive* (English Works, II, pp. 70 f.); or among works we may more confidently suppose Locke to have read, Antony Ascham, 1649, part II, ch. x, p. 104, or Dudley Digges, 1644, who (pp. 14 ff.) declares himself 'unwilling' to weary his readers with the 'unprofitable debate' of 'the originall power', by which he means the debate between the two theories Locke specifies in the next sentence. And cf. Sanderson, 1660, VII, sect. xiv *et seq.*; and above, p. 76.

† Filmer apart, the normal device is rather to reinterpret one of these theories in terms of the other; thus Hobbes, *Leviathan*, II, xx, contrives to conclude that dominion paternal is 'not by generation but by contract'. Digges, 1644, accepts a patriarchal origin but proposes a contractual present basis for government. On the other hand, Sanderson, 1660, VII, xvi, states an unqualified theory of the patriarchal origin of government; as he does again in his preface to Ussher's *The Power Communicated by God to the Prince* (1661).

‡ For a discussion of these seemingly Hobbesian views cf. above, p. 76. But see, too, Digges, 1644, who, much in the manner of Locke, announces his willingness to adopt the 'scheme' of the contract theory for purposes of argument and then builds,

existed and never could, and laws derived from any but the highest power cannot bind; for who would have the right to determine anything against his superiors, or those who were equally free? Now that power is sovereign which has no superior on earth to which it is bound to give an account of its actions.* But such a power can never be established unless each and every individual surrenders the whole of this natural liberty of his, however great it may be, to a legislator, granting it to him who with the authority of all (by proxy, as it were), empowered by the general consent of each, makes valid laws for them.† Whence it follows that whatever any individual is permitted to do that, too, the magistrate is permitted to command. For he concentrates in his person the authority and natural right of every individual by a general contract; and all indifferent things, sacred no less than profane, are entirely subjected to his legislative power and government.

To these a third way of constituting civil power may perhaps be added:‡ One in which all authority is held to come from God but the nomination and appointment of the person bearing that power is thought to be made by the people. Otherwise a right to govern will not easily be derived from the paternal right nor a right of life and death from the popular.

However, I offer no conclusion about these theories, nor do I consider it of any relevance to our present controversy whether one or other of them be true.§ Rather I say: God wished there to

before Hobbes, a 'one body' theory of government on his concession, and concludes, 'What the supreame Power, that is the State, does is truly the act of all, and none can have just quarrel with what they themselves doe'.

* Compare this definition with that of Bodin, *summa in cives ac subditos legibusque soluta potestas*, Republic, I, viii, and of Sanderson, 1660, VII, sect. vi, *Supremus scilicet Magistratus; solo Deo minor, quique in gubernando commisso sibi populo nec superiorem habet nec parem.*

† Cf. above, p. 77, and Ascham, 1649, for whom again subjects are 'fastened to a state by the ligaments of our own wills'.

‡ Sanderson, 1660, VII, sect. xv, though subsequently favouring the paternal derivation of government also concludes his discussion with the distinction Locke advances here—between government as such, which proceeds from God, and particular governors in whose selection the people may partake. Digges, 1644 (p. 28), adopts this *mediante populi consensu* theory. But the best known and best argued recent statement of this view was that of Edward Gee, *The Divine Right and Original of the Civil Magistrate from God* (1658), p. 295.

§ The remarkably concise statement that follows is surely the sum of Locke's political philosophy at this time. His theory sets out from the will of God; cf. above, p. 79, and English *Tract*, pp. 1–3, 36, *Essay Concerning Toleration* (MS Locke c. 28, fol. 21), *Third Letter for Toleration*, ch. 11, for Locke's remarkable consistency in the use of this particular strategy.

be order, society and government among men. And this we call the commonwealth. In every commonwealth there must be some supreme power without which it cannot truly be a commonwealth; and that supreme power is exactly the same in all government, namely, legislative.* The object and matter of legislative power we have shown above to be all indifferent things, and we repeat once more that either the power of the supreme magistrate is over these, or else it is nothing. But since it is certainly agreed that the magistrate has power over civil things indifferent, and most people grant this to be so, it would follow from their own arguments that if religion did not exist all indifferent things would [p. 12] be subject to the authority of the magistrate, and therefore, since our religion is Christian, it follows that if no law can be deduced from the Christian religion by which any part of indifferent things is withdrawn from the magistrate's control, and by which the magistrate is forbidden to determine this or that sort of indifferency in this or that respect, then power in all indifferent things is of exactly the same extent as if there were no religion at all, since the authority of the magistrate is denied in many indifferent things only on the pretext of a Christian law of this sort.

But whether any law of this sort opposed to civil power can in fact be found established among the precepts of the Gospel will appear from the following arguments of the dissenting schools.

(1) The first among them are those who, proceeding directly, maintain that the law of the Gospel takes this authority from the magistrate to itself and keeps the civil governor at a distance from holy matters. They claim that the New Testament forbids him to presume to intermingle himself and his power with holy worship.† They exult in their present emancipation from this slavery and chatter about nothing but their Christian liberty. Determined to make good their case, they pile up Scriptural texts, quote the testimony of the Apostles, marshal an army of instances and, with complete faith in these forces, look for an easy and certain victory. As it would be tedious to go through each of these cases individu-

---

* Cf. *Two Treatises*, II, sect. 134.

† Cf. Bagshaw, 1660 (a); his 'second argument' is that imposing is 'directly contrary to Gospel precept' and he proceeds to make his case on the strength of a string of Scriptural texts; in the *Second Part*, this becomes his principal theme; cf. too, Milton, *De Doctrina Christiana*, pp. 153–5; and 1659, pp. 7, 55.

ally, let alone to discuss and refute them in detail, I shall briefly reply thus: truly, great liberty is given to mankind by our Saviour and is often proclaimed in the Gospel, but on looking at that evidence a little more carefully it will be agreed that this liberty provides very little support for their argument. For that liberty of which mention is so frequently made in the Gospel has two senses only.* One is that Christ frees his subjects from the dominion and slavery of the devil. The other is that he removed from the necks of the Jews that grim yoke of the ceremonial law which, as the Apostle Peter observes,† neither they nor their fathers could support; and, after nullifying that law under which, straitened and oppressed, they had long groaned, he set them free to enjoy the common destiny of his subjects and of his most welcome kingdom.

However, the New Testament nowhere makes any mention of the controlling or limiting of the magistrate's authority since no precept appointed for the civil magistrate appears either in the Gospel or in the Epistles. In truth it is for the most part silent as to government and civil power, or rather Christ himself, often lighting on occasions of discussing this matter, seems to refuse deliberately to involve himself in civil affairs and, not owning any kingdom but the divine spiritual one as his own, he let the civil government of the commonwealth go by unchanged. And the Apostle Paul, the teacher of the Gentiles, confirms the point, I *Cor.* c. 7, where he teaches that the civil condition of men is not to be altered at all by Christian religion and liberty, but that bondservants, even though they were made subject to Christ, should still continue bondservants in their civil state and owe the same obedience as before to their masters. Nor is the argument at all different in [p. 13] the case of the prince and his subjects, since there appears not the faintest trace in Holy Scripture of any commandment by which the power of the magistrate is diminished in any indifferent matters.

(2) Others deny that the magistrate is allowed to impose indifferent things in divine worship on the ground that Scripture itself

* The only other major writer on indifferency and conscience to take Christian liberty in quite so limited a sense is Taylor, *Ductor Dubitantium*, Bk. III, i, sect. 28.

† Acts xv. x; cf. Sanderson, 1660, v, sect. xxxi, having presented the 'conclusion' that human laws *rite constitutae...obligant subditorum conscientias*, goes on to discuss the objections to this view, *quorum primum et praecipuum est illud quod a Christiana libertate petitur: cui confirmando pleraque Scripturae loca quae ad astruendam illam libertatem spectant, magna cum in medium afferuntur, et objectiones inde varie efformantur.*

is a perfect rule both of life and conduct.* I reply:† that by this argument the perfection of Scripture abolishes the magistrate's power in civil as much as in ecclesiastical things. For if Scripture is so far a perfect rule of conduct that it is an offence to introduce other laws regarding the reform and discipline of conduct, civil edicts would, on this account, be as unlawful henceforth as religious ones. Nor would it be right for the magistrate to enact a law about anything at all, since no law can be introduced which is not in some sort a rule of life and conduct. By what greater right could he prescribe a style of dress to judges and lawyers than to priests and ministers of religion? Or how should he presume to determine place, manner and time of speaking for a lecturer any more than for a preacher of the Gospel, since the argument is the same in each case and that perfect rule of life neither needs nor allows any other rule for determining the conduct of the Christian lecturer or public speaker? But I suggest that this rule can be called perfect in two ways. First, Scripture can be called a perfect rule in so far as it provides general standards of conduct from which all other particular rules derive and can be deduced. Nor can any just command be discovered, whether of magistrate, parent or master, which is not contained and grounded in Scripture, as, for example, that precept, Let all things be done decently and in order,‡ encompasses the particular laws regarding the ceremonies of divine worship subsequently to be enacted by the governors of the church. Secondly, that may be called a perfect rule of conduct which embraces each particular duty of our lives and prescribes what should be done and what left undone by each of us in every circumstance—a perfect rule of life such as there never was or could be. Or, if they like, Scripture is a perfect rule of the inward and necessary worship, but it has nowhere delivered or described the number and kind of ceremonies and circumstances but has left them to the churches themselves so that the custom of each place

---

* By 1660 this was 'the characteristic principle of the Congregationalists': Nuttall, *Visible Saints*, ch. 11; cf. Bradshawe, 1660(*b*) '*In primis* they hold and maintain that the Word of God contained in the writings of the Prophets and Apostles is of absolute perfection'; but see, too, the Fifth Monarchist, Aspinwall, *The Legislative power is Christ's Alone* (1656): 'My intention in this small tractate is to shew the perfection of the whole word of God.'

† Locke's answer is rather more substantial than, though in effect the same as, that of Sanderson to the same objection, 1660, VI, sect. xxviii, 2.

‡ I Cor. xiv. 40; cf. above, p. 20, and Sanderson, 1660, VI, sect. xxviii.

might be taken into account and all things established in the light of the necessity of the times, the opinions of men and the dignity of the things themselves.

(3) It is objected that to mix the contrivances of human wit with divine worship is 'superstition';* that acts of worship which ought to be performed according to the purpose and rule of the divine will do not allow of human ceremonies, nor are presumptuous men lightly permitted to violate that holy sphere and the realm in which God is sole legislator. Hence if any rite is prescribed in divine worship which is distasteful to their palate, they at once launch a bitter attack on the legislator and pass sentence with severe censure on both the thing itself and its author. But because 'superstition' is a word which has an evil sound, by this means, as though with some spectre, those who seek either to decry or to [p. 14] change the outward worship of God are accustomed to alarm the ignorant minds of the crowd, and they apply this designation as a mask to things that are quite inoffensive and proper.

In Latin the word means the worship of those remaining alive after death and it corresponds to the word δαιμονία, which has various meanings in Greek:† first, it is synonymous with the worship of demons, that is, of spirits; second, the worship of heroes; third, fear (which they consider slavish) of the one true God, as a result of which, terrified no doubt, we represent the deity as harsh, implacable and cruel; fourth, the worship of each sect and religion is called 'superstition' by others since the initiates of every sect, condemning all other ways of worshipping the deity but their own, are in the habit of labelling them 'superstition'. Thus, Festus calls the Christian religion a superstition, *Acts*, c. 25, v. 19, *But had certain questions against him of their own superstition, and*

---

* Cf. above, p. 41, and Bradshawe, 1660(*b*); the fourth tenet is 'that it is grosse superstition for any mortal man to institute or ordain as parts of Divine Worship any mysticall rite and Ceremonie of Religion'; superstition is the first and major objection presented by Bagshaw, 1660 (*a*), p. 4.

† Cf. G. J. Vossius, *Etymologica Linguae Latinae* (1662), p. 504. But Locke's discussion is closer to that of Hammond, 1644, 4, Of Superstition, sects. ii–xxvi: superstition 'in Latine is most clearly according to the use of the word *Superstitium Cultus*, the worship of some departed from this World supposed yet to have life in another'; and he proceeds to the Greek word to which he gives four meanings: worship of demons, worship of heroes, fear of evil spirits, and fear of the supernatural in general. Locke's own later definition of superstition is an extension of the third position he states here, 'apprehension of evil from God and hopes, by formal and outward addresses to him to appease him without real amendment of life', etc. (MS Film 77, p. 30).

of one Jesus, who was dead, whom Paul affirmed to be alive.[*] Whence we conclude that the same liberty is granted to these objectors as was allowed Festus: they may call the institutions of the Church and the religious ceremonial prescribed by law 'superstition', but the worship itself is not thereby rendered in any way less lawful. Nor is it any more to be repudiated on that account than the Christian faith had to be abandoned by blessed Paul once he had heard it called 'superstition'. When, in short, they claim that God is the sole legislator this is to be understood in the same way as the argument that Scripture is the only and perfect rule of life. Namely, that God alone has power over the consciences of men, that he alone enacts laws on his own authority, and that all just commands, public as well as private, proceed from his will and are founded on it.[†] However, that text, *One only is the Lawgiver able to save and to destroy,* taken from the Epistle of St James,[‡] is not wholly relevant to the present issue, as appears from the context.

(4) Scandal is raised as an objection; that is to say, the magistrate is not allowed to impose ceremonies because they are stumbling-blocks.[§]

In the first place, I reply that that is not a scandal which annoys another, or which another considers improper to be performed—which is habitually the state of mind of those who take the opposite view and who usually sin, not by imitating, in which the nature of scandal consists, but by taking offence.[¶]

Second, I hold that all that which is called scandalous, at which a man may stumble and so fall, is not directly evil; for Christ himself is often called a stumbling-block and many are said to have been offended by him.

[*] Locke's use of this story is eccentric and mal-contrived; his concern to emphasize his own dominant sense of human partiality has led him to offer a particularly tendentious gloss; Festus, after all, uses the word in the quite strict sense of Locke's first definition; Hammond uses the text in this connexion: 'Festus...putting him under the vulgar notion of dead Heroes.'

[†] Taylor, *Ductor Dubitantium,* III, i, sect. 34, 'The difference of Divine and Human laws in their Obligation'. [‡] James, iv. 12; cf. Sanderson, 1660, VI, sect. xxvii.

[§] Scandal was the most usual objection of all parties; cf. above, p. 46, also Bagshaw, 1661 (*a*), p. 16; Bradshawe, 1660 (*a*), *Twelve General Arguments Proving that the Ceremonies...are Unlawfull,* no. 12, 'Ceremonies are...directly against the law of Charity...', etc.; Locke's answers are standard too.

[¶] Locke follows the Anglican models here; cf. Morton, 1619; Hammond, 1644, II, Of Scandal, etc.; Morton opens with the proposition, 'scandal...is not every kind of grieveing or angring of any Brother'; Hammond, sect. xvii, similarly makes sin reside in the imitation, not in the example.

Third, I hold that he who takes offence always errs, but not so he who gives it.*

Fourth, I say that if the magistrate were not allowed to establish anything but what cannot offend anyone he could not justly enact any law at all, since nothing is so pleasing to everyone, nothing seems so just and reasonable to every eye, that someone will not discover in it something which he will denounce and consider in his judgment unlawful.†

And, fifth, I hold that because it may happen that a man is genuinely offended by ceremonies established by the magistrate it does not therefore follow that the law is sinful and on that account does not oblige, since the ill will of an individual inferior or a private opinion or scruple does not in the least prejudice the public [p. 15] right of the magistrate. Nor can any condition of an inferior possibly suspend the power of a superior. For in such a case the obligation of laws would depend, not on the will of the magistrate but on our assent, and a subject might at will nullify all the laws enacted by the magistrate. It can never be that the magistrate should know the minds and wishes of all his subjects, since the perverting influence of customs, the frivolity of opinions, the allurements of pleasures, the violence of passions and the enthusiasm of parties confuse and mislead our feeble minds in such diverse ways. Nor, even if he did know, could he or should he consult the opinion and scruples of all concerned.‡ It suffices for the legality and obligation of a law if in free and indifferent contexts he establishes whatever appears to him, as bearing responsibility for the commonwealth, to be in some way conducive to public peace and the welfare of the people.§

(5) Others,¶ to withdraw themselves from the reach of the

---

* Hammond, 1644, II, Of Scandal, 'no man is offended or scandalized but...he falls into some sin'; Bagshaw, 1661 (a), p. 16, treats this *scandalum acceptum non datum* theory with some scorn; so does Milton, 1659, pp. 58 ff.

† Morton, 1619, ch. v, reaches the same general conclusion, 'If every pretence of God's feare might chalenge favour of transgressing Man's law...', etc.

‡ The Latin seems to be slightly unsatisfactory here; to have the sense which is surely intended one must suppose a negative or an interrogative form.

§ Cf. Taylor, *Ductor Dubitantium*, III, i, rule vii, 'that a law should oblige does not depend on the acceptance of the people'; and above, p. 42.

¶ This is the position not only of Bagshaw but more particularly of the Vanists or Seekers; Locke may have had contact with this group through his Christ Church colleague and correspondent Henry Stubbe. Stubbe wrote a defence of the Vanist position in 1659 and Sir Henry Vane was his patron; cf. Sir Henry Vane, *The Retired Man's Meditations* (1655), p. 388; and J. Willcock, *Life of Sir Henry Vane the Younger*

magistrate and to flout the obligation of the laws established by him, retire into themselves and seek an asylum where they may safely hide in the depths of their own conscience, not to be profaned in the least degree by the laws and ceremonies of the church. This liberty of conscience is altogether divine and under obligation only to the will of God, so that if the magistrate asserts that it lies within the scope of his power, he culpably perpetrates an affront to the divine majesty and does violence and injustice to his fellow men. Hence all laws which in any way constrain or circumscribe this liberty are held to be *ipso facto* unlawful and void.

But, in order to understand what laws are indeed opposed to the liberty of conscience—it being apparent that all the just laws of the magistrate, civil as well as ecclesiastical, do oblige the consciences of subjects—some distinction must first be made between obligation and liberty.*

I maintain, then, that the obligation of human laws may be of two sorts, (1) Material, (2) Formal.†

(1) Obligation is 'material' when the thing itself which is the subject-matter of a human law obliges the conscience of itself; when, that is, it was already unquestionably necessary by virtue of the force of the divine law before the introduction of a human law. (2) Obligation is 'formal' when a thing otherwise indifferent is imposed on the people by the lawful power of the magistrate and obliges the conscience. One of these obliges of its own nature, the other by virtue of the extent of the magistrate's command.

It follows that the liberty with which we are concerned here is also twofold:‡ (1) a liberty of the judgment, (2) a liberty of the will.

(1) Liberty of the judgment exists when the approbation of the judgment is not necessarily required that this or that is in its own nature 'necessary'; and in this consists the whole liberty of the conscience. (2) Liberty of the will exists when the assent of the

---

(1913), has drawn attention to Locke's ownership of a copy of this work. The same view is found in Milton, 1659, p. 21, and Owen, 1826, xv, p. 452, 'A Christian God's Temple'.

* Cf. Sanderson, 1660, vi, sect. iv; Locke is more precise than Sanderson in specifying his categories, but the content of their arguments is identical.

† Sanderson, 1660, vi, sect. iv, *scilicet praeceptionem Legis humanae posse sumi dupliciter: vel formaliter, pro ipso actu praecipiendi; vel materialiter pro re praecepta.*

‡ Sanderson, 1660, vi, sect. v; Taylor, *Ductor Dubitantium*, iii, i, 'The laws of God bind the will and the understanding...human laws meddle not with the understanding'.

will is not required to this or that act; and this can be removed without infringing the liberty of the conscience.

These points being made, I now hold:

(1) That if the magistrate commands what has already been enjoined by God—for example, that a subject should refrain from theft or adultery—the obligation of this law is both material and formal so that the liberty of both the judgment and the will is removed and thereby that of the conscience itself. Such a law, [p.16] however, is not unjust, since it throws no new shackles on the conscience, nor does the magistrate set other or narrower limits to the liberty of the conscience than does God himself.*

(2) That if the magistrate, in so far as he is provided with legislative power, on his own authority commands a free and indifferent action of his subjects by decree, then that law—since its obligation is merely formal and not material, that is, the matter is made necessary not of its own nature but by virtue of the command of the civil magistrate—certainly binds the conscience. But it does not remove its liberty since to be obeyed it requires the assent of the will only. It does not require the assent of the judgment that it has any necessity in itself.† And hence I say that all the magistrate's laws, civil as well as ecclesiastical, those that concern divine worship as much as those that concern civil life, are just and valid, obliging men to act but not to judge; and, providing for both at the same time, unite a necessity of obedience with a liberty of conscience.

(3) That if the magistrate chooses to impose a thing indifferent by material obligation on his subjects; that is to say, if he legislates as if the thing was in itself necessary before the law was proposed by him when in fact it was not but was quite indifferent, then by such a law he ensnares the liberty of the conscience and sins in commanding it. But in truth ecclesiastical laws, by which acts are transformed into ceremonial practices, are not proposed in this manner, nor so much ordered because they are necessary as called necessary because they are ordered.‡

* Locke has somewhat rearranged Sanderson's argument here, cf. 1660, Praelect. VI, sect. ix; Sanderson's argument is actually more subtle as he allows that there is a *new* obligation effected in such cases.

† Cf. Sanderson, 1660, VI, sect. iv, *Quod si obligationem eam non aliunde ducat, quam a praeceptione suae legis formaliter accepta . . .etsi obligatio sequatur, quae parendi necessitatem conscientiae imponat, illaesa tamen et integra manet interna Conscientiae libertas.*

‡ Sanderson, 1660, VI, sect. iv, *longe enim alia res est, cum quid propterea a Magistratu praecipitur, quod putetur esse necessarium; aut prohibetur, quia putatur esse illictum,*

Finally, at the end of the column, come those who forbode ill of the authority of the magistrate and say that so great a power is neither lawful nor tolerable on this ground: that it can be extremely productive of misfortune, that it can be full of hazards, that it is impossible to know where the magistrate will finally restrain himself. What burden or absurdity, they repeatedly cry, may not a headstrong magistrate impose on us, if he is endowed with an almost infinite power of this sort?* Why has God bestowed reason on us, and why religion, to what purpose are we born human, to what end made Christians, if neither our reason nor our religion will suffice to establish practices for fulfilling the worship of God?† And a great many similar complaints and bugbears‡ of various kinds are conjured up in the empty heads of these foolish men.

But it is appropriate to observe here, that these objections, as those mentioned before, oppose and uproot the power of the magistrate in civil indifferencies as much as in those of religion, whence again we may perceive how close the affinity and association is between all things indifferent, those regarding ceremonies no less than those regarding manners.§ So that if the authority of the magistrate is withdrawn, even in part, from the one, it collapses in the other. But, briefly, I reply: in the nature of things there is nothing so utterly perfect and harmless that from it no evil can, or is accustomed to, derive, or at least be feared; and many just and [p. 17] lawful things are regularly felt by some to be senseless and onerous. But in truth those inconveniences which befall me, or

etc. Bagshaw, 1661 (a), p. 13, inveighs against this distinction between freedom of practice and freedom of judgment, a distinction which, he notes, is 'the Summe of what many Learned men both in their Writings and Discourses do affirm'.

* Among whom Bagshaw is conspicuous, 1660 (a), p. 10; it is, he argues, 'impossible to fix a point where the imposer's power will stop', once Locke's view is granted; cf. Bradshawe, 1660(a), *A Treatise of Divine Worship*, p. 10, 'Those that have power upon their own will and pleasure to bring into God's service some indifferent thing, may bring in any indifferent thing; those that bring in without special warrant from God, pyping into his Service, might as well bring in dancing'.

† Cf. Henry Stubbe, 1659, pp. 17 f., the work 'reviewed' by Locke in MS Locke c. 28, fol. 12: 'to what purpose is there so much liberty permitted as may begett our torture?...', etc., and again, 'God did ill to endow us with reason which ought to have no further use in us than that we quit it in its principal exercise...'; it seems quite likely that Locke had this passage in mind here.

‡ Hooker, I, vii, 6, in a very similar context describes the inflammatory devices of political rhetoric as 'bugs words'.

§ Cf. Sanderson, 1660, VI, sect. xxviii.

can befall me, from the right of another in no way impede his right.*

And so I have now displayed and described the forces of the enemy in this slight sketch and in passing have touched lightly on the heads of their arguments. To review all their devices and examples and authorities would be a tedious business, nor does time allow, or the weight of the arguments demand, a detailed examination. Whoever now takes arms against us will find his place in the ranks set out above. [p. 18]

* Bagshaw, 1660 (a), pp. 10–15, argues that inconveniences *should* be considered as limitations on the rights of Christian magistrates; but Locke is not altogether fair here; there is a sense in which his whole argument can itself be taken as an argument from inconvenient consequences, cf. above, p. 20.

APPENDIX I

SUPPLEMENTARY PAPERS: THE LOCKE MSS
AND THE SOURCES OF LOCKE'S THOUGHT

In this section I have reproduced three subsidiary manuscripts from Locke's papers which in different ways throw light on the context, occasion and meaning of the two *Tracts*. Secondly, I have drawn on the Locke MSS as a whole to present an account of works read by the author before or soon after 1660 which might have influenced his political and moral philosophy. In this context I have taken the opportunity to discuss some of the manuscript sources of the present study in general; for more detailed treatment see Von Leyden, 1954, and Abrams, 1961.

(A) THE LETTER TO 'S.H.'

This manuscript (MS Locke c. 27, fols. 12–13) is a draft version of the letter that Locke presumably sent to Stubbe after reading the latter's *Essay in Defence of the Good Old Cause*. It contains what are obviously alternative versions of many sentences, phrases and words. I have included here all those passages that bear on Locke's early political thinking. I have eliminated a number of duplications and deletions and have modernized Locke's spelling and punctuation. A few phrases remain illegible.

S. H.

The same messenger that carried my letter the last week to Bristol returned with your book, which I have read with infinite satisfaction and the only pauses I made in my hasty perusal were to reflect with admiration the strength and vigour of your style, seasoned with many poignant passages of wit and sharp sallies, and that clearness of reason and plenty of matter wherewith every page is stuffed. The only deficient I complain of, if I may be permitted to complain after satisfaction, which I do, [is] not that I think your weapon less sharp if you do not everywhere show where the point lies or think you no good champion because you do not hold it in that posture and manage it with that regulated motion which a pedantical fencer would prescribe you, but because that party you more particularly design it against are so blinded with prejudice and ignorance that they will not be able to discover them unless a figure or hand in the margin direct their purblind observation; you must tell them what is arguing *ab impossibile*, what *ab incongrue*, if you will have them take notice, and they will never believe you have any forces unless you draw them up into battalions and show them where they lie encamped; they are so general habituated to that play of *primus secundus tertius*, the only thing one may confidently presume they learned at school, that unless you deal with them in the same method they will not think themselves concerned, they will not conceive it possible they should be met with by a man that travels not in the same track.* I am sorry that you continued not your history of toleration down to these times and given us an account of Holland, France, Poland, etc, since nearest examples have the greatest influence and we are most easily persuaded to tread in those fresh steps which time has least defaced, and men will travel in that road which is most beaten though carriers only be their guides; when you have [shown?] the authority of antiquity the testimony of daily experience will demonstrate that men of different professions may quietly unite under the same government and unanimously carry the same civil interest and hand in hand march to the same end of peace and mutual society though they take different ways towards heaven.† You will add no small strength to your cause and be very convincing to those to whom what you have already said has left nothing to doubt but whether it be now practicable.

The only scruple I have is how the liberty you grant the Papists (which I consent with you ought to be denied them only in reference to the State), can consist with the security of the Nation (the end of government) since I cannot see how they can at the same time obey two different authorities carrying on contrary interests, especially where that which is destructive to ours is backed with an opinion of infallibility and holiness supposed by them to be immediately derived from God founded in the Scripture and in their own equally sacred tradition, not limited by any contract and therefore not accountable to anybody, and you know how easy it is under the pretence of spiritual jurisdiction to [take?] in all secular affairs since in a commonwealth wholly Christian it is no small difficulty to set limits to each and to define exactly where one begins and the other ends.‡ Besides, I cannot apprehend what

* Locke here proceeds to a long satirical illustration of the hazards of formalism —an illustration drawn not from academic life but from the prevalence of the manner of the 'school of complements' in ordinary social discourse.

† This was always Locke's ideal; the irony here is, of course, obvious; the cases of 'daily testimony' that he asks Stubbe to consult are all instances of anarchy, destruction and violence of the most brutal sort caused by religious differences. The impossibility of men living quietly together while holding contrary beliefs was, indeed, the theme of two despondent histories of the world published in 1659; cf. Sir Henry Wotton, *The State of Christendom*, and J. Parival, *The History of this Iron Age* (London, 1659). ‡ This is precisely what Locke asks Bagshaw to do in the English *Tract*.

security you can truly have of their fidelity and obedience from all their oaths and protestations, when that other sovereignty they pay homage to is acknowledged by them to be owner of a power that can acquit them of all perfidy and perjury, and that will [be?] ready to pardon and court them to it with dispensations and rewards, and you will have but small reason to repose trust in one who, whenever it shall be his interest (which it always will be), shall by deceiving you not only obtain the name of Innocent but meritorious, who, by throwing off his obligations (whereof he will always keep the key himself), shall not only possess himself of your portion of earth but purchase additional a title to heaven and be canonized saint at the charge of your life and liberty; and seeing you yourself (if I remember aright) make the apprehensions of interest and the justice of the cause the rule and measure of constance to, activity for, and obedience under any government, you can never hope that they should cordially concur with you to any establishment whose consciences and concearnments both for this world and hereafter shall always bias them another way. These are those tares have started up in my thoughts amongst those better seeds you have sown there, and possibly are only owing to the 'temper of the soil', and must grow or wither as you please to order them, yet however deserve weeding.* Thus you see how I make use of the liberty you allow me out of a belief that you have as much ingenuity as learning, and it is in this confidence that I appear perhaps in the head of your assailants, but not with the thoughts of a duellist but doubter, being resolved not to be an opponent but your   Admirer

(B) THE LETTER OF JAMES ALLESTRY TO SAMUEL TILLY

This document (MS Locke c. 3, fol. 21) is a short letter addressed to Tilly at 'Mr Prats near Carfax in Oxford'.

In answer to yours of the 7th instant I assure you that the Treatise you left in my hand will be put to the press tomorrow and all Expedition used in its dispatch. Wherefore I earnestly entreat you to send me the Title page and what other additions you shall think fitting to add to make it complete, by the first opportunity, as also to specify how many Copies you desire, that I may accordingly acquaint my friend who hath undertaken the printing it from whom you may expect all ingenuous and candid dealing.†

May 14th, 1661.

---

* The last four words are, however, deleted. The reference to Stubbe's 'learning' in the following sentence is no idle gesture. Stubbe was not made assistant keeper of the Bodleian for nothing. His books, including the *Essay in Defence of the Good Old Cause*, are invariably clogged with displays of semi-relevant erudition.

† 'Expect' is deleted before 'desire'.

(C) THE 'ADVERSARIA 1661'

It is suggested in the Introduction (chapter II) that orderly method and systematic procedure were for Locke necessary technical conditions for the pursuit of philosophical understanding. I suggest that this concern for an orderly method of work may well have been a consequential factor in his intellectual development from scholasticism to empiricism. This was certainly the case with Locke's friend and collaborator Robert Boyle, who has left us descriptions (Boyle, 1744) of the sequence of experiments that led to a similar transformation of his thought. Insistence on disciplined procedure is one of the plainly unchanging elements of Locke's thought. The enthusiasm for measuring, tabulating, arranging, comparing spreads through all his work. We may take the elaborate tabulation of concepts and categories that appears on pp. 1–3 of the *Adversaria 1661* (Bodleian Library, MS Film, 77) as a true map of his thought world at the time he wrote the *Tracts* —the ultimate intellectual background against which those works should be read:

Nat 29 Aug: 32   *Adversaria 1661*

	Theologia	Historica vel Rationalis
	Spiritus	Angeli
	Immortalitas	Anima separata. Resurrectio
	Cultus	Ritus. Ceremoniae. Sanctorum invocatio. Sacerdotes
	Ethica	Lex naturae — virtutes et vitiae

	Politia		*Prudentia*	
		Finis est		
Fundamenta	Ius paternum	Felicitas	Caelestis quae
	Consensus populi	Tranquilitas	pertinet ad Theologiam
		Sanitas	quae pertinet ad
		Opes	Physicam
Forma	Monarchia	Potestas	quae pertinet ad
	Aristocratia	Fama	oeconomiam
	Democratia	Gratia	quae pertinet ad
	Mixta		Politiam
	Constitutiones	Media ad hos fines	
	fundamentales	Sui cognitio	
		In passiones suas imperium	

Administratio Leges Civiles Ingeniorum Cognitio
                               Consiliorum indagatio
                               Animorum Gubernatio Rhetorica
                               Oeconomica
                               Venditio et Comptio—Historia
                               Artis exercitum   mercatura
                                                    cuiuslibet

Physica sive Corporum Scientia

Materia
    Extensio et numerus Geometria
    Motus   Mechanica
    Universum   Mundus Creatio

Caelestis
    Ignis   Astronomia
    Aer   Meteora
    Aqua   Mare
    Terrestria Geographia physica

Fossilia

Vegetabilia

Animalia Insecta Volatilia Grissilia natantia

Homo

Anima: Intellectus voluntas passiones—quae pertinere etiam possunt
              ad Theologiam

Corpus humanum: Medecina: Anatomia sive hist partium; Pathologia
              sive historia affectuum et Therapeutia sive hist
              curationum

Sensus   Obiecta sensum
        Numerus   Arithmetica
        Extensio   Geometria

Quantitas Motus Gravitas pondus mechanica
          Colores pictoria et tinctura

Motus   Soni musici
         Odores
         Sapores Coquinaria
         Tactiles qualitates   Calor frigus et de his omnes artes
                       mechanicae

Relatio

His omnibus addenda nomina Relationum quae solum sunt nostri de
rebus inter se comparatis conceptus.

(D) MS EVIDENCE OF THE SOURCES OF LOCKE'S POLITICAL IDEAS

I have drawn together in this section the works with any sort of political bearing which, on the evidence of Locke's own early notebooks and correspondence, he may be supposed to have read or known in some detail before or soon after 1660. The MS from which each title is taken has been indicated, but the degree of reliability with which the different notebooks can be dated varies considerably. It seems reasonable to infer that Locke maintained something like parallel series of notebooks throughout this period of his life. Thus, we have an early volume used for miscellaneous purposes and headed *Lemmata*. Then we find a book dated 1659 but which was apparently used for notes made at three different stages in his career: around 1660, around 1680 and around 1694; this is headed *Lemmata Ethica*; a companion volume of medical and chemical materials is headed *Lemmata Physica*. Similarly there is a general notebook under the title *Adversaria*, dated 1661 but actually used rather later and regularly; one volume of an *Adversaria Pharmacopeia* series; and indications of an *Adversaria Physica* series. I have assumed all books in the general *Lemmata* volume to have been read by Locke before 1660; at the back of the *Lemmata Ethica* is a book list which I have also taken to indicate books Locke had read when he wrote the *Tracts*; one at least of these titles (Bergerac, *Comicall History of the World in the Moon*) is discussed in contemporary correspondence between Locke and Strachey. Most of the works mentioned in the account book, MS Locke f. 11, have indications of specific dates at which Locke either bought them or recommended them to his pupils. MS Locke f. 27 is dated between 1664 and 1665, and works listed in it are not noted here; MS Locke f. 14, however, which is dated 1667, has been used as the dating is somewhat ambiguous. On page 19 of this volume the entries are reorganized on Locke's standard commonplace system; I have assumed that works entered after this point were read in 1667 or later but that the miscellaneous entries before page 19 could belong to a rather earlier period. There is, for example, a reference to Edward Bagshaw on page 16 and Locke is not very likely to have been interested in making points against Bagshaw as late as 1667; the titles listed in the *Lemmata Ethica* are also listed again here on page 8; and a work we know Locke to have bought in January 1661 is listed on page 3. On this basis the political works we may confidently suppose Locke to have read by the time he wrote the Latin *Tract* would be:

ALLESTREE, RICHARD, 1659. *The Whole Duty of Man*, London. (MS f. 11.)

ASCHAM, ANTHONY, 1649. *Of the Confusions and Revolutions of Governments*. London. (MS f. 11—but the entry is simply 'Mr Ascham's book'.)

BALZAC, JEAN LOUIS DE, 1648. *The Prince*. London. (MS e. 6.)

BARCLAY, JOHN, 1630. *Argenis*. Leyden. (MS e. 6.)

BARCLAY, WILLIAM, 1600. *De regno et regali potestate adversus... Monarchomachos*. Paris. (MS f. 14.)

BODIN, JEAN, 1576. *Methodus ad facilem historianum cognitionem*. Basle. (MS e. 6.)

CICERO, 1617. *Opera*. Cologne. (MS e. 6, MS f. 11.)

CRASHAW, RICHARD, 1646. *Steps to the Temple*. London. (MS f. 11.)

DIGBY, SIR KENELM, 1651. *Letters between the Lord George Digby and Sir Kenelm Digby concerning Religion*. London. (MS e. 6.)

DIGGES, SIR DUDLEY, 1642. *An Answer to a printed book entitled observations upon his Majestie's late answers*. Oxford. (MS f. 14.)

——, 1643. *The unlawfulness of subjects taking up arms against their Sovereigne*. Oxford. (MS f. 14.)

DU BARTAS, GUILLAUME DE SALUSTE, 1641. *Divine Weeks and Works*, translated by T. Sylvester. London. (MS e. 6.)

FILMER, SIR ROBERT, 1648. *The Anarchy of a Limited or Mixed Monarchy*. London. (MS d. 10 and MS f. 14 where there are three references, pp. 5, 7, 16, and where the author is given as Sir Thomas Filmore.)

GEE, EDWARD, 1658. *The Divine Right and Original of the Civil Magistrate*. London. (MS f. 14.)

GROTIUS, HUGO, 1632. *De iure belli ac pacis*. Amsterdam. (MS f. 14.)

——, 1639. *De veritate religionis Christianae*. Oxford. (MS f. 11 and MS f. 14.)

HALES, JOHN, 1659. *Golden Remains*. London. (MS f. 14; this entry is endorsed 'pure agt Bagshaw'; cf. above, chapter 11.)

HERBERT, GEORGE, 1656. *The Temple: sacred poems and private ejaculations*. London. (MS f. 11.)

HOOKER, RICHARD. *The Laws of Ecclesiastical Polity*, Preface and Book 1; no edition specified. (MS c. 28 and MS e. 7.)

MAXWELL, JOHN, 1646. *The Burden of Issachar*. Oxford. (MS e. 7.)

MILTON, JOHN, 1641. *Of Reformation touching Church-Discipline in England*. London. (MS d. 10 and MS f. 14.)

——, 1644. *Areopagitica*. London. (MS f. 14.)

OSBORNE, FRANCIS, 1656. *Advice to a Son*. Oxford. (MS c. 24.)

PEARSON, ANTHONY, 1658. *The great case of tithes truly stated.* London. (MS d. 10 and MS f. 14.)

RICHARDSON, GABRIEL, 1627. *The State of Europe.* Oxford. (MS e. 6.)

SANDERSON, ROBERT, 1660. *De Obligatione Conscientiae, Praelectiones Decem.* London. (MS c. 28, MS e. 6 and MS e. 7.)

SENECA, 1649. *Opera.* Leyden. (MS e. 6; with Du Bartas, Seneca is the main source of references and observations in this first notebook.)

TAYLOR, JEREMY, 1648. *Treatises: the Liberty of Prophesying,* etc. London. (MS f. 11.)

WOTTON, SIR HENRY, 1654. *Reliquae Wottonianae, or a collection...* London. (MS e. 6.)

WREN, MATTHEW, 1659. *Monarchy Asserted.* Oxford. (MS f. 14.)

In addition we may note that Locke refers to a number of published state papers in these early years: the *Remonstrance* of 15 December 1651 (MS f. 14); an unspecified collection of statutes (MS f. 11); the 'Commonwealth Statute' of 1649 (MS f. 11) and a 'declaration of Parliament' of the same year (MS f. 11); and an 'act of Parliament' in 1650 (MS f. 11).

APPENDIX II

BIBLIOGRAPHY

The bibliography is divided into four sections and includes: (A) works by Locke and Bagshaw, (B) works on the 'Great Question' of indifferent things, (C) works on the general ideology of seventeenth-century England with particular reference to the theme of order, and (D) works on John Locke and general historical works.

(A) WORKS OF LOCKE AND BAGSHAW

Unless otherwise stated I have used the fourth edition of Locke's *Works*, 1740, 3 vols.

LOCKE, JOHN, 1660. *Tracts on Government*. MSS Locke, c. 28, fol. 3; e. 7.

―― 1662-4. *Essays on the Law of Nature*, edited by W. Von Leyden, Oxford, 1954.

―― 1667. *An Essay Concerning Toleration*. MS Locke c. 28, fol. 21; an earlier draft is printed by Fox Bourne, 1876, I, pp. 174-94.

―― 1690. *An Essay Concerning Human Understanding*.

―― *Of Ethic in General*. MS Locke c. 28, fol. 146.

―― 1690. *Two Treatises of Government*, edited by Peter Laslett, Cambridge, 1960.

―― 1689. *Letter Concerning Toleration*.

―― 1690. *Second Letter for Toleration*.

―― 1692. *Third Letter for Toleration*.

―― 1695. *The Reasonableness of Christianity, as delivered in the Scriptures*.

―― 1705. *A Paraphrase and Notes on the Epistles of St. Paul to the Galatians, I and II Corinthians*.

―― 1706. *Of the Conduct of the Understanding*.

BAGSHAW, EDWARD, 1657. *Dissertationes duae anti-Socinianae*. London.

―― 1659 (*a*). *De Monarcha Absoluta Dissertatio Politica*. Oxford.

―― 1659 (*b*). *A Practical Discourse concerning God's decrees*. Oxford.

―― 1660 (*a*). *The Great Question Concerning Things Indifferent in Religious Worship*. Oxford.

―― 1660 (*b*). *Saintship No Ground of Sovereignty*. Oxford.

―― 1661 (*a*). *The Second Part of the Great Question....* Oxford.

―― 1661 (*b*). *Exercitationes Duae: Orationes habitae in Aede Christi...* Oxford.

―― 1661 (*c*). *Letters...upon the Bishop of Worcesters Letter*. Oxford.

―― 1662 (*a*). *The Necessity and Use of Heresies, or the Third Part....* London.

―― 1662 (*b*). *A Letter to the Lord High Chancellor of England*.

―― 1664. *The Case and Usage of Mr Edward Bagshaw...* London.

APPENDIX II

(B) THE DEBATE ON INDIFFERENT THINGS
General works

AMES, WILLIAM, 1643. *Conscience with the Power and Cases Thereof.* London.

AQUINAS, ST THOMAS, 1920–5. *Summa Theologica*, translated by the Fathers of the English Dominican Friars, 22 vols. London.

CALVIN, JOHN, 1875. *Institutes of the Christian Religion*, translated by H. Beveridge. Edinburgh.

GREVILLE, ROBERT, LORD BROOKE, 1640. *The Nature of Truth, its Union and Unity with the Soul.* London.

—— 1641. *A Discourse Opening the Nature of Episcopacy...* London.

HALES, JOHN, 1765. *The Works of the Ever Memorable Mr John Hales.* Glasgow.

HALL, JOSEPH, 1649. *Resolutions and Decisions of Divers Cases of Conscience.* London.

HOOKER, RICHARD, 1622. *Of the Lawes of Ecclesiastical Politie, eight bookes...* London.

LUTHER, MARTIN, 1896. *Luther's Primary Works*, translated by Wace and Buckheim. London.

MILTON, JOHN, 1931–8. *De Doctrina Christiana*, in *The Works of John Milton*, XVI, ed. Patterson, Abbott and Ayres, 18 vols. New York.

OWEN, JOHN, 1826. *Two Questions Concerning the Power of the Supreme Magistrate about Religion*, in *The Works of John Owen*, XIX, ed. T. Russell, 21 vols. London.

PERKINS, WILLIAM, 1621. *A Golden Chaine, or the Description of Theologie*, translated by Robert Hill. London.

—— 1651. *The Whole Treatise of Cases of Conscience.* London.

PRESTON, J., 1631. *The Law Outlawed.* London.

RALEGH, SIR WALTER, 1677. *History of the World*, Part I, Bk II.

SANDERSON, ROBERT, 1660. *De Obligatione Conscientiae, Praelectiones decem.* London.

—— 1657. *XXXV Sermons*, and *XXI Sermons* (published together). London.

SIBBES, RICHARD, 1639. *The Excellency of the Gospel above the Law.* London.

STILLINGFLEET, EDWARD, 1660. *Irenicum, a Weapon Salve for the Church's Wounds.* London.

SUAREZ, FRANCESCO, 1944. *Tractatus de Legibus* in *Classics of International Law*, ed. J. B. Scott. New York.

TAYLOR, JEREMY, 1847–54. *The Liberty of Prophesying, Ductor Dubitantium*, in *The Whole Works of...Jeremy Taylor*, ed. Heber, Eden and Taylor. London.

Specific works, 1600–1640

The selection of polemical writings taken as typical of the whole debate on indifferency in this essay is that launched by the so-called *Lincoln Abridgment*:

An abridgment of that booke which the Ministers of Lincolne diocese deliverd to his Majestie upon the first of December 1605. London, 1617.

MORTON, THOMAS, 1619. *A defence of the Innocencie of three ceremonies of the Church of England.* London.

AMES, WILLIAM, 1622. *A reply to Dr Morton's generall defence of three nocent ceremonies.* London.

BURGES, JOHN, 1631. *An Answer rejoyned to the much applauded pamphlet, a Reply to Dr Morton's General Defence of the Innocencie of Three Ceremonies.* London.

AMES, WILLIAM, 1633. *Triplication, a Fresh Suite against Ceremonies.* London.

The three ceremonies disputed in this controversy were the sign of the cross, kneeling at communion, and 'in particular' the surplice; a similar polemical sequence of a slightly more general character is listed in the next section, below.

Specific works, 1659–60

In addition to the set of pamphlets just listed I have used the literature of indifferency published in the eighteen months prior to the writing of Locke's English *Tract*; these works are listed separately here to emphasize the dramatic acceleration and concentration of the debate in the year of the Restoration:

JEANES, HENRY, 1659. *A Treatise Concerning Indifferency in Human Actions.* Oxford.

This work is a direct continuation of the controversy detailed above and reiterates the case of Ames against Burges; in its turn it provoked:

HAMMOND, HENRY, 1659. *A Vindication of Uniformity in Humane Doctrinall Ceremonies.* Oxford.

JEANES, HENRY, 1660. *A reply unto Dr Hammond, or Uniformity ungrounded in I Cor: 14. 40.* Oxford.

Jeanes was a Somerset minister who published in Oxford; another Somerset minister also entered the debate early in 1660:

BURGESS, CORNELIUS, 1660. *Reasons shewing the Necessity of Reformation of the Publick Doctrine, Worship, Rites and Ceremonies, Church government and Discipline of the Church of England.* London, 3 August.

This provoked:

PEARSON, JOHN, 1660. *No Necessity of Reformation*... Oxford, 20 August.

SAVAGE, HENRY, 1660. *Reasons shewing that there is no need of such a Reformation*... Oxford, 5 September.

HAMILTON, WILLIAM, 1660. *Some Necessity of Reformation*...*a reply to Dr Pearson*. London, 11 September.

BURGESS, CORNELIUS, 1660. *A Postscript to Dr Pearson*. Oxford, 13 September.

PEARSON, JOHN, 1660. *An Answer to Dr Burges* [*sic*]. Oxford, 20 September.

Jeanes, in his first 'tractate', had linked the name of William Bradshawe with that of Ames in his case against John Burges; in 1660 Bradshawe's pamphlets on indifferent things were republished:

BRADSHAWE, WILLIAM, 1660 (*a*). *Severall Treatises of Worship, and Ceremonies*. London, 11 September 1660. (Originally published Amsterdam, 1604–5.)

—— 1660 (*b*). *English Puritanisme*. London. (Originally as above.)

Meanwhile, the year had also seen the publication of:

WESTFIELD, THOMAS (Bishop of Bristol), 1660. *The White Robe, or the Surplice Vindicated*. London, August.

PARRY, JOHN, 1660. *A Resolution of a Seasonable Case of Conscience*. Oxford, July.

ANON., 1660. *A modest discourse concerning ceremonies*...*shewing the unlawfulness of them in the worship of God*. London, July.

MILTON, JOHN, 1659. *A Treatise of Civil Power in Ecclesiastical causes*. London.

COLLIER, THOMAS, 1659. *The Decision and Clearing of the Great Point now in Controversie*. London.

REYNOLDS, EDWARD, 1659. *Two Sermons*...*touching the composing of Controversies*. London, in *Works*, ed. Chalmers, 1826, 6 vols.

DURHAM, JAMES, 1659. *Of Scandal*. Edinburgh.

and finally produced:

BAGSHAW, EDWARD, 1660 (*a*). *The Great Question Concerning Things Indifferent*... London, September.

Other works

The four following seventeenth-century works are of major importance for the discussion of indifferency and have also been used extensively, although they do not fit into any of the above categories:

HAMMOND, HENRY, 1644. *Tracts: Of Conscience, Of Scandall, Of Will-worship, Of Superstition, Of Resisting the Lawful Magistrate under colour of Religion.* Oxford.

OWEN, JOHN, 1659. *A Discourse concerning Liturgies,* in Owen, 1826, XIX, p. 398.

POWEL, GABRIEL, 1606. *De Adiaphoris: Theological and Scholastical positions concerning the Nature and Use of Things Indifferent.* London.

WILLIAMS, ROGER, 1644. *The Bloudy Tenent, of Persecution for cause of Conscience discussed.* London.

Also particularly the following among many later works:

BAKER, H., 1952. *The Wars of Truth: Studies in the Decay of Christian Humanism.* London.

BARKER, A. E., 1942. *Milton and the Puritan Dilemma.* Toronto.

BOSHER, R. S., 1951. *The Making of the Restoration Settlement.* London.

CRAGG, G. R., 1950. *From Puritanism to the Age of Reason.* Cambridge.

HALLER, W., 1950. *Liberty and Reformation in the Puritan Revolution.* New York.

HASTINGS, W., 1908. *Encyclopaedia of Religion and Ethics.* London.

HENSON, H. H., 1903. *Studies in English Religion in the Seventeenth Century.* London.

JORDAN, W. K., 1932–40. *The Development of Religious Toleration in England,* 4 vols. London.

KIRK, K. E., 1921. *Some Principles of Moral Theology.* London.

—— 1925. *Conscience and its Problems.* London.

LECKY, W., 1882. *History of the Rise and Influence of the Spirit of Rationalism in Europe,* 2 vols. London.

LECLER, J., 1960. *Toleration and the Reformation,* 2 vols., translated by T. L. Westow. London.

LYON, T., 1937. *The Theory of Religious Liberty in England.* Cambridge.

McADOO, H. R., 1949. *The Structure of Caroline Moral Theology.* London.

McNEILL, T. L., 1954. *The History and Character of Calvinism.* New York.

PIERCE, C. A., 1955. *Conscience in the New Testament.* London.

SEATON, A. A., 1911. *The Theory of Toleration under the Later Stuarts.* Cambridge.

SMITH, H. F. R., 1911. *The Theory of Religious Liberty in the Reigns of Charles II and James II.* Cambridge.

SPICQ, R. P., 1938. 'La Conscience dans le Nouveau Testament', *Revue biblique.* Paris.

TULLOCH, J., 1872. *Rational Theology and Christian Philosophy in England in the Seventeenth Century.* London.

WHEWELL, W., 1862. *Lectures on the History of Moral Philosophy.* Cambridge.

WOODHOUSE, A. S. P. (ed.), 1938. *Puritanism and Liberty.* London.

(C) THE IDEA OF ORDER

In this section I have listed (i) seventeenth-century works which display or explore that antithesis of order and chaos, and the related problems of knowledge, postulated as the centre of Locke's early thought in my introductory essay, and (ii) secondary works in which this theme is expounded and documented. I have not, however, repeated references to books already listed although some of these—the works of Brooke, Hooker, Raleigh and Taylor and of Baker and McAdoo for example—are of major importance in the present context.

Primary works

These are works by Locke's contemporaries or predecessors in which the root problem of moral philosophy, politics or science is seen, as it was by the young Locke, as one of extracting principles of order from a manifest chaos:

ALLESTREE, RICHARD, 1659. *The Whole Duty of Man*. London.

ANDREWES, LANCELOT, 1631. *XCVI Sermons by the . . . late Lord Bishop of Winchester*. London.

BAXTER, RICHARD, 1655. *The Arrogancy of Reason*. London.

—— 1667. *The Reasons of the Christian Religion*. London.

BOYLE, ROBERT, 1744. *The Christian Virtuoso*, and *Of the Usefulness of Natural Philosophy*, in *The Works of Robert Boyle*, 5 vols., ed. Birch. London.

BROWNE, SIR THOMAS, 1835. *The Works of Sir Thomas Browne*, ed. Wilkin. London.

BUNYAN, JOHN, 1666. *Grace abounding to the chief of sinners*. London.

CAMPANELLA, THOMAS, 1927. *Apologia pro Galileo* (Frankfurt, 1622), ed. McColley. New York.

CHILLINGWORTH, WILLIAM, 1638. *The Religion of Protestants a Safe Way to Salvation*. Oxford.

COWLEY, ABRAHAM, 1668. *The Works of Mr A.C.* London.

DIGBY, SIR KENELM, 1658. *Two Treatises*. London.

GLANVILL, WILLIAM, 1664. *Scepsis Scientifica*. London.

HAKEWILL, GEORGE, 1627. *Apologie, or Declaration of the Power of God in the Government of the World*. London.

HOBBES, THOMAS, 1650. *Humane Nature: Or the fundamental Elements of Policie*. London.

—— 1650. *De Corpore Politico: Or the Elements of Law, Moral and Politic*. London.

—— 1651. *Leviathan, or the Matter, Forme and Power of a Common-wealth Ecclesiastical and Civil*. London.

JONSTON, JOHN, 1657. *A History of the Constancy of Nature . . .* London.

MILTON, JOHN, 1641. *The Reason of Church-government urg'd against Prelaty*. London.
—— 1649. *The Tenure of Kings and Magistrates*. London.
MORE, HENRY, 1662. *Collection of severall philosophical writings*. London.
PARIVAL, J., 1659. *The History of this Iron Age*, translated by B. Harris. London.
PEARSON, JOHN, 1659. *An Exposition of the Creed*. Oxford.
POWER, HENRY, 1664. *Experimental Philosophy, in Three Books*. London.
SANCHEZ, FRANCESCO, 1649. *Tractatus Philosophicus quod nihil scitur*. Rotterdam.
SANDERSON, ROBERT, 1615. *Logicae Artis Compendium*. Oxford.
STILLINGFLEET, EDWARD, 1662. *Origines Sacrae*. London.
TAYLOR, JEREMY, 1660. *Unum Necessarium*, in Taylor, 1847, VII.
WILKINS, JOHN, 1693. *Of the Principles and Duties of Natural Religion*. London.
WOTTON, SIR HENRY, 1659. *The State of Christendom*. London.

Secondary works

BETHELL, S. L., 1951. *The Cultural Revolution of the Seventeenth Century*. London.
BOAS, MARIE, 1954. 'An Early Version of Boyle's Sceptical Chymist', *Isis*.
BREDVOLD, L. I., 1934. *The Intellectual Milieu of John Dryden*. Michigan.
BROAD, C. D., 1947. 'From Bruno to Descartes', *Cambridge Historical Journal*.
BURTT, E. A., 1924. *The Metaphysical Foundations of Modern Science*. New York.
CASSIRER, E., 1953. *The Platonic Renaissance in England and the Cambridge School*. New Haven.
DE WULF, M. 1926. *History of Medieval Philosophy*, translated by E. C. Messenger, 2 vols. London.
HARRIS, V., 1949. *All Coherence Gone*. Chicago.
HOWELL, W. S., 1956. *Logic and Rhetoric in England, 1500–1700*. Princeton.
JONES, R. F., 1936. *Ancients and Moderns*. Washington University Studies.
KOYRÉ, A. 1957. *From the Closed World to the Infinite Universe*. Oxford.
LOVEJOY, A. O., 1936. *The Great Chain of Being*. Cambridge, Mass.
MEYER, R. W., 1952. *Leibnitz and the Seventeenth Century Revolution*. Cambridge.
NICOLSON, M. H., 1950. *The Breaking of the Circle*. Evanston, Illinois.
PAGEL, W., 1942. 'The Debt of Science and Medicine to a Devout Belief in God', *Transactions of the Victoria Institute*.

PAGEL, W., 1935. 'Religious Motives in the Medical Biology of the Seventeenth Century', *Bulletin of the Institute of the History of Medicine.*

TILLYARD, E. M. W., 1950. *The Elizabethan World Picture.* London.

WESTFALL, R. K., 1959. *Science and Religion in Seventeenth Century England.* New Haven.

WHITEHEAD, A. N., 1925. *Science and the Modern World.* Cambridge.

WILLEY, B., 1934. *The Seventeenth Century Background.* London.

(D) SECONDARY WORKS
(i) *Works on Locke*

AARON, R. I., 1937. *John Locke.* Oxford.

AARON, R. I., and GIBB, J., 1936. *An Early Draft of Locke's Essay, together with Excerpts from his Journals.* Oxford.

ABRAMS, P., 1961. *John Locke as a Conservative* (unpublished dissertation in the Cambridge University Library).

BASTIDE, C., 1907. *John Locke, ses Théories Politiques et leur Influence en Angleterre.* Paris.

BROWN, J., 1882. *Locke and Sydenham.* London.

CHRISTOPHERSEN, H. O., 1930. *A Bibliographical Introduction to the Study of John Locke.* Oslo.

COX, R. H., 1960. *Locke on War and Peace.* Oxford.

CRANSTON, M., 1956. 'Men and Ideas: John Locke', *Encounter,* no. 39.

—— 1957. *John Locke: a Biography.* London.

DE MARCHI, E., 1953. 'Le origine dell'idea della tolleranza religiosa nel Locke', *Occidente,* IX, 6. Turin.

DEWHURST, K., 1962. *John Locke, a Medical Biography.* London.

FOX BOURNE, H. R., 1876. *The Life of John Locke,* 2 vols. London.

FRASER, A. C., 1901. *Locke.* Edinburgh.

GOUGH, J. W., 1950. *John Locke's Political Philosophy.* Oxford.

KING, LORD, 1830. *The Life of John Locke with Extracts from his Correspondence, Journals and Commonplace Books.* London.

LAMPRECHT, S. P., 1918. *The Moral and Political Philosophy of John Locke.* New York.

LASLETT, P., 1960. *John Locke's Two Treatises of Government.* Cambridge.

LONG, P., 1959. 'A Summary Catalogue of the Lovelace Collection of the Papers of John Locke in the Bodleian Library', *Oxford Bibliographical Society,* n.s., VIII.

MACLEAN, A. H., 1947. *The Origins of the Political Opinions of John Locke* (unpublished dissertation in the Cambridge University Library).

APPENDIX II

Molyneux, W. E., 1957. *The Development of Locke's Theory of Toleration* (unpublished dissertation in the Bodleian Library, Oxford).

Monson, C. H., 1958. 'Locke and his Interpreters', *Political Studies*, VI, 2.

Neilson, F., 1951. 'Locke's Essays on Property and Natural Law', *American Journal of Economics and Sociology*, X, i.

Simon, W. M., 1951. 'John Locke: Philosophy and Political Theory', *American Political Science Review*, XLV, ii.

Singh, R., 1961. 'John Locke and the Theory of Natural Law', *Political Studies*, IX, 2.

Strauss, L., 1953. *Natural Right and History*. Chicago.

—— 1958. 'Locke's Doctrine of Natural Law', *American Political Science Review*.

Viano, C. A., 1960. *John Locke, dal Razionalismo all'Illuminismo*. Turin.

—— 1961. *John Locke, Scritti Editi e Inediti sulla Tolleranza*. Turin.

Von Leyden, W., 1954. *John Locke: Essays on the Law of Nature*. Oxford.

—— 1956. 'John Locke and Natural Law', *Philosophy*, XXVI, 1.

Waldman, M., 1959. 'A Note on John Locke's Concept of Consent', *Ethics*, LXVIII, 1.

Wild, T., 1953. *Plato's Modern Enemies and the Theory of Natural Law*. Chicago.

Yolton, J. W., 1956. *John Locke and the Way of Ideas*. Oxford.

—— 1958. 'Locke on the Law of Nature', *The Philosophical Review*, LXVII, 4.

(ii) *Seventeenth-century works*

Ascham, A., 1649 (*a*). *Of the Confusions and Revolutions of Government*. London.

—— 1649 (*b*). *Of the Original and End of Civil Power*. London.

Digges, Sir D., 1642. *An Answer to a printed book entitled Observations upon his Majesty's late answers*. Oxford.

—— 1644. *The Unlawfulness of subjects taking up arms against their Sovereign*. Oxford.

Fell, J., 1659. *The Interest of England Stated*. London.

Filmer, Sir R., 1652. *Observations concerning the Originall of Government*. London.

Gee, E., 1658. *The Divine Right and Original of the Civil Magistrate*. London.

Goodwin, J., 1644. Θεομαχια: *or the Grand Imprudence of men running the hazard of Fighting against God, in suppressing any Way, Doctrine or Practice concerning which they know not certainly whether it be from God or no*. London.

Reynolds, E., 1660. *Of Brotherly Reconciliation*, in Reynolds, 1826, V, 135.

RICHARDSON, S., 1647. *The necessity of Toleration in matters of Religion.* London.

ROBINSON, H., 1643. *Liberty of Conscience: or the sole means to obtain Peace and Truth.* London.

STUBBE, H., 1659. *An Essay in Defence of the Good Old Cause, or a Discourse concerning the Rise and Extent of the power of the Civil Magistrate in reference to Spiritual Affairs.* London.

TOWERSON, G., 1663. *A Brief account of some expressions in St Athanasius, his Creed....* Oxford.

—— 1676. *An Explication of the Decalogue.* Oxford.

TYRRELL, J., 1692. *A Brief Disquisition of the Law of Nature.* London.

VANE, SIR H., 1655. *The Retired Man's Meditations.* London.

USSHER, J., 1661. *The Power Communicated by God to the Prince and the Obedience Required of the Subject.* London; first published 1640, this edition by James Tyrrell with a Preface by R. Sanderson.

WALTON, I., 1678. *Life of Dr Sanderson.* London.

WALWYN, W., 1644. *The Compassionate Samiritan unbinding the Conscience.* London.

WHITLOCK, SIR B., 1660. *Monarchy Asserted to be the Best, most ancient and legal form of Government.* London.

(iii) *Other works*

BAMBOROUGH, R., 1956. 'Plato's Political Analogies', in Laslett (ed.), *Philosophy, Politics and Society.* Oxford.

CROMBIE, A. C., 1954. *Oxford's Contribution to the Origins of Modern Science.* Oxford.

FINLEY, M. I., 1962. 'Athenian Demagogues', *Past and Present*, 28.

GIERKE, O. VON, 1934. *Political Theories of the Middle Age* (tr. Maitland). Cambridge.

—— 1938. *Natural Law and the Theory of Society* (tr. Barker), 2 vols. Cambridge.

HOOPES, W., 1950. 'Voluntarism in Jeremy Taylor and the Platonic Tradition', *Huntington Library Quarterly*, 4.

MALLET, C. E., 1924. *History of the University of Oxford*, 3 vols. Oxford.

OXFORD UNIVERSITY, 1654. *Musarum Oxoniensum.* Oxford.

—— 1660. *Britannia Rediviva.* Oxford.

PLATO, 1941. *The Republic*, Cornford (ed.). Oxford.

Register of the Visitors of the University of Oxford, 1647–1658. Camden Society, London.

Register of the Visitors of the University of Oxford, 1660–1662. Camden Society, London. [*Register*]

SCHLATTER, J., 1940. *Social Ideas of Religious Leaders.* New York.

SHAW, W. A., 1900. *History of the English Church during the Civil Wars*, 2 vols. London.

THOMPSON, H. L., 1901. *Christ Church*. Oxford.

WOOD, A. à, 1891–1900. *Life and Times*, Clark (ed.), 5 vols. Oxford.

—— 1889–99. *Survey of the Antiquities of the City of Oxford*, Clark (ed.), 3 vols. Oxford.

—— 1813. *Athenae Oxonienses*, Bliss (ed.). Oxford.

WOOD, F. A., 1903. *A History of Chew Magna*. Bristol.

INDEX